Pacifying the Plains

Pacifying the Plains

General Alfred Terry and the Decline of the Sioux, 1866-1890

JOHN W. BAILEY

CONTRIBUTIONS IN MILITARY HISTORY, NUMBER 17

GREENWOOD PRESS
WESTPORT, CONNECTICUT • LONDON ENGLAND

Library of Congress Cataloging in Publication Data

Bailey, John W   1934
    Pacifying the plains.

    (Contributions in military history; no. 17 ISSN 0084-9251)
    Bibliography: p.
    Includes index.
    1. Dakota Indians—Government relations—1889-1934.
2. Dakota Indians—Wars, 1866-1895. 3. Indians of North
America—The West—Government relations—1869-1934.
4. Terry, Alfred Howe, 1827-1890. 5. Generals—United
States—Biography. 6. United States. Army—Biography.
I. Title. II. Series.
E99.D1B17   970'.004'97   78-19300
ISBN 0-313-20625-2

Library of Congress Catalog Card Number: 78-19300
ISBN: 0-313-20625-2
ISSN: 0084-9251

First published in 1979

Greenwood Press, Inc.
51 Riverside Avenue, Westport, Connecticut 06880

Printed in the United States of America

10 9 8 7 6 5 4 3 2 1

FOR SHERRY

Contents

Illustrations

Maps

Preface

The soldiers and the Sioux have been the subject matter of books too numerous to mention. Some volumes have become period pieces, and in this sense, they are valuable works. Others, aimed at a popular audience, have glorified the western experience at the expense of factual evidence and scholarship. Some were serious efforts that fell short. In the past twenty-five years several books on military-Sioux relations have merited the attention of serious students. Edgar I. Stewart's *Custer's Luck* (1955) was an effort to separate the myth and legend from the actual events of the Battle of the Little Bighorn. His detailed account of the Indians' "last defiant gesture" has stood the test of time. In 1956 Robert G. Athearn published *William Tecumseh Sherman and the Settlement of the West,* in which he portrayed the post-Civil War army's role as protector of frontier settlers. This fine work illustrated the problems of a top military official during the years 1865 to 1883.

Two of the finest works to appear in recent years on the military and the Indians are by Robert M. Utley. In his excellent synthesis, *Frontier Regulars* (1973), the author tried to reach a middle ground between the eastern humanitarian view of the soldier as butcher of Indians and the military's picture of themselves as the "advance guard of civilization." In an earlier work, *The Last Days of the Sioux Nation* (1963), Utley masterfully described the military and psychological conquest of the Sioux that culminated in the Ghost Dance delusion and the Wounded Knee tragedy of 1890-1891. In another recent book, James C. Olson's *Red Cloud and the Sioux Problem* (1965), the author told the story of Red Cloud's people and their transition from "warriors to wards of the Government." In both Utley's book on the Sioux and Olson's book on Red Cloud, the point of view is primarily that of the Indians.

General Alfred H. Terry appeared in all of the works mentioned above but only as a minor personage. Yet he was a significant figure who served for eighteen years during the critical period in the development of military-Sioux relations. He commanded the Department of Dakota from 1866 to 1869 and from 1873 to 1886 and the Division of the Missouri from 1886 to 1888. When Terry came to the northern plains after the Civil War, the Teton Sioux roamed Dakota, Nebraska, Wyoming, and Montana. By the late 1880s the Tetons had been relegated to a portion of South Dakota and forced to subscribe to the practices of the white man's civilization.

By using the general's correspondence and official reports as well as other materials, I have tried to determine Terry's role in the decline of the Sioux. While top army officers moved from department to department, Terry remained in Dakota. Through his long experience on the northern plains, the general was in an excellent position to make wise decisions on the management of Indian affairs. His keen legal mind and his humane character led him to seek the best treatment available for the Sioux in the context of late nineteenth-century America.

The research and writing of this work have been made possible by the concern of a number of helpful people. To the librarians and archivists of Marquette University, the Milwaukee Public Library, the National Archives, the Library of Congress, Yale University Library, Carthage College Library, the Nebraska Historical Society, Minnesota Historical Society, State Historical Society of North Dakota, Custer Battlefield National Monument, the Virginia State Library, and the Virginia Historical Society, I owe many thanks. Research grants from the Lutheran Church of America and the Carthage College Research fund were greatly appreciated. The maps were improved significantly with the help and advice of Bill Miller and Bill Lovitt. Phil Hultgren has enhanced the illustrations with his technical skill. I have benefited immensely from thoughtful comments by Frank Kelment, Karel Bicha, Bob Hay, Athan Theoharis, and especially Paul Prucha. Support from my colleagues John Neuenschwander, Tom Noer, and Jon Zophy is appreciated. Researching and writing the manuscript was truly a family project. My children, Steve and Lisa, helped with their understanding and support. To my wife, Sherry, I dedicate this book with love and appreciation.

Abbreviations in Notes

AAAG	Acting Assistant Adjutant General
AAG	Assistant Adjutant General
ACP	Appointment, Commission, and Personal
AGO	Adjutant General's Office
CO	Commanding Officer
COM	Commissioner
HQ	Headquarters
LC	Library of Congress
LR, LS	Letters Received, Letters Sent
NA	National Archives
RG	Record Group
TR, TS	Telegrams Received, Telegrams Sent

Pacifying
the Plains

1 Civil War and Reconstruction Duties

The life of Alfred Howe Terry was in many respects a microcosm of American history from 1850 to 1890 in that he was a participant in many of the central events of his time. As a young man he had many of the experiences that an upper-class New England family could afford. He received a good education and then dabbled in civil engineering, law, and the military. He traveled in Europe and grew to be a cultured and respected person in his community of New Haven, Connecticut. In 1861 when the Civil War broke out, he patriotically joined in the war effort and led local volunteers in many of the important battles of the war. The culmination of his part in the struggle came when he personally commanded his troops in an important and brilliant victory over the Confederates at Fort Fisher toward the end of the war.

Terry remained in the regular army after the war and served in Virginia and Georgia for four and a half years during the Reconstruction period. His most important work, however, was on the northern plains, where he labored to solve the problems of another minority group, the American Indian. The general negotiated with the natives and helped draw up perhaps the most important treaty made with the Sioux. He fought to uphold the treaty, and he attacked those Indians who sought to disregard the document. He strove for a just settlement of the Indian problem but ended up leading the most famous military expedition of the century against the natives. In the end his role was one of subjugating and managing the northern plains Indians who fell before the onslaught of the American westward movement.

This soldier of Civil War and frontier days came from an old and distinguished Connecticut family. Originating in England, the family had its start in America when young Samuel Terry, an indentured servent, came to New England in 1650. Alfred was descended from four of the founders of Hartford: Reverend Thomas Hooker, who led his people to Hartford

in 1636, Elder William Goodwin, John Talcott, and William Wadsworth.[1]
One ancestor was active in colonial times when he assisted in ousting an
English official, Sir Edmund Andros, who hoped to consolidate several
New England colonies into a confederation. Another ancestor, General
Jeremiah Wadsworth, held an important position in the colony during the
American Revolution. In the War of 1812, Terry's maternal grandfather,
General Hezekiah Howe, was a bookseller and respected citizen who com-
manded the defense of New Haven against a British attack upon the city.[2]

Terry's parents, Alfred, Sr., and Clarissa Howe, married in 1825 and
settled in Hartford, where Alfred was born on November 10, 1827. Two
years later the family moved to New Haven, where the senior Terry
entered the book and stationery business. The Terrys had three other
boys and five girls in the following years. Alfred was very close to his
brother Adrian, who served by his side during the Civil War and afterward became a businessman in Knoxville, Tennessee. J. Wadsworth,
another brother, attended Yale, where he studied medicine, and served
as an army surgeon during the Civil War; later he practiced medicine in
Englewood, New Jersey. Little is known of Robert Goldsborough Terry,
the youngest brother, who died in 1878. Alfred remained close to his
sisters, and since he never married, they proved a valued source of com-
panionship. Clara married Robert P. Hughes, who became Terry's aide-de-
camp and a close friend for many years. Harriet was a housemother at
Vassar College from 1871 to 1877. Little is known of the other sisters—
Jane, Frances, and Eliza.[3]

Alfred grew up in New Haven and attended that town's public schools.
In his teens he took a job in civil engineering, but a few years later he
became a clerk in the office of E. K. Foster, judge of probate for that
district. At age twenty-one, Terry went to Yale Law School, and the
following year, 1849, he was admitted to the Connecticut bar. He became
a fine trial lawyer, and with his family connections and immense capacity
for work, he had prospects for a superior court judgeship in the future.
A conservative Republican by political inclination, in 1850 he became
city clerk, a job he held for four years until he was appointed clerk of
the superior court.[4]

During this period Terry filled his leisure moments with many outside
interests. In 1860 when his father died, he inherited a small fortune and
had time and money to partake of some of the finer things in life. He
enjoyed music and seems to have been a flautist at one period in his life.

He also devoted time to building model ships and studying military science. He read histories of campaigns and studied battle plans, fortifications, and offensive and defensive movements. He loved to read, and he learned two foreign languages, French and German, in order to translate works on the European military campaigns that he devoured when time permitted. His military interests drew him to the local militia, the New Haven Greys, which he joined in 1849. He started as a private and advanced up the ranks to colonel by 1860. That summer he spent in Europe, traveling from England to Italy and studying military fortifications, ships of war, and any other military sites that were open to the public. He returned to Connecticut in 1861 in time to respond to Lincoln's urgent call for volunteers in the Civil War crisis.[5]

With the outbreak of the rebellion, the governor offered Terry the colonelcy of the Twenty-first Regiment of the Second Connecticut Volunteers. He accepted, organized the men, and on May 7, 1861, moved his unit off to the Washington area to defend the capital. For the colonel it was a frustrating experience. He participated in the Battle of First Bull Run and suffered through the inglorious retreat of the Union forces from Manassas Junction. At the end of his ninety-day enlistment, Terry returned to New Haven. He was exhausted and had lost seventeen pounds from his already lean body. He lamented that the rebel privates were inferior to his men but that Confederate gentlemen officers were superior to the politicians who commanded Union forces.[6]

Upon the completion of his three months' duty with the volunteers, Terry reenlisted with the Seventh Connecticut for three years. During that time he took part in the capture of Port Royal, South Carolina, and the siege and reduction of Fort Pulaski, Georgia, which guarded the mouth of the Savannah River. In April 1863, he was appointed brigadier general of volunteers and served in various military operations around Charleston, South Carolina. Terry suffered the effects of malaria during the summer of 1863 and was given a leave of absence for twenty days. In early 1864, he returned to command the First Division of the Tenth Army Corps of the Army of the James under the command of General Benjamin Butler. Most of his duty now was in and around Richmond and Petersburg, Virginia.[7]

President Abraham Lincoln chose Butler for this position of leadership more for political reasons than for any military attributes Butler possessed. The president from time to time had to placate Radical Republicans in

Congress with military appointments, and some of them were a detriment to the army. On one occasion in the lines outside Petersburg, Terry witnessed the bungling efforts of Butler and could contain himself no longer. A signal officer standing nearby Terry overheard the incident and described how

> Butler in his feeble way was sending a regiment at a time to
> assault the rebel lines and as I happened to be with General
> Terry and his staff as they sat on their horses just in the rear
> of our lines, heard an aide as he galloped up say, "compliments
> of General Butler to General Terry, you will send another regi-
> ment to the relief of the assaulting party." General Terry re-
> plied, "my compliments to General Butler and say to him I
> will send no more troops to the front unless the whole army is
> sent."[8]

Terry realized that he was putting his military career on the line, but he refused to allow his men to be destroyed piecemeal in a futile effort to overcome a strong Confederate position. It was a gamble on Terry's part, but he got away with his strong stand against Butler. Evidently other Union commanders also failed to follow Butler's orders, and he could not punish them all.[9]

By December 1864, Butler was off to his last military expedition of the war. His objective was a coastal stronghold, Fort Fisher, at the mouth of the Cape Fear River in North Carolina. The fort was a key defensive position for Wilmington, the only remaining Confederate port of any significance along the Atlantic coast and a lifeline of subsistence for General Robert E. Lee's forces in Virginia. Butler was to conduct an amphibious landing in conjunction with Rear Admiral David Porter's fleet and destroy the fort. There was no joint planning by the two commanders, however, and this lack of coordination spelled defeat for the Union forces. Butler lost only three men and ten were wounded by their own supporting gunfire, but the general saw little possibility of dislodging the Confederates from their strong position and gave up the campaign.[10]

General Ulysses S. Grant was openly disappointed at their failure to destroy Fort Fisher, but he was not ready to give up. He requested Butler's transfer, placed General Terry in command of virtually the same force that the disposed general had used, and ordered another effort to subdue the fortress. This time Terry and Porter worked together closely and coordinated their movements perfectly. The navy laid down a devastating bombardment on the fort, and Terry landed his men without difficulty. He immediately set up a defensive line across the peninsula and west of the fort to guard against an attack from the rear by troops stationed near Wilmington.[11]

When the Federals completed their defensive line, Terry began the assault on Fort Fisher with thirty-three hundred soldiers. Two thousand sailors and marines landed at another point and participated in the attack. The navy laid down a barrage in front of the soldiers' advancing line, and the Confederates were helpless. As the soldiers gained ground, the barrage moved with them, always keeping well ahead of Terry's men. The general repeatedly sent messages to naval personnel pointing out new targets for their guns and encouraging them in their work. This cooperation between the army and the navy proved to be the key to victory. Fort Fisher fell on January 15, 1865, and with it the northerners took some two hundred Confederate prisoners. The Union had suffered about one thousand casualties, but the way was now open to Wilmington.[12]

Terry and his men next pushed to that key port city and occupied it on January 22 with the support of General John Schofield and his men, who advanced from Tennessee into Carolina. During this time General William T. Sherman had completed his march through Georgia and was now moving through South Carolina and into North Carolina. At Bentonville on March 21, Sherman met the Confederates under the command of General Joseph Johnston. It was an indecisive battle, but it proved to be the last time these combatants faced each other in a major battle. Sherman marched his sixty thousand men to Goldsboro, where he joined with Schofield's forty thousand troops, which included Terry's corps. The end of the Civil War came in early April before Sherman could move his combined force into Virginia.[13]

Alfred Terry emerged from the Civil War with an enviable record. The thirty-eight year old bachelor had received a wound that left him with a slight limp, but he completed his service as a major general of volunteers and gained a brigadier general's commission in the postwar regular army. His spectacular victory at Fort Fisher in the closing days of the war won him the admiration of many. Admiral Porter pronounced him the "beau ideal of a soldier and a gentleman."[14] One of the highest honors that a soldier could receive was the thanks of Congress, which Terry received for gallantry and skill in his Fort Fisher victory. He valued this recognition and was one of only five or six to be so honored by name.[15]

Terry's victory at Fort Fisher made him one of many Civil War heroes for the Union, and it won him the praise of Grant and Sherman, the two highest-ranking men in the army following the war. They admired this vigorous, active young officer whose outstanding characteristic was his ability to cooperate with superiors, equals, and subordinates. Grant wrote of him as "a man who makes friends of those under him by his considera- tion of their wants and their dues. As a commander, he won their con- fidence by his coolness in action and by his clearness of perception in taking in the situation under which he was placed at any given time."[16] This was high praise from the general-in-chief and future president of the United States. Terry was amply rewarded for his Civil War achievements with his position in the regular army, the highest rank any non-West Point graduate earned in the postwar period.

The general from Connecticut was an imposing figure at the close of the war, standing six feet two inches in height. His slender build resulted in a nickname, "No Hips," which the Sioux Indians later gave him. He had clear blue eyes, a pleasant, if somewhat serious, expression on his face, and a full beard that complemented his head of brown hair. He dressed and conducted himself as a well-bred gentleman, which would help him gain acceptance among the people of the South where he served in his next military assignment.[17]

Terry served in Reconstruction duty from June 1865 to August 1866. He commanded the Department of Virginia and faced the task of smooth- ing over the road to reconciliation with the former Confederates. It was not an easy job. On one occasion he ordered his soldiers to take possession of the *Richmond Examiner* offices as a result of inflammatory articles printed in that newspaper. The editor published the love story of a beauti- ful southern belle and an unnamed general of the Union Army. The story had an unhappy ending when the general's wife arrived from the North a few days before the wedding was scheduled to take place. Although Terry was not the unnamed guest, he managed to have the editor jailed for a short period of time. Even more disturbing to Terry was the lack of respect for law and order that he sensed in the actions of the judges and juries of the civil courts in Virginia. He was appalled at their decisions and the double standard of laws they rendered between blacks and whites. The general sometimes wondered if he had made the right decision by remaining in the military rather than returning to law practice. When he witnessed the travesty of justice that permeated the civil courts of Virginia, however, he could not but respect the role of the soldier as the more honorable.[18]

After fourteen months in Reconstruction duty, Terry was transferred to the northern plains. Here he served for about three years until he returned to Reconstruction duty in May 1869, this time in the Department of the South. For the next three years and four months, his responsibility encompassed the states of Florida, South Carolina, North Carolina, Alabama, Georgia, Kentucky, Tennessee, and Mississippi, although not all at one time, because some were accepted back into the Union and others were assigned to the department at a later date.[19] Terry replaced Colonel Thomas H. Ruger at the Atlanta headquarters, where he was on temporary duty. It was not the last time their paths would cross, because Ruger later served under Terry in the West.[20]

It took Terry only a short time to become aware of the complexities of his new post in Georgia. He had too few soldiers to police such a vast region. He faced election frauds, riots, yellow fever epidemics, violence on United States internal revenue collectors, and all types of crimes, including murder. The main violators of law and order were members of the Ku Klux Klan and other similar organizations that stood for white supremacy in the South.[21] The army gradually withdrew from the region as the southern states rejoined the Union and military control was phased out.

The end of Terry's Reconstruction duty opened the door for his return to Dakota and his work with the Sioux. He looked forward to this duty, and he anticipated accomplishing significant and lasting work among the whites and Indians of the northern plains. He was pleased that Grant and Sherman had shown such confidence in him that they had placed him in positions where the nation needed its best people. Virginia, immediately after the Civil War, and the Department of the South, in the late 1860s and early 1870s, were key spots where difficult decisions were made and crucial policies were implemented. On the post-Civil War frontier, the Sioux were recognized as the most potent Indian force that the United States faced, and Terry was given the difficult job of subduing this formidable adversary.

NOTES

1. Harriet Terry to Stephen Walkley, November 1, 1901, Terry Papers, Yale University Library, New Haven, Connecticut.

2. L. P. Bradley to Terry, February 12, 1883, Terry Papers; newspaper clipping, n.d., Terry Papers. For biographical information, see also Carl W. Marino, "Gen. Alfred Howe Terry: Soldier from Connecticut" (Ph.D. diss., New York University, 1968), pp. 1-36.

3. This family information was taken from many letters and papers in the Terry Family papers.

4. Newspaper clipping, n.d., Terry Papers; Alfred Terry to Little Fanny, November 28, 1870, Terry Papers; John Niven, *Connecticut for the Union: The Role of the State in the Civil War* (New Haven: Yale University Press, 1965), pp. 45, 122-123.

5. Niven, *Connecticut for the Union,* pp. 45, 122-123.

6. Adrain Terry to Isadore, August 8, 1861, Terry Papers. See Niven, *Connecticut for the Union,* for Terry's Civil War career.

7. Terry to Lt. Col. Charles L. Halpine, May 10, 1863, ACP, Terry, AGO, RG94, NA; proceedings of the Army Retiring Board, April 4, 1888, Terry, AGO.

8. Lester L. Swift, ed., "The Recollections of a Signal Officer," *Civil War History* 9 (March 1963): 50.

9. Ibid., pp. 50, 52.

10. Jay Morten Luvaas, "The Fall of Fort Fisher," *Civil War Times Illustrated* 3 (August 1964): 5-7.

11. Ibid., pp. 7-9.

12. Ibid., pp. 31-33.

13. John G. Barrett, "Sherman and Total War in the Carolinas," *North Carolina Historical Review* 37 (July 1960): 368-376; Jay M. Luvaas, "Johnston's Last Stand—Bentonville," *North Carolina Historical Review* 33 (July 1956): 332-346.

14. *Erie Daily Dispatch,* May 25, 1865.

15. Terry to Sherman, September 3, 1879, ACP, Terry, AGO.

16. U. S. Grant, *Personal Memoirs of U. S. Grant* (New York: Century Co., 1885), pp. 540-541.

17. *Erie Daily Dispatch,* May 25, 1865.

18. Terry to Bvt. Maj. Gen. J. A. Rawlins, March 19, 1866, LR, Records of the HQ Army, 1825-1903, RG 108, NA; Alfred Terry to Adrian Terry, November 27, 1868, Terry Papers; Terry to Bvt. Col. T. J. Bowers, AAG, January 11, 1866, LR, HQ Army; *Richmond Examiner,* March 22, 1866.

19. Annual report of Terry, October 10, 1870, LR, AGO.

20. Ibid., October 31, 1869, LR, AGO.

21. See the annual reports of Terry from 1869 to 1872.

2 Guarding the Routes to Montana, 1866-1868

General Terry faced an awesome task when he moved to Fort Snelling, Minnesota, in 1866 to become the first commander of the new Department of Dakota. His major focus during the first three years was to organize the department so that it might best protect settlers in the region and to provide security for those who traveled across the Sioux lands in search of wealth in the rich mining areas of Montana and Idaho. That he succeeded in accomplishing these jobs on this raw frontier was a tribute to his skill as a leader and to the fortitude of the men who served under him. For the Indians of the northern plains, however, it signaled the beginning of a movement that would eventually destroy their traditional way of life.

Essential to Terry's success was knowledge of the geographical makeup of the department and information concerning the people who lived there. Congress created the Department of Dakota on August 6, 1866, as part of a general military reorganization of the command system in the West. It comprised the state of Minnesota and the territories of Dakota and Montana, an extensive area of some 378,918 square miles of wilderness that made up the northern plains of the United States.[1]

Minnesota, the easternmost region of the department, was an area of rich soil and sufficient rainfall. It had numerous lakes and rivers and luxuriant growth of grasses and forests. This attractive area gave way on its western border to Dakota Territory, where the soil was not so rich and the rainfall not so abundant. The area was subject to periodic drought conditions, and the rainfall average was between fifteen and twenty-five inches annually. The dry east gradually changed to the arid western part of the territory. Several geographical features dominated Dakota: the Red River and its fertile valley in the northeast, the James River in the east, and the Missouri River, the white man's highway into the northern plains, in the central part of the territory. The western wastelands were broken by the oasis-like feature of the Black Hills in the southwestern corner of the region.[2]

West of Dakota lay Montana Territory. Its eastern region was little more than an extension of western Dakota. The central area yielded to rolling lands, foothills, and the Rocky Mountains, which dominated the western portion of the territory. Two important waterways, the Yellowstone and the Missouri, flowed from these mountains and provided early transportation routes into the territory.

Native Americans who inhabited the northern plains were basically eastern woodland Indians who had migrated there. Because of the pressures of whites and of Indians with more advanced technology, natives such as the Sioux, the Crows, and the Cheyennes were forced onto the plains. With this new environment came a new culture centered around the horse and the bison. The introduction of the horse on the northern plains stimulated a transportation revolution for these natives and changed their life-style to that of the nomadic buffalo hunter. The bison, which roamed the region in countless numbers, provided the Indians with the necessities of food, shelter, and clothing. The natives' very existence depended upon the successful hunting of this shaggy beast.[3]

The dominant native peoples of the northern plains were the Sioux (map 1). There were three main divisions of the Sioux: the Santees who lived in southwestern Minnesota, the Yanktons who inhabited the area in Dakota east of the Missouri River, and the Tetons who roamed the area west of the Missouri in the present states of North Dakota, South Dakota, Montana, Wyoming, and Nebraska. On occasion they traveled to the central and southern plains to visit and hunt with the Cheyennes and Arapahos, who in turn visited them in the north.[4]

The Teton division of the Sioux, the most warlike, was divided into seven tribes. The Hunkpapas, Sans Arcs, and Blackfeet lived along the North and South Dakota state boundary and westward into the Powder, Tongue, and Bighorn river area along the south bank of the Yellowstone. The Miniconjous resided in a small area in northwestern South Dakota west of the Two Kettle tribe, which stayed along the Grand and Moreau rivers in north central South Dakota. The Brulés controlled the Cheyenne, White, and Niobrara river areas in southern Dakota and northwestern Nebraska. To their west the Oglalas dominated the Black Hills and northeastern Wyoming, including the headwaters of the Powder River. It was these Teton Sioux whom General Terry and the army of the northern

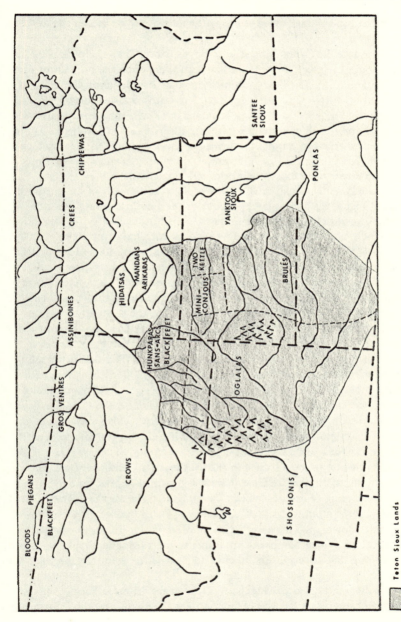

Teton Sioux Lands

Map 1   NORTHERN PLAINS INDIAN TRIBES

plains had to subdue before white settlement would be safe in the northern plains.

Generally the Sioux did not function as tribes. They rather divided into a number of bands that varied in size depending upon the number of families it contained. The band occupied much of its time in procuring food by hunting buffalo and other wildlife. The warriors also enjoyed raids on neighboring Indians, such as the Mandans or Crows, their enemy, in order to steal ponies and count coups on their adversaries. On certain occasions they called tribal gatherings for special ceremonies, such as the sun dance, or perhaps to organize a mammoth buffalo hunt. For most Teton Sioux it was a satisfactory existence, which held many virtues.

White Americans had mixed feelings about settlement in the northern plains. There was little question about the desirability of settlement in Minnesota with its rich resources. Settlers had trickled into the area during the 1840s, and its population had grown spectacularly from 6,000 in 1850, to 172,000 in 1860, and to 440,000 in 1870. But Dakota and Montana were not as desirable as Minnesota to white settlers. Fur trappers had visited the area since the early 1800s, when Lewis and Clark had brought back stories of the abundance of fur-bearing animals in the region. They had built stockade posts along the Missouri, but the population was not permanent. During the 1850s farmers from Minnesota spilled over into the Red River Valley of northern Dakota, but their success as farmers was dependent upon the varying amount of rainfall. Population actually decreased in this region from 5,000 in 1860 to 2,500 in 1870 because of drought conditions. St. Paul businessmen encouraged settlement and welcomed the establishment of the town of Pembina near the Canadian border. For Minnesota merchants, the Red River country seemed the gateway to the trade of interior Canada, with St. Paul the city most likely to benefit from this endeavor.[5]

Other white farmers settled in the southeastern corner of southern Dakota during the 1860s. Here there was plentiful rainfall for agriculture, and the trading center of Yankton developed on the Missouri River. Settlers came in numbers that reached close to 12,000 by 1870. Aside from the slowly growing agrarian population on the fringes of eastern Dakota and a small number of volunteer soldiers living in dilapidated stockades along the Missouri, the Indians had Dakota for themselves in the mid-1860s.

Farther to the west, the scene was somewhat different because of the discovery of gold in the Montana mountains. Beginning in 1862 prospectors

flooded into southwestern Montana and made settlements at Bannock,
Virginia City, and Helena during the next few years. By 1866 at least
10,000 people lived in these towns and hundreds of camps in the surrounding area. Wealth abounded, but there were few articles for purchase. Profit
awaited those who could supply the miners of these distant goldfields.[6]

Almost constant warfare with the Sioux in the early 1860s blocked the
merchants of such towns as Sioux City, Iowa, and St. Paul, Minnesota,
from supplying the needy Montana miners. The army had attempted to
force peace on the Sioux after the uprising of 1862 in Minnesota, but to
little avail. Generals Alfred Sully and William Harney unsuccessfully cam-
paigned against the Sioux in the two years following the uprising, and thus
the transportation routes to Montana from the East remained unsafe.[7]

With the conclusion of the Civil War in the spring of 1865, the people
of Minnesota and Dakota expected a greatly strengthened military buildup
in the area. The volunteer soldiers had done a creditable job in the absence
of the regular army, but permanent peace and a solution to the Sioux problem remained the goal that settlers had set for the postwar military in the
northern plains.

General Terry was the man whom Grant and Sherman chose to meet
the challenge of organizing the new department, protecting the settlers
of the region, providing safe routes to Montana, and gaining peace with
the Sioux. To accomplish this, Terry drew from an army that was greatly
reduced in size from its Civil War numbers and one that was undergoing
tremendous organizational changes. At the end of the war, the United
States had an army of over one million men. A year later Congress had
reduced it to 54,302—5 percent of its size during the war. The top echelon
of officers in the new army included seventeen positions. The two highest
ranks were those of general of the army and lieutenant general. These
were filled by Grant and Sherman until 1869 when Grant became president. Then Sherman held the top military position, and Philip H. Sheridan
moved into the second slot. Below these two positions were five major
generals and ten brigadier generals. Terry was one of the latter.[8]

The general left Virginia and his Reconstruction responsibilities and
headed for St. Paul, Minnesota, to assume his new command with the
sound of praise ringing in his ears. Secretary of War Edwin M. Stanton
had written to the general, expressing his belief that Terry's ability,
integrity, and wisdom in the administration of the Department of Virginia had entitled him to commendation for success.[9] With this boost,
Terry lost little time in preparing for his new adventure in the West. He

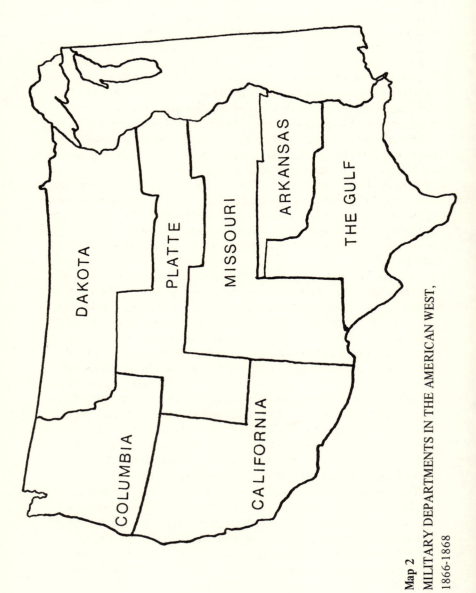

Map 2
MILITARY DEPARTMENTS IN THE AMERICAN WEST,
1866-1868

arranged for his mother and Eliza, one of his sisters, to spend the winter in St. Paul, and then he reported for duty at St. Louis. He planned to travel up the Missouri River to inspect some of the posts in his department on the way to Fort Snelling, located just outside St. Paul.[10]

Terry spent September and October traveling from St. Louis along the Missouri and overland to St. Paul. He made short visits to Omaha and Sioux City talking with people and learning about the country to the north, the Indians, and the forts he would visit. From Iowa the new commander steamed to Fort Randall in southern Dakota. The post seemed well located, but he noted that most of the cottonwood logs from which the fort buildings were constructed were rotten. The next stop along the river was Fort Thompson near Crow Creek Indian Agency. He found the Indians well behaved and the post in a suitable location.[11]

From the river forts Terry traveled eastward toward Fort Wadsworth. While on the trail buffalo were spotted, and the general participated in a spirited chase over the plains. But while he was riding at full speed, his horse fell, and he tumbled to the ground. Terry painfully injured his right arm; as a result he spent little time at Fort Wadsworth and bypassed Fort Abercrombie altogether in his haste to reach the comforts of St. Paul. In his new quarters he wrote his reports, recuperated from his fall, and studied the available information on post locations within his department.[12]

Terry concluded from his observations that the Indians were surprisingly peaceful in Minnesota and southeastern Dakota. There were numerous stories of horse-stealing raids, but few white men died in clashes with the Indians in Dakota during this time. Many of the Santee and Yankton Sioux seemed peaceful and willing to try agriculture, while the more hostile Teton Sioux roamed west of the Missouri River hunting buffalo. There were hints of trouble in northwestern Dakota where Terry received reports of attacks on woodcutters and other citizens who were traveling through the area. He realized that action might be necessary in the future.[13]

Terry was aware of peace efforts made during the past four years after the Sioux uprising in Minnesota in 1862. Military expeditions under Generals Alfred Sully and Patrick Connor and Colonel Henry Sibley in 1863, 1864, and 1865 were unsuccessful in breaking the military strength of the Teton Sioux.[14] Failing to force peace on the Sioux through military action, the government next sent a commission to negotiate with the natives. Governor Newton Edmunds of Dakota Territory headed the group, which also included Edward B. Taylor and Colonel Sibley. They met with various bands of the Sioux in October 1865 and early 1866 and successfully gained treaties with the Two Kettles, Blackfeet, Sans Arcs, Hunkpapas, Yanktonais, and the Oglalas. Members of these Sioux bands agreed to live in peace, remove from the overland routes, and withdraw to permanent reservations.[15] Those Indians who refused to accept reservation life and continued to hunt and live where they pleased gradually were considered hostiles by government officials. Sherman perceived that these natives must either be forced to comply with federal orders or be killed. But Terry felt that in time, the hostiles would accept reservation life, particularly when the number of buffalo diminished.[16]

The general's first problem was to obtain peace with the estimated twenty-six thousand to thirty-three thousand Indians within his department in order to secure the routes to the Montana gold and silver fields.[17] Sherman proposed that Terry should make the Missouri River as safe as possible and that he should "open and protect the new route from Minnesota to Montana and afford the stages and wagons that travel that long and exposed route, all the assistance in his power." Terry felt this policy was much more enlightened than that of annual summer warfare against the Indians. With a war policy it would make sense to concentrate the troops at one or two locations within the department and send them on extended expeditions into hostile territory to conduct search-and-destroy missions. Terry believed that numerous small posts for protective purposes and a peace policy with the Sioux was the best choice.[18]

Sherman did not oppose war with the Sioux, but he thought that peace was a more practical solution for the moment. Thousands of prospectors were making their way to the Montana mines, and they needed protection. Others were taking advantage of the Homestead Act passed by Congress in 1862, which allowed farmers 160 acres of free land in the West. Terry and Sherman realized the importance of guarding the routes to Montana and settled on the policy of small military posts along the Missouri River and a chain of forts along a road or roads from the Minnesota settlements to the upper Missouri.[19]

The white citizens of Dakota Territory strongly supported this policy. The merchants and farmers of Dakota, Iowa, and Minnesota had benefited financially from the Sully and Sibley expeditions against the Sioux in the early 1860s, but they understood that a greater profit might be gained under Sherman's policy. Extermination of the Indians was not the answer, but a system of reservations and annuities for the Indians and a chain of forts separating the whites and the natives would benefit both interests: the Indians would survive, and the area's politicians, farmers, and merchants would become prosperous. This cordon of forts would be mobile and gradually push the Indians from desirable soil onto less desirable land around which their permanent reservations would be established. Through a program of government subsistence for the Indians and the constant need to obtain provisions for the soldiers, the civilian population could make honest profits from the trade and still enjoy the opportunity to practice fraud and wrongdoing on the Indians and the United States government if they were so inclined.[20]

Another source of income for whites would be to supply the immigrant trains heading for Montana. Thus towns in Nebraska, Iowa, Dakota, and Minnesota competed for the distinction of being at the head of a route that led to the Montana mining country. Travelers tried several routes outside of Terry's department through Nebraska and Wyoming, but Red Cloud and his Oglala braves protested that their hunting grounds were being violated.[21]

The general was more interested in routes through his own department, since they would help determine his decisions on troop allocations. Newton Edmunds, the Dakota governor, encouraged development of the Cheyenne River route. Military protection was nearby, and travelers could follow the north branch of the river along the north edge of the Black Hills, across the Powder River region to the Yellowstone River and Virginia City. Since this route traversed Teton Sioux hunting grounds, it would be a difficult road for the army to secure.[22]

The safest route was to travel the Missouri River by steamboat as far on the river as it was navigable. An additional few days of stagecoach or wagon travel brought miners to the Montana goldfields. Terry, Sherman, Edmunds, and other public officials all supported the protection of this route as the key to travel to Montana.

The people of Minnesota clamored for a road from their state to link up with the Missouri River route to Montana, and it seemed practical to Terry. Although it would be costly to build new forts and furnish escort services for immigrant trains, it was a policy that the government committed itself to accomplish.[23] Terry had traveled along the Missouri in 1866, and the following year he had thoroughly inspected the rest of his department, including Montana. The result was the recommendation of a comprehensive and costly building program, but one Terry felt would get the job done.

The general had divided his department into four military districts: Minnesota, which included eastern Dakota; South Eastern Dakota; the Middle District, which encompassed northern Dakota; and Montana. Terry had four infantry regiments of about one thousand men each for his department, and he stationed the Tenth Infantry under Colonel E. B. Alexander in Minnesota, the Twenty-second Infantry in South Eastern Dakota under Colonel David S. Stanley, the Thirty-first Infantry under Colonel Regis de Trobriand in the Middle District, and the Thirteenth Infantry under Colonel I. V. D. Reeve in Montana.[24]

Terry had specific recommendations about each fort in the districts (map 3). In the District of Minnesota there would be five forts. Fort Snelling, the department headquarters, and Fort Ripley were located in the settled area of the state; because they were under no threat of Indian attack, they received only one company of about seventy soldiers. Fort Abercrombie, newly built Fort Ransom, and Fort Wadsworth, all located in eastern Dakota, divided the remaining eight companies of infantry. Their job was to guard the immigrant trains on the Minnesota road that were passing through to the Missouri River. Terry recommended abandoning Fort Ridgely in southern Minnesota, for the post had outlived its usefulness by 1867. The nearby Santee Sioux had settled down to agricultural pursuits and were content to live in peace.[25]

In South Eastern Dakota Terry also called for changes. He ordered the abandonment of Fort James in 1866 and Fort Thompson in 1867 because the farmers of the area were now secure from Indian attack. Terry retained the four remaining posts in the district, stationing one company each at Fort Dakota and Fort Randall to provide protection and supplies for the region. To the north along the Missouri River, he retained Fort Sully and Fort Rice, where he dispatched the remaining eight companies to guard the river traffic.[26]

In the Middle District of northern Dakota, the general established three new forts. He located Fort Totten, a three-company post, near Devils Lake to guard the Minnesota road in that area. To the west on the Missouri River, he replaced Fort Berthold with Fort Stevenson at a better site twenty-five miles down river from the old post. With two companies there and an additional five at Fort Buford at the confluence of the Yellowstone and Missouri rivers, the water traffic was sufficiently guarded along its winding path into Montana.[27]

Terry organized the Montana District around three new posts built in 1866 and 1867. Fort Shaw on the Sun River in the northwestern part of

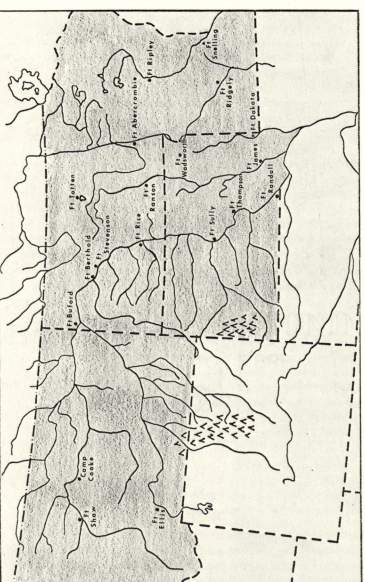

Map 3
THE DEPARTMENT OF DAKOTA, 1866-1868

Department of Dakota

the state was a four-company post and the headquarters of the district. East of it at the confluence of the Judith and Missouri rivers, he located Camp Cooke with three companies. South of Shaw was Fort Ellis, a three-company post situated near the Yellowstone River. These forts formed a cordon to protect the mining centers and farmers of the region.[28] Although miners were considered good Indian fighters, Terry preferred to have the regular army responsible for the protection of the entire populace rather than rely on volunteers.[29]

The general had done a good job in organizing his new department and in affording military protection for the Missouri River and Minnesota Road routes to Montana. He had traveled through Dakota with a company of mounted infantry and had used the advice of his engineers expertly in choosing the new fort locations.[30]

Terry had also traveled by steamer on the Missouri River to the Montana mining towns and farm communities. He had an unusual experience about 125 miles above the mouth of the Yellowstone when his steamer reached a favorite buffalo crossing on the river. Snorting and bellowing, the bison plunged into the swift-running current and swam to the opposite shore. The buffalo were so thick in the river that the boat could not move and the engines had to be stopped. One observer explained:

> In front the channel was blocked by their huge, shaggy bodies, and in their struggles they beat against the sides and stern, blowing and pawing. Many became entangled with the wheel ... As they swept toward the precipitous bank of the north shore and plunged over into the stream, clouds of dust arose from the crumbling earth while the air trembled with their bellowings and the roar of their myriad hoofs. The south bank was turned to a liquid mass of mud by the water streaming from their sides as they scrambled out and thundered away across the prairie. . . . No one on board cared to shoot among them, for the sight of them was too awe-inspiring a demonstration of physical might of untamed brute creation.[31]

It took several hours before the boat could break through the unending herd and continue up the Missouri River. As the passengers on the vessel passed out of view the mighty beasts were still seen crossing the river. Terry could only wonder, perhaps, if the supply of these bison would ever be exhausted. The shaggy animals meant life or death to the northern

Plains Indians and their very existence would play a significant part in future treaty negotiations between the natives and the whites.[32]

As Terry toured his department, he became aware of the inadequacy of his force; four infantry regiments were hardly sufficient to police such a vast area. He requested more men and expressed the need for cavalry units. If these were not available, then perhaps he could obtain more horses for his foot soldiers. The Dakota forces were limited primarily to garrison and escort duty because there were not enough horses to wage an offensive campaign against the Indians. Congress had authorized the establishment of four more cavalry regiments in July 1866, but these units were not destined for Dakota at this time.[33]

Terry had many other problems that were time-consuming, and though they were a nuisance, their solution played a part in the army's role of harbinger of white civilization in the Department of Dakota. The commander was concerned over the recent order from the Department of Interior prohibiting the sale of powder and lead by traders to the Indians. Terry pointed out that many natives had lost their skill with the bow and arrow since they now used guns exclusively. Other Indians had no horses, and it seemed to Terry that they must either starve or rely on the government for subsistence. The general felt that the Indians would be pleased if the policy were reversed and put more in line with promises made by white treaty makers in 1865-1866.[34]

The severe winter of 1868 brought desperate conditions to many Indians. Colonel de Trobriand reported that four natives had "literally died of starvation" at Fort Berthold Agency.[35] Reports from Fort Totten described the Devils Lake Sioux as being in poor condition, and Terry hurriedly directed that the army provide provisions for the natives from the fort's amply provisioned storehouses.[36] When the Indians could not obtain food, they raided nearby forts or settlements and stole cattle, horses, and mules. This was a common occurrence, and Terry constantly received complaints.[37]

Many times the soldiers were unable to go after Indians who had made cattle raids because they were engaged in constructing their own shelters. The labor force that was utilized in building new forts in the department was made up primarily of soldiers. Because the workers used the soft cottonwood that was readily available, the quarters did not last long and had to be rebuilt every few years.[38]

Other problems nagged Terry. On one occasion in 1867 he sought permission to pursue hostile Indians across the border into uninhabited areas of Canada. The general was concerned with the difficulty of protecting the Minnesota road when it passed within the proximity of the British Possessions. Terry's request was denied, and again he had to do his best with what he had.[39] The border problem was closely tied with that of illegal whiskey trade with the Indians. It was difficult to stop the trade, but Terry must have relished the predicament in which he found the traders when their steamer, the *Amelia Poe* with about 150 barrels of whiskey on board, sank in the Milk River in northern Montana. He sent a detachment of soldiers to prevent the lawbreakers from salvaging the contraband intended for the Indian trade.[40]

White woodcutters were also a frequent bother. Many times they would cross the Missouri River to the west side to chop wood to sell to the river steamer captains. The Indians resented the whites' taking their wood, which they needed for their own use. But the whites felt the wood was there for the taking and refused to stop cutting it. The result was usually an Indian ambush of the whites and a call for help to the military officials in the area. Terry had little sympathy for these people and usually ordered the logs turned over to the Indians.[41]

Most of the time the general required the army to escort civilians to white settlements. The Black Hills was the exception, for here he ordered the military to forbid white entrance into these Sioux lands. This region was desirable to whites because of rumors that rich farmland, abundant wood, and precious metals could be found in the area. Whenever Terry learned of proposed expeditions by whites into the hills, he wrote Sherman asking permission to stop these encroachers. The general was concerned that the Indians not be excited by such a move and was pleased to receive approval from the divisional commander. Terry wrote to Governor Andrew J. Faulk in Yankton warning that these undertakings were unauthorized and that no military protection was available for the adventurers.[42]

One problem that particularly frustrated Terry was how to determine the validity of reports of Indian depredations. Rumors constantly circulated throughout the department. In 1867 Terry received false reports of massacres at Forts Rice and Buford. Casual remarks were taken and exaggerated until few knew the truth of the matter. Merchants spread some massacre stories so that people would be afraid to use certain routes to Montana and thus hurt the business of one town to the betterment of their village on another route. Many frontier communities fell into the practice of fabricating stories of massacres in order to get the military to call for volunteer units from the threatened community. In this way miners could tide themselves over the winter with militia salaries gained at the expense of the federal government.[43]

Such was the case in Montana in 1867. Governor Green C. Smith was in Washington on business, and he left territorial affairs in the hands of the acting governor, Thomas F. Meagher. During the spring there was the usual Indian scare, and Meagher sought permission from General Grant to call out the volunteers to protect the citizens of Montana. During the past two summers there had been similar Indian scares, and the governor or acting governor had called up the volunteers, only to find that no real war existed. Much more disappointing to them was the fact that the government refused to pay the expenses the volunteers incurred.[44]

In 1867 the same pattern emerged. This time Meagher did not wait for Grant's reply before he mustered the volunteers into the service of the United States. Terry had planned a visit to Montana in order to check on the defensive arrangements that had been made for the farmers and ranchers of the Gallatin Valley, and he also investigated the Indian scare. He arrived in early August and immediately arranged to meet with Smith, who had returned from the East. From the governor he learned of the unfortunate death of Meagher, who had drowned at Fort Benton during the night of July 1 when he accidently fell from the deck of a steamer.[45] Terry met with Smith in Helena on August 4 and learned that about six hundred volunteers were still in the field. The general inquired among some of the leading citizens of Helena and got a mixed reaction as to whether there was a need for the volunteers in the first place. Terry concluded that Indians had not been encountered and that there had been no need to call out the six hundred.[46]

As Terry returned to Fort Snelling from his visit in Montana, he must have reflected over his first two and a half years in the Department of Dakota. They had been challenging and productive years in which he had traveled extensively throughout the northern plains and had organized the construction of seven new forts. The role of the army as guardian of the routes westward and of protector of civilization on the northern plains had been the central issue in the Department of Dakota during its first years of existence. Terry and his sturdy soldiers had given a good account of themselves, but the important question of establishing peace with the Sioux remained.

NOTES

1. *United States Statutes at Large* (Boston: Little, Brown, 1869), 14: 24.

2. Herbert S. Schell, *History of South Dakota* (Lincoln: University of Nebraska Press, 1968), pp. 5-14; Elwyn B. Robinson, *History of North Dakota* (Lincoln: University of Nebraska Press, 1966), pp. 6-11.

3. Robert H. Lowie, *Indians of the Plains* (New York: McGraw-Hill, 1954), pp. 184-193; see also Frank Gilbert Roe, *The Indian and the Horse* (Norman: University of Oklahoma Press, 1955).

4. For the Sioux, see Royal B. Hassrick, *The Sioux: Life and Customs of a Warrior Society* (Norman: University of Oklahoma Press, 1964), pp. 3-31, 61-75.

5. For Dakota settlement, see Schell, *History of South Dakota,* pp. 65-84; United States Department of Commerce, *Historical Statistics of the United States: Colonial Times to 1957, A Statistical Abstract Supplement* (Washington, D.C.: Government Printing Office, 1960), pp. 12-13.

6. William S. Greever, *The Bonanza West: The Story of the Western Mining Rushes, 1848-1900* (Norman: University of Oklahoma Press, 1963), pp. 215-220.

7. For northern plains military activity in the early 1860s, see Robert M. Utley, *Frontiersmen in Blue: The United States Army and the Indian, 1848-1865* (New York: Macmillan Co., 1967), pp. 261-280; Robert H. Jones, *The Civil War in the Northwest* (Norman: University of Oklahoma Press, 1960), pp. 57-96; Richard N. Ellis, *General Pope and U.S. Indian Policy* (Albuquerque: University of New Mexico Press, 1970), pp. 52-105.

8. Russell F. Weigley, *History of the United States Army* (New York: Macmillan, 1967), pp. 262-263, 266-267; William A. Ganoe, *The History of the United States Army* (New York: D. Appleton, 1924), pp. 307-308, 312.

9. Stanton to Terry, August 18, 1866, Terry Papers, Yale University Library.

10. Alfred Terry to Adrian Terry, September 8, 1866, Terry Papers.

11. Terry to Bvt. Brig. Gen. W. A. Nichols, HQ Mil. Div. of Missouri, November 8, 1866, LS, Records of the U.S. Army Continental Commands, RG393, NA.

12. Ibid.; Terry to Sherman, November 6, 1866, LS, Records of the U.S. Army Continental Commands.

13. Ibid.

14. Ellis, *General Pope,* pp. 37-38, 52-105.

15. Charles J. Kappler, ed., *Indian Affairs: Laws and Treaties* (1904; reprint ed., New York: Interland Publishing, 1973), pp. 896-908; Howard

R. Lamar, *Dakota Territory, 1861-1889* (New Haven: Yale University Press, 1956), p. 105.

16. Annual Report of Sherman, November 5, 1866, LR, AGO, RG94, NA, pp. 532, 619; William T. Sherman, *The Sherman Letters: Correspondence Between General Sherman and Senator Sherman from 1837 to 1891* (1894; reprint ed., Da Capo Press, 1969), pp. 321-322.

17. *Annual Report of Gov. Newton Edmunds, Dakota Territory,* October 14, 1865, H. Ex. Doc. 1, 39 Cong., 1 sess., Serial 1248, p. 175.

18. Annual Report of Sherman, November 5, 1866.

19. Ibid.

20. George H. Phillips, "The Indian Ring in Dakota Territory, 1870-1890," *South Dakota History* 2 (Fall 1972): 345-367; Lamar, *Dakota Territory,* pp. 100, 103, 106.

21. Annual Report of Sherman, November 5, 1866; W. Turrentine Jackson, *Wagon Roads West: A Study of Federal Road Surveys and Construction in the Trans-Mississippi West, 1846-1869* (New Haven: Yale University Press, 1965), pp. 281-282, 287, 291.

22. Jackson, *Wagon Roads West,* pp. 285, 301-302.

23. Ibid., p. 304. Maintenance of each soldier on the plains, including pay, subsistence, and transportation, cost the government a thousand dollars annually.

24. Annual Report of Terry, September 27, 1867, and ibid., October 5, 1868, LS, AGO.

25. Terry to Gen. J. H. Rawlins, Chief of Staff, December 15, 1866, LS, Records of the U.S. Army Continental Commands.

26. Ibid.

27. Ibid.; Francis Paul Prucha, *A Guide to the Military Posts of the United States, 1789-1895* (Madison: State Historical Society of Wisconsin, 1964), p. 113.

28. Terry to Rawlins, December 15, 1866.

29. Hazen to Bvt. Maj. H. G. Sitchfield, AAAG, Department of Platte, October 16, 1866, LR, Records of the U.S. Army Continental Command.

30. Terry to Reeve, April 6, 1867, and to Bvt. Col. S. B. Hayman, May 24, 1867, LR, Records of the U.S. Army Continental Commands.

31. Joseph M. Hanson, *The Conquest of the Missouri, Being the Story of the Life and Exploits of Captain Grant Marsh* (Chicago: A. C. McClurg, 1909), pp. 97-98.

32. Ibid.

33. Terry to Bvt. Brig. Gen. Nichols, March 8, 1867, and to Nichols, April 20, 1867, LS, Records of the U.S. Army Continental Commands; Lucile M. Kane, trans. and ed., *Military Life in Dakota: The Journal of*

Philippe Regis de Trobriand (St. Paul: Alvord Memorial Commission, 1951), p. 138.

34. Terry to Rawlins, Chief of Staff, November 12, 1866, LS, Records of the U.S. Army Continental Commands.

35. Kane, *Life in Dakota,* p. 231.

36. Terry to Bvt. Col. J. W. G. Whistler, Commanding Fort Totten, January 25, 1868, LS, Records of the U.S. Army Continental Commands; *Annual Report of Benj'n Thompson, U.S. Indian Agent, Lake Traverse Agency,* October 31, 1868, H. Ex. D. 1, 40 Cong., 3 sess., Serial 1366, pp. 654-655.

37. Annual Report of Terry, 1868; Captain Dickey, Ft. Buford, to Terry, September 10, 1868, LS, Records of the U.S. Army Continental Commands.

38. *Report of General Grant,* November 21, 1866, H. Ex. Doc. 1, 39 Cong., 2 sess., serial 1285, pp. 17-18.

39. Terry to Nichols, March 4, 1867, LS, Records of the U.S. Army Continental Commands.

40. Terry to Col. I. V. D. Reeve, September 3, 1868, LS, Records of the U.S. Army Continental Commands.

41. Terry to Nichols, July 31, 1868, LS, Records of the U.S. Army Continental Commands; Kane, *Life in Dakota,* pp. 310-311, 336.

42. Terry to Nichols, May 20, 1867, and to Faulk, June 1, 1867, LS, Records of the U.S. Army Continental Commands.

43. Annual Report of Sherman, 1867; J. B. Bassett to Terry, August 17, 1868, and Terry to Nichols, May 13, 1867; LS, Records of the U.S. Army Continental Commands. See also Robert G. Athearn, "The Fort Buford Massacre," *Mississippi Valley Historical Review* 41 (March 1955): 675-685.

44. Robert G. Athearn, *Thomas Francis Meagher: An Irish Revolutionary in America* (Boulder: University of Colorado Press, 1949), pp. 156-167; James L. Thane, Jr., "The Montana Indian War of 1867," *Arizona and the West* 10 (Summer 1968): 154; Annual Report of Terry, September 27, 1867, LS, AGO. The narrative of the 1867 Montana war is taken from Terry's report except where otherwise noted.

45. Proclamation of Governor Smith, July 3, 1867, Territorial Papers of Montana, LS, Records of the Department of State, RG59, NA.

46. Terry to Nichols, July 23, 1868, September 27, 1867, LS, Records of the U.S. Army Continental Commands.

3 General Terry's Indian Apprenticeship

In 1867 General Terry was still a newcomer to the frontier in terms of his knowledge of the Sioux. He had served as commander of the Department of Dakota for only a short time, and he had little firsthand knowledge of the Indian problem he faced in his department. The general had traveled throughout much of his department, visiting forts and talking with soldiers, merchants, politicians, and other settlers, but he had not talked with any Indians. Much of his job of gaining peace with the Sioux was tied in with the mood of the Indians who lived within his department. Terry needed to learn about these natives, who were a key to his success or failure as a department commander on the northern plains.

Terry was aware of prior government treaties with the Indians of the plains. He could date his knowledge back to midcentury shortly after gold had been discovered in California. In 1851 commissioners had met with Indians at Fort Laramie and had signed a treaty that opened a vast roadway through the central plains to the Pacific. Indians agreed to keep out of this area except to hunt, and the whites obtained rights to construct roads, forts, and trading posts there. The Senate ratified the treaty, which provided a payment to the Indians of fifty thousand dollars annually for ten years. New gold discoveries in the late 1850s in Colorado, however, made a new treaty necessary, because that area still belonged to the Indians. In 1861 at Fort Wise in Kansas, the Indians surrendered more land to the whites in return for annual payments of thirty thousand dollars over the next fifteen years, which they would use for houses, agricultural tools, stock animals, mills, and skilled technicians to teach them modern ways of subsisting.[1]

The races had lived in relative peace until the early 1860s when isolated cases of Indian-white conflict occurred. When the government failed to meet its promises, southern plains Indians left their reservations. In retaliation John M. Chivington, a Methodist minister and colonel of Colorado volunteers, with seven hundred men attacked a peaceful Cheyenne village and brutally killed about two hundred Indian men, women, and children. A few years later in 1867, General Winfield Scott Hancock took a large force and surprised a Cheyenne village, burning three hundred lodges belonging to these unfortunate natives.[2] The government did not fare as well in the northern plains where Red Cloud and his Oglala Sioux successfully drove the army out of three forts along the Powder River that had been established to protect travelers on their way through Wyoming to the Montana mining towns.[3]

Thus the plains were in turmoil in early 1867. The southern Indians were still suffering from the injustices of the Chivington massacre and Hancock's foray, and the northern Indians sought to keep their lands in the Powder River valley. There seemed no place for the Indians to go where they would be free from the miners, soldiers, and peace commissioners.

Congress had been concerned about the declining state of affairs with the Indians when it sought a peaceful solution by creating in March 1865 the Joint Special Committee on the Condition of the Indian Tribes. The committee, made up of three senators and four congressmen, divided into three groups in order to visit and to study conditions on the northern and southern plains and on the Pacific slope. In January 1867, the committee submitted its report of nearly five hundred pages of testimony taken from frontiersmen and Indians. The document revealed a sad story of poverty, disease, and a declining population among the Indians brought on by fraudulent agency practices and military aggression on the part of the whites.[4]

In order to correct these abuses, Congress took a further step toward better relations with the natives when it passed a bill on July 20, 1867, creating the Indian Peace Commission. The legislation stipulated that President Andrew Johnson appoint three military men, and the law itself named the four civilians that would comprise the group.[5]

Terry was a logical choice to serve on the commission. He was commander of the department where many of the troublesome Indians lived, and he was familiar with the military situation in the northern plains. His background as a lawyer and his reputation as a cooperative and fair-minded individual supported his appointment. Another presidential choice was General William T. Sherman, a Civil War veteran and commander of the Division of the Missouri. Sherman held a top policy-making position on

Indian affairs and advocated peace with the natives, even if it meant the use of military force to obtain it. The general was disappointed by his appointment to the commission because he felt he would be extremely busy trying to keep peace on the frontier while the commissioners did their work. Terry's other military associate on the commission was Major General William S. Harney, commander of the Department of the Platte and a veteran of the 1862 Sioux war in Minnesota. Harney, an experienced Indian negotiator, also took the responsibility of managing the details of travel and defense for the commission.[6]

Nathaniel G. Taylor was one of the civilians named to the commission. He had served as President Johnson's commissioner of Indian affairs and was a warm friend of the Indians. Humanitarians would applaud the choice of this graduate of Princeton and former Methodist minister. Senator John B. Henderson of Missouri, the author of the bill that created the commission and chairman of the Senate Committee on Indian Affairs, was another fine choice for the civilian group. He became the commission spokesman to the Indians and proved to be an able representative of the government. Henderson's counterpart in the House was William Windom, but he refused the appointment and recommended Samuel F. Tappan in his place. Tappan was a former abolitionist and free-soiler in Kansas, and Indian reform would prove to be another outlet for this Christian crusader. A former lieutenant colonel of the Second Colorado Cavalry and a loyal follower of Taylor, he was a quiet person who seldom entered into the commission discussions, instead whittling on a stick or contemplating the ground. John B. Sanborn, a Minnesota lawyer and former major general of volunteers during the Civil War, rounded out the civilian element of the commission. He had gained recognition for his work as a member of the treaty makers on the Little Arkansas in 1865. These men generally supported a peace policy with the Indians and opposed the use of force against them unless absolutely necessary.[7]

This was an excellent array of talent on the peace commission, and westerners and easterners alike wished them success in gaining peace and a fair settlement with the Indians. With the combined skills of the statesman, the soldier, the lawyer, the frontiersman, and the veteran Indian negotiator, the commission expected to produce a final solution to the Indian problem for those who lived east of the Rocky Mountains. They had a rich variety of experience and skill in their group and a fifty thousand dollar budget with which to carry out their plans.

The commissioners held their initial meeting in St. Louis in early
August in spite of Terry's absence due to department business. By way
of organization they elected two civilians, Taylor and Sanborn, as president and as vice-president, respectively. Taylor appointed A. S. H. White,
a Department of Interior clerk, as secretary.[8] The commissioners discussed
their travel agenda and decided to send messengers to the various Indian
camps to notify them of important meetings to be held at Fort Laramie,
Wyoming, on September 13 and at Fort Larned, Kansas, on October 13.
The commissioners made it known that they expected the Indians to
attend the closest meeting and promised presents for those who participated.[9]

After hiring a photographer and taking care of other details, the commissioners prepared for their journey on board the steamer *St. John* westward on the Missouri River to Fort Leavenworth, Kansas. Here on August
13 the commissioners heard testimonies from Father Pierre J. de Smet,
a Jesuit missionary to the Indians, General William S. Hancock, and Kansas
Governor Samuel J. Crawford. At the next day's meeting held at the
Planters House in Leavenworth, they gathered more testimony, this time
from Indian agents. Also they reached an agreement to allow additional
members of the press from the *Chicago Tribune* and the *Cincinnati Com-
mercial* to join the entourage at their own expense.[10]

From Leavenworth the commissioners made their way to Omaha on
August 16, where they interviewed General Christopher C. Augur, the
new commander of the Department of the Platte, Nebraska Governor
David Butler, and Indian superintendent Henry B. Denman. Moving north
along the Missouri River, they were met by Terry on August 25 near Fort
Sully, Dakota Territory. The general had missed some of the preliminary
sessions, but he had arrived in time to participate in the talks with the
Indian delegations.[11]

By August 31, the commissioners were ready to meet with a number
of Sioux tribes who were gathered near Fort Sully. With council tents
raised and Indians and agents gathered around the commissioners, the
great drama of the talks was about to begin. This was a scene that was to
be repeated time and again across the plains as the commissioners sought
to achieve three objectives: they hoped to make peace with the Indians
and to remove the causes of their militancy; they sought to ensure the
safety of the frontier settlements and to remove the warrior impediments
from the building of the transcontinental railroads; and they determined

to develop a plan for civilizing the Indians and thus ensure perpetual peace.[12]

Present at Fort Sully were members of six Sioux tribes: the Brulés, Blackfeet, Hunkpapas, Oglalas, Miniconjous, and Two Kettles. Most of the hostile Indians belonging to these tribes still were roaming the country to the west while their more peace-loving brethren met with the commissioners. Commissioner Sanborn opened the council. He told the assembled Indians that the commissioners were sent by the president of the United States to determine if the Indian lands were fertile enough to be made into a permanent reservation. Sanborn explained that he was pleased to see the Indians and was willing to hear anything that they might have to say.[13]

Several chiefs spoke from each tribe, with Long Mandan and Two Lance of the Two Kettle band touching on matters that concerned the Indians. They described how they had visited Washington to see the president and how he had made them chiefs. They cherished the papers that government officials had given them proclaiming them leaders of their people, and they still retained these crumpled documents after many years. More to the point, they expressed their desire to farm as the whites did and pleaded for implements with which to work the soil and whites to teach them how to farm. The government had promised provisions and farm implements to these Indians, but the natives had received little. All the chiefs seemed in agreement that they wanted to live in peace and be happy and prosperous like the whites.[14]

Burnt Face, a Sans Arc chief, summed up much of the Indian frustration when he described how he had sent messengers to the hostiles to persuade them to come and talk with the peace commissioners. They would not come, he reported, and he did not blame them. His fingernails were worn out from planting corn and digging up the ground, he explained. He had nothing else as he did not receive provisions from the whites. He was poor and needed help, but all the whites gave him was advice.[15]

The Shield, a Two Kettle chief, added that he thought the hostile Indians were the ones who would suffer, but "they are better off than I am." He believed the white men wanted to starve him to death. He described a scene he had heard about where Indian goods were sent in untied boxes, which resulted in the theft of half of the goods. He complained that the provisions that arrived safely at the reservation were distributed during hunting season and that the Indians had to return to the agency in order to receive their goods, thus disrupting the hunt. Since the grasshoppers had destroyed much of that year's crops, it was essential that the natives hunt to survive. The Shield also pointed out that Indian provisions were sent in the worst boats available, which sometimes sank halfway up the river, while boats carrying provisions for the soldiers at the forts never had these troubles. Above all, the Sioux chiefs demonstrated their poverty and their dependence on the whites.[16] Terry must have been struck by their helpless situation and concerned that the Indians receive their annuities as provided for in treaties.

When the Indians had finished their speeches, Senator Henderson made some concluding remarks. He pointed out that the buffalo and the Indian were dying out because the Indians relied upon the chase and not their own labor. He added that the natives claimed too much land, which only made them poor. "The white men who are happiest," he explained, "are the ones who have a small portion of land, and who cultivate it the best." The senator told the assemblage that if they cultivated the ground and raised corn, wheat, and barley, they could live as well as the white man. He promised the natives that the government would furnish them with plows and other farm implements and provide teachers for their children. He told them to learn to live like the white man, and to this end he would send them clothes like the whites wore. He explained that they would get no more paint for their faces and bodies and that the government would build sawmills and send men to build fences and houses. He promised to send cattle so that the Indians would always have more meat than they needed. All of this would be done, he pledged, if the natives would settle in the area around Fort Thompson and cultivate the soil. With these pronouncements the council ended.[17]

Terry had listened and had tried to understand the different points of view. It seemed clear to him that some of the agents were dishonest and that the Indians were in a hopeless situation as far as the enforcement of the treaties that they signed.

The commissioners had hoped to continue on to Fort Rice on the Missouri River in northern Dakota Territory, but they were forced to turn back at a point about twelve miles above the mouth of the Big Cheyenne River because of shallow water. On their return trip they met with Sioux at Fort Sully and Fort Thompson in central Dakota before they moved south to visit the Yankton Agency on the eastern bank of the Missouri River. Sanborn opened the proceedings of September 4 with an address to the gathered Yankton Sioux:

My friends: The six commissioners before you have been
sent by the Great Father to your country to see what is best
for you and to induce all the Indians who are now hostile to
come in and make peace. We also came up here to examine
the Country as to its adaptability to the purposes of agriculture. We have called at the various reservations and agencies
along the river. We are glad to learn that you are trying to
help yourselves and that you have been engaged in planting
corn. You have made good progress, considering the short
time you have been engaged in agriculture. You should use
every endeavor to bring up your children to use the hoe and to
cultivate the ground. A long time ago, you could all live by the
chase but now the game is disappearing and you are no longer
sure of subsistence. Before your children are as old as you are
all the game will have been destroyed. Our people desire to
help you, if you only will help yourselves.

In closing he invited comments by the Indian chiefs.[18]

Strike the Ree and Medicine Cow made several points in their speeches
that followed. One concerned the corruption of the agents and the system in general. They complained that so many promises had been broken.
They had no school and had not been paid for their lands. The chiefs explained that in the past, fifty Indian scouts had fought hostile Indians
and had not received any pay. Their biggest complaint, however, centered
around the agents who did not distribute all of the goods but kept some
in the warehouse. Agent Conger explained that seldom was the whole
tribe there for the issuance of goods at any one time, and thus it was
necessary to keep a small portion in reserve for the absentees. Medicine
Cow was suspicious that the Indians received no receipt for their goods
and wondered why the warehouse door was always locked. Other grievances centered around the agent's and agency farmer's habit of keeping
all the wagons and most of the cattle, while the Indians had none. It also
disturbed the chief that the agency farmer usually took the best land for
his own farm and sold the goods he harvested for a profit.[19]

Finally Medicine Cow got to the crux of the matter: "I do not think
your great father is a liar and a thief. I see the goods and the money. The
men he sends up here are the thieves. They steal."[20] This was a reference
to Dr. Walter A. Burleigh, a Dakota doctor, lawyer, Indian agent with the
Yankton Sioux, and territorial delegate from 1865 to 1869. He was an

opportunist who aimed to make or steal a fortune as quickly as he could. While an Indian agent he padded the payroll and practiced graft and nepotism. Burleigh's father-in-law, Andrew J. Faulk, served as the third governor of Dakota Territory from 1866 to 1869.[21] Terry knew these Dakota politicians and corresponded with them on official business from time to time.

White corruption was a concern for the Yankton chiefs, but the resultant poverty that the Indians suffered was their real fear. To add to the natives' burden were the grasshopper attacks that destroyed the crops they had planted that year. Strike the Ree had little food left. He begged that something be done for them before they all starved to death.[22]

Senator Henderson closed the council by showing his sympathy for the Indians over the destruction caused by the grasshoppers during the past year, but he strongly advised the Yankton to continue their efforts at farming. He encouraged them to make the young men farm rather than hunt. "You must not think that labor is degrading or dishonorable. That is not so," he stressed. "Among the whites, the man who works is the most honorable." The senator promised that next year the Indians would have a school where their children could learn to speak English. He encouraged them to wear clothing similar to white people and to "act like white people in every respect." He warned them to stop painting their faces, to abandon the tent, and to build houses.[23]

Terry, no doubt, was appalled by the poverty of the Indians and angered by the greedy actions of spoilsmen Indian agents. These were Indians of the Department of Dakota and thus his problem as well as that of the Interior Department in Washington.

During the following days the commissioners met with the Poncas, Santees, and others, who made the same complaints that Terry had come to expect.[24]

It was apparent to the commissioners that a second visit up the Missouri would be necessary to gain their objectives with these Indians. Meanwhile they moved south along the Missouri to Omaha, where the commissioners rested for a few days and met to discuss their progress. General Terry agreed to help the Indians of his department who suffered crop destruction as a result of the grasshopper invasion. On September 11, the commissioners discharged their steamer and made arrangements to proceed on the Union Pacific Railroad to North Platte, Nebraska.

At this Nebraska railroad junction, the commissioners became aware of recent troubles with the hostile Sioux and Cheyennes. They received reports of fighting near Fort Phil Kearny and Fort C. F. Smith on the Powder River Road in Wyoming and Montana. The commissioners also heard of Northern Cheyenne action near Plum Creek, Nebraska, where the Indians had wrecked a train and killed several people. Captain Frank North and his Pawnee scouts had come to the rescue, putting to chase the Cheyennes and killing fifteen and capturing two. During the council at North Platte, the Cheyenne chief, Turkey Leg, negotiated a trade: six captive white women and children for Turkey Leg's nephew and his wife, whom the Pawnee Scouts had seized.[25]

With news of the recent conflicts in their minds, the commissioners met with the Oglala Sioux and the Northern Cheyennes on September 19. After the usual preliminaries, Commissioner Taylor inquired as to the cause of the war between the Indians and the soldiers. Chief Spotted Tail, a friendly Sioux, was quick to point out that the forts along the Powder River Road and the railroad along the Smoky Hill River brought white men, who drove away the game that the Indians so desperately needed for subsistence. Other chiefs elaborated on this theme and at the same time asked for guns and powder with which to hunt. Because this was a long session, the commissioners decided to adjourn for the day and to continue the next morning. That night they considered their strategy for the next day, and a feeling of disagreement flared when Tappan supported Taylor's pacifist approach to the Indians while Terry moved to allow Sherman to present a more militant stand. Terry's motion passed as the commissioners decided on a tough policy with the general delivering the punch.[26]

The next day Sherman made it clear to the natives that the railroad along the Smoky Hill route would be built and that the Indians "must not interfere." The Cheyennes would be paid if the railroad disrupted their hunting. He also explained that the Powder River Road was used to supply Montana gold miners and that no white settlements other than the forts had been made along the road. He contended that the president "supposed that the Indians in that country had consented to this road," and, if not, that they would be reimbursed. Because the natives had asked for powder and ball and other supplies, Sherman allowed that only the peaceful bands would receive these. The others would not because of the killing and looting. They would have to continue to hunt with the bow and arrow until such time that their actions proved a peaceful countenance.[27]

After these comments, Sherman answered specific questions of the Indians and gave them advice. He stressed that whites worked hard for all

they had and that the Indians must abandon the hunt, work hard as farmers and stockmen, and adopt the ways of the whites. The general pointed
out that the Indians could not stop the white man's progress and that if
the natives persisted in troublemaking, the Great Father would hold back
the soldiers no longer but allow them to sweep the Indians "out of existence." He encouraged the Indians to pick out a suitable reservation in
Dakota before the whites took all the land. Sherman promised that the
United States would help in any way possible if peace was the desire of
the Indians. He closed by saying:

> This Commission is not a Peace Commission only. It is also
> a War Commission. The Great Father wishes us to be kind and
> liberal to the Indians of the plains, if they keep peace, but if
> they will not hear reason, but go to war, then he commands
> that these roads be made safe by a war, that will be different
> from any you have ever before had.[28]

Silence greeted the end of Sherman's militant speech. The chiefs smoked
their pipes, and then Chief Pawnee Killer left the lodge, put war paint on
his face, and rode away on his horse. Other chiefs followed until only the
friendly Brulés and Oglalas remained. The council was adjourned after the
civilian members of the commission prevailed upon Sherman to lighten
the sting of his message by agreeing to the distribution of guns, ammunition, camp equipment, and blankets. The commissioners promised that
they would return in November for a final settlement.[29]

Terry and his associates had not been successful in gaining their objectives in the northern plains. The hostile Sioux had not come in for the
councils, and the peaceful Indians had only proved that they were generally
not able to emulate the white man in his agricultural and civilized ways.
The Powder River Road question had not been settled nor had permanent
locations for reservations been established. Terry had learned a great deal
about the people who lived in Dakota. He learned of the poverty that the
peaceful Indians claimed and usually demonstrated. He had heard their
peaceful pronouncements and could only wonder about the so-called
hostiles to the west. He had learned also about certain whites who desired
wealth and power no matter what the cost to Indians and fellow whites.
Some agents appeared to be honest, but there was much evidence that
many were not and that their greed was taking a frightful toll on the
natives of Dakota.

The commissioners had not been able to make arrangements to meet the northern Sioux at Fort Laramie in September, so they prepared to move south. During this same time Sherman was called back to Washington. The journalists covering the commission were convinced that Sherman was censored for his outspoken and blunt statements to the Sioux at North Platte. Another explanation concerned persistent rumors that the president had offered Sherman the position of secretary of war but that the general had declined, preferring to remain in a subordinate position to Grant. The president appointed Major General Christopher C. Augur to take Sherman's place on the commission. The new general, who sported grey muttonchop whiskers and often had a cigar in his mouth, proved to be a rather ineffectual member, and the leadership of the military faction passed on to Terry in Sherman's absence.[30]

From Nebraska the commissioners moved south to parley with the Osages, Comanches, Kiowas, Arapahos, Cheyennes, and Apaches at Medicine Lodge Creek located in south central Kansas near the Indian Territory border. They held a number of meetings with approximately five thousand Indians in the latter part of October in which the commissioners pointed out that the natives had broken the peace treaty signed two years ago. The Indians countered by saying that the whites had broken the treaty by not sending the provisions they had promised. The natives explained that they feared the reservations and wanted to continue to live the free life that they enjoyed as long as the buffalo lasted. Then they would consider the alternative.[31]

Terry entered more and more into the questioning of the Indians at this time, uncovering fraud on the part of the Osage agent named Snow.[32] Terry also bettered his relationship with the press one evening when he called them out of their tents to view a spectacular meteor streaking across the sky.[33] The commissioners needed moments like this to ease the tension they lived under. Senator Henderson and General Harney quarreled on several occasions. Their concern centered on the absence of the Cheyennes who were in the midst of their four-day Medicine Arrow ceremony. Henderson, always in a hurry to get things done, called for drastic action to bring in the Cheyennes. But Harney, wise to Indian ways, was determined to wait out the delay rather than offend the Indians. When Henderson, in a fit of restlessness, proclaimed he was leaving for St. Louis, Harney lost his temper and threatened to have the senator arrested and held until the Cheyennes arrived.[34] Taylor usually stepped in at moments like this to restore order and determine the course of action, but the commissioner had returned to Washington on personal business. Terry smoked cigars, while Harney and Sanborn eased their tensions during the noontime meals by passing a whiskey bottle rather than squabble over the comings of the Cheyennes.[35]

Eventually the Indians appeared, and the commissioners gained a peace treaty from all the tribes at Medicine Lodge. According to the treaty the whites received the right to travel across the southern and central plains in peace and gained a promise for the protection of the railroad laborers in the area. The Indians settled for a reduced reservation, and the commissioners promised a resident Indian agent, schools, a physician, a blacksmith, and other props of the white man's civilization. This time they agreed to provide the natives twenty thousand dollars annually for twenty-five years, to be spent by the secretary of the interior for the benefit of the Indians.

After the signing of the treaty, the commissioners had the presents distributed, which included thirty wagon loads of provisions. Ammunition needed for the hunt was handed out, and Terry saw to it that revolvers purchased for the Indians but then in the possession of their agent, Colonel Jesse H. Leavenworth, were also delivered to the Indians. Westerners were not sure that the guns and ammunition were for the hunt, speculating that they would be used for warfare against white settlers.[36]

The commissioners completed their work on the southern plains with the successful conclusion of talks at Medicine Lodge. In Kansas they had gained a peace agreement with the Cheyennes and other troublesome southern plains Indians. It was up to the Senate to ratify the treaty and the House to appropriate the funds needed to carry out the annuity payments promised in the treaty. If Congress failed at this juncture, warfare, no doubt, would spread across the plains as it had in the past.

In the northern plains, however, the commissioners had reached a standstill in their negotiations. Although they had met with peaceful Indians, such as those under Spotted Tail, they had not talked with the hostile northern Sioux under Red Cloud and others. Even the peaceful Indians were reluctant to move from their lands to reservations in Dakota. The government policy of concentration seemed a long way off. Trouble persisted in the Powder River region, and the commissioners realized that they had much hard work ahead to solve that problem.

It had been over two months since Terry had joined the commissioners. He had gained a great deal of knowledge to go along with the frustration he must have felt. Now he could see the Indian question in a much broader context than he had in Dakota. He also had learned much about the art of Indian negotiating and bribery. One can only sense his concern with dishonest Indian agents and his desire to formulate a fair policy to provide and protect Indian treaty lands and to see to their subsistence until they gave up the hunt and practiced agriculture. As the commissioners got ready to return to the northern plains to negotiate with the Sioux, Terry prepared to take a more active part in the negotiations. His apprenticeship was over.

NOTES

1. Report of the Indian Peace Commissioners, January 7, 1868, from Report of the Commissioner of Indian Affairs, H. Ex. Doc. 1, 40 Cong., 3 sess., Serial 1366, pp. 491-493; Charles J. Kappler, ed. and comp., *Indian Affairs: Laws and Treaties* (1904; reprint ed., New York: Interland Publishing, 1972), pp. 588-596. For elaboration, see LeRoy R. Hafen and Francis M. Young, *Fort Laramie and the Pageant of the West, 1834-1890* (Glendale: Arthur H. Clark Co., 1938, pp. 177-196.

2. Kappler, *Indian Affairs*, pp. 492-495. For background see Stan Hoig, *The Sand Creek Massacre* (Norman: University of Oklahoma Press, 1961); Robert M. Utley, *Frontiersmen in Blue: The United States Army and the Indian, 1848-1865* (New York: Macmillan, 1967); Henry E. Fritz, *The Movement for Indian Assimilation, 1860-1890* (Philadelphia: University of Pennsylvania Press, 1963); Robert W. Mardock, "The Plains Frontier and the Indian Peace Policy, 1865-1880," *Nebraska History* 49 (Summer 1968): 187-201.

3. Report of the Indian Peace Commissioners, Serial 1366, p. 501. The best books on the Powder River Road trouble are James C. Olson, *Red Cloud and the Sioux Problem* (Lincoln: University of Nebraska Press, 1965), and Dee Brown, *Fort Phil Kearny: An American Saga* (New York: Putnam, 1962).

4. *Condition of the Indian Tribes,* S. Report 156, 39 Cong., 2 sess., Serial 1279.

5. *United States Statutes-at-Large* (Boston: Little, Brown, 1869), 15: 17-18.

6. Robert G. Athearn, *William Tecumseh Sherman and the Settlement of the West* (Norman: University of Oklahoma Press, 1956), pp. 171-173; Henry M. Stanley, "A British Journalist Reports the Medicine

Lodge Peace Councils of 1867," *Kansas Historical Quarterly* 33 (Autumn 1967): 253-254.

7. Robert Winston Mardock, *The Reformers and the American Indian* (Columbia: University of Missouri Press, 1971), pp. 25-26; Douglas C. Jones, *The Treaty of Medicine Lodge* (Norman: University of Oklahoma Press, 1966), pp. 81, 99, 208; Fritz, *Movement for Indian Assimilation,* pp. 48-49, 64.

8. Report of Indian Peace Commissioners, Serial 1366, pp. 486-487; Indian Peace Commission, Special File No. 3A, vol. 1, Records of the Office of the Secretary of the Interior, RG48, NA, p. 1; Athearn, *Sherman,* pp. 176-177. Sherman had nominated both men so that the military was in agreement with these selections.

9. Indian Peace Commission, vol. 1, p. 3; Report of Indian Peace Commissioners, Serial 1366, pp. 486-488; *Report of P. J. de Smet,* June 1, 1867, H. Ex. Doc. 1, 40 Cong., 2 sess., Serial 1326, pp. 241-242.

10. Report of Indian Peace Commission, p. 486.

11. Ibid., p. 488, vol. 1, pp. 10-14.

12. Ibid., vol. 1, pp. 20-26.

13. Ibid., p. 41.

14. Ibid., pp. 41-52.

15. Ibid.

16. Ibid.

17. Ibid., pp. 53, 57-58.

18. Ibid., p. 59.

19. Ibid., pp. 60-63.

20. Ibid., p. 63.

21. Howard Roberts Lamar, *Dakota Territory, 1861-1889: A Study of Frontier Politics* (New Haven: Yale University Press, 1956), pp. 109, 112; Langdon Sully, "The Indian Agent: A Study in Corruption and Avarice," *American West* 10 (March 1973): 4-9.

22. Indian Peace Commission, vol. 1, pp. 61, 63.

23. Ibid., pp. 68-69.

24. Ibid., pp. 70-81.

25. Donald F. Danker, ed., *Man of the Plains* (Lincoln: University of Nebraska Press, 1961), pp. 60-61; George B. Grinnell, *Two Great Scouts and Their Pawnee Battalion* (1928; reprint ed., Lincoln: University of Nebraska Press, 1973), pp. 146-147.

26. Indian Peace Commission, vol. 1, pp. 82-88.

27. Ibid., pp. 88-90.

28. Ibid., pp. 88-92.

29. Remi Nadeau, *Fort Laramie and the Sioux Indians* (Englewood

Cliffs, N.J.: Prentice Hall, 1967), pp. 240-242; George E. Hyde, *Spotted Tail's Folk: A History of the Brulé Sioux* (Norman: University of Oklahoma, 1961), pp. 122-125.

30. Athearn, *Sherman,* p. 183; Stanley, "A British Journalist," p. 261; Jones, *Medicine Lodge,* pp. 81, 100.

31. Indian Peace Commission, vol. 1, pp. 98-109.

32. Ibid., p. 110.

33. Jones, *Medicine Lodge,* p. 189.

34. Ibid., pp. 80, 141; Stanley, "A British Journalist," pp. 290-291.

35. Jones, *Medicine Lodge,* pp. 41, 208.

36. Indian Peace Commission, vol. 1, pp. 98-126; Donald J. Berthrong, *The Southern Cheyennes* (Norman: University of Oklahoma Press, 1963), pp. 290-298.

4 The Peace Commission of 1868

The year 1868 was notable in the decline of the Sioux, for this was the time when the peace commissioners made their final foray into Indian country to negotiate the treaty of Fort Laramie. That they successfully obtained the signatures of hostile and friendly natives in return for generous presents and promises of actions that would bring the trappings of the white man's civilization to the Indian agencies only deepened the gloom of those who cherished the old way of life among the Sioux. Terry and the other commissioners were well meaning when they forced the treaty on the Indians. To them it seemed a humanitarian settlement and the sharing of the benefits of Christian civilization. For the Sioux it was advisable to take the presents because the white man seemed determined on his course of action. For friendly Indians the treaty meant the confinement of reservation life and the rejection of their old way of existence. For the hostiles it meant harassment by the soldiers until they were forced to accept the lot of the friendlies.

The year 1868 was also memorable for Terry. It was a time when he clarified his thinking on the Sioux question and the course of Indian-white relations that he felt the government should follow. It was a time when he had the opportunity to help shape the course of events with his part in drawing up the treaty and his recommendations to the president on the conduct of federal policy as carried in the peace commission's final report.

The background to these events began in November and December 1867 when the commissioners once again made the grueling trip to the northern plains to negotiate with the Sioux. They maintained the same set of objectives that Congress had assigned to them in July: peace, safety for frontier settlers and railroad laborers, and a formula for civilizing the Indians, which included the establishment of permanent reservations.

The talks began at Fort Laramie and continued at North Platte with friendly natives, since the main body of the Sioux was not present. They heard from Spotted Tail at one talk when he advised the commissioners: "We want to live as our fathers have lived on the buffalo and the deer that we now find on our hunting grounds. We love to roam over the plains. We love our wigwams. We love to hunt. We do not want to live like the white man. The Indian cannot be a white man."[1] Red Cloud also sent word saying he would not make peace until the whites abandoned the forts on the Powder River Road. Thus the talks floundered again.[2]

This last outrage was more than some of the commissioners could take. Harney and Sanborn became quite angry and proposed a military expedition against Red Cloud and his hostiles. Terry estimated that it would take ten thousand infantry and ten thousand cavalry from the Department of Dakota, and Augur estimated the same number from the Department of the Platte to subdue the natives. Since a majority of the soldiers were still needed in Reconstruction duty in the South, they were not available for service in the West. The infuriated commissioners could only wait and hope to negotiate with the elusive Red Cloud at another time.[3]

It was now late in the year and time for the winter season. The commissioners realized that their chances of further fruitful negotiations during the harsh weather that lay ahead were negligible. They thus returned to the nation's capital to write up a report of their year's activities. By early January 1868, the commissioners had reached verbal agreement on the issues and had selected Henderson, Taylor, and Sherman to write the report. With Taylor doing most of the writing, they submitted the document to the full commission for its approval. By January 7 the commissioners signed the accepted report and forwarded it to President Johnson.[4]

The report was long and detailed. Appended to it was the journal containing the minutes of their meetings, a mass of evidence taken from Indians and whites in the councils, copies of treaties made with the Indians, and an accounting of monies received and disbursed by the commission. The report itself set forth the commission's objectives, a brief summary of the councils held with Indians, and the reasons and accounts for the various outbreaks made by the plains Indians during the 1860s, especially those of Chivington's attack on the Cheyennes and Red Cloud's war on the Powder River forts.[5]

Clearly the most significant part of the report was the last section, where the commission made its recommendations on how to achieve a lasting peace with the Indians. As exhibited by the report, Commissioners Taylor and Henderson had clearly won the day. They had set out to "conquer by kindness" and the report was a reflection of their determination.

The commissioners concluded that American efforts to render fair treatment to the Indians had failed. They characterized congressmen as learned on most issues except the Indian question. Although much legislation concerning the Indian had been well intentioned, it had proved "erroneous in fact or perverted in execution." Congress seemed interested only in Indian lands and not in the Indians themselves. The commissioners also found religious groups guilty of neglect of the Indians. While they collected and spent thousands of dollars for charitable efforts in Africa and Asia, "scarcely a dollar is expended or a thought bestowed on the civilization of Indians at our very door." Instead Americans took Indian lands by force or fraud and left the Indians paupers begging for government provisions.

The commissioners speculated as to why the Indians and whites could not live together in peace. They concluded that the various removal policies had been detrimental to Indian civilization and that had it not been for the "antipathy of race," and the difference of tribal customs and Indian languages, the two peoples could live as one. They believed that education and civilization, arm in arm, would do much to eradicate these differences and soften the blow of racism.

The report continued with a characterization of the Indian as a noble savage:

> He is the very embodiment of courage . . . and at times he seems insensible of fear. . . . When the contact came the Indian had to be removed. He always objected, and went with a sadder heart. His hunting grounds are as dear to him as is the home of his childhood to the civilized man. He too loves the streams and mountains of his youth; to be forced to leave them breaks those tender chords of the heart which vibrate to the softer sensibilities of human nature, and dries up the fountains of benevolence and kindly feeling, without which there is no civilization.[6]

The tone of the report, no doubt that of Taylor, must have been difficult for Terry and other military men of the commission to accept.

After lamenting the cruelty of Andrew Jackson's removal policy in the

1830s and noting the fact that many of the Indians east of the Rockies lived in an arid region unfit for cultivation, the commissioners made their recommendations to Congress. They stressed the need for the establishment of two Indian territories, each with a territorial governor who would be a man of "unquestioned integrity" and be paid a salary large enough so that he might remain honest. Schools, with required attendance, would be established where "barbarous dialects should be blotted out and the English language substituted." Congress would establish courts, perhaps military courts at first until civil courts could be established. The commissioners encouraged missionaries to work among the Indians in order to spread Christianity and punish polygamy. In an effort to break down tribal organization, they encouraged Indians to build permanent dwellings on homesteads that belonged to individual Indians. Agriculture would provide them with their subsistence in conjunction with government annuities, which would consist of domestic animals, agricultural and mechanical implements, and clothing. The commission recommended that money annuities, a means of corruption in the agency program, be abolished.

The two territories as envisaged by the commissioners were Indian Territory and the Great Sioux reservation. The first was bounded by Kansas on the north, Arkansas and Missouri on the east, Texas on the south, and the 100th or 101st meridian on the west. Here would live many of the tribes that Terry had negotiated with at Medicine Lodge, plus the Five Civilized Tribes, formerly of the southeast, and other tribes, with a total population estimated at 86,425. The northern reservation was to be bounded by the 46th parallel on the north, the Missouri River on the east, Nebraska on the south, and the 104th meridian on the west. Northern Indians including the Sioux, Cheyennes, Arapahos, Crows, and Piegans, for a total population of about 54,126, would live here. If this policy of concentration were accomplished, Kansas and Nebraska would be cleared of Indians, and American railroad laborers and settlers would be safe from Indian attacks.

The commissioners also sought to draw up a plan for civilizing the Indians. In an eleven-point program the commissioners called for a vast revamping of the government bureaucracy in dealing with the Indians. The key question centered around the transfer of the Indian Bureau to the War Department. Until 1849 the Indian Bureau had been under the War Department, but in that year the Department of Interior had been created, and Indian affairs were transferred to the new department. With the alleged and sometimes proven Indian agency corruption, there had been a strong movement in favor of transfer. The commissioners reached a compromise on this issue with their recommendation that Indian affairs be turned over to an independent bureau or department, with Congress determining its cabinet status. The commissioners reasoned that there were peaceable as well as hostile Indians in the West and thus neither solely the responsibility of the War or Interior department.

On the matter of Indian agents, they advised that Congress declare a time no later than February 1, 1869, as a date when all superintendents, agents, and special agents in the Indian service be vacated with the purpose of eliminating the unfit and untrustworthy personnel. Those who had proved themselves "competent and faithful" would then be re-appointed.

The commissioners recommended that territorial governors, who served as ex officio superintendents of Indian affairs within their territories, be relieved of the power to call out and equip territorial militia for the purpose of making war against the Indians. Several unfortunate incidents had already resulted from actions of this nature in Colorado and Montana by governors who perhaps had ulterior motives in stirring up an Indian war.[7]

With these recommendations the commissioners hoped to undo two hundred years of Indian history and perhaps achieve civilization as they knew it for the Indian in the next twenty-five years. It was an optimistic view and one that was better than alternative programs of annihilation or full absorption into white society. It did not seem to bother the commissioners that they had roundly criticized removal policies of the past and in the same breath had recommended removing the Indians to two large reservations in Indian Territory and Dakota. They now hailed this new concentration policy as the salvation of the Indian.[8]

Except for negotiations with the Navajos and Sioux, the commissioners had completed their task. To accomplish this they next met in Omaha on April 1, 1868. Present were Sanborn, Sherman, Harney, Terry, Tappan, and Augur, as well as invited guests Philip H. Sheridan, commander of the Missouri Division, Governor Andrew J. Faulk of Dakota Territory, and Father Pierre de Smet. Authorities called Sherman to Washington in the midst of the meetings, but he promised to rejoin the commissioners as soon as possible. Henderson and Taylor were detained in Washington at the time and were unable to attend these sessions. From Omaha the commissioners traveled westward across Nebraska to Fort Laramie.[9]

With them the commissioners carried a peace treaty that they desired to have the northern tribes sign. The commissioners wished to persuade the hostiles, particularly Red Cloud's and Sitting Bull's people, to sign it, as well as the friendlies, who would sign almost any treaty in return for a few presents.[10]

The treaty, which consisted of seventeen articles, in essence accomplished the commission's goals as set forth by Congress. Article I called for peace and for the punishment of those, white or Indian, who broke the peace. The commissioners also set up a Great Sioux Reservation, which would become the private domain of the Indians. Unauthorized whites would never be permitted "to pass over, settle upon, or reside in the territory." This Sioux reserve included roughly all of present-day South Dakota west of the Missouri River and included the Black Hills.[11]

Several of the articles set forth the formula for civilizing the Indians. The United States agreed to construct a number of buildings, including a warehouse, storeroom, agency building, residence for the physician, buildings for the carpenter, farmer, blacksmith, miller, and engineer, and a schoolhouse. A number of whites would live on the reservation, including a resident agent and schoolteacher. The commissioners set provisions for private ownership of land and compulsory education for all Indian children from ages six to sixteen years.[12]

In article XI the Indians gave up their rights to occupy permanently the lands outside their reservation and, although they retained the right to hunt outside the reservation, it was only for as long as the buffalo existed in numbers large enough to justify the chase. It would be very difficult to change any of the land agreements once the treaty was signed. According to article XII, at least three-fourths of all adult male Indians had to agree to make such a change. The Indians also agreed not to attack railroad workers or wagon trains or to carry off white women and children from the settlements. It was understood that this Treaty of 1868, once signed or ratified by both sides, would annul all other treaties that had been made between the two parties.[13]

To the Indians article XVI was extremely significant. It set off the land north of the North Platte River and east of the summits of the Bighorn Mountains as an unceded Indian territory. No whites were to pass through this area, and indeed the forts on the Powder River Road were to be abandoned. The president had ordered the closing of the forts in March, but it took several months to complete the task. Thus Red Cloud and his following had won a great victory over the whites, and his hunting lands would once again be free of the disrupting activities of the whites.[14] The western Montana towns would still be supplied, but since Union Pacific railroad construction had pushed farther west, it was actually more convenient to supply the miners by another route west of the unceded Indian territory.

The commissioners were pleased with the treaty document. If it were adhered to, peace would be restored, the Indians would accept civilization in the guise of a Jeffersonian yeoman farmer, and Kansas and Nebraska would be free of the Indians, who would be settled on two permanent reservations to the north and south of these central states. The trick was to corral the hostile Sioux and entice them with generous gifts to sign the treaty. Once they did, the major problem would become one of enforcement.

During April and early May, the commissioners met with the Brulé, but the hostile tribes of the Sioux were not present to negotiate.[15] Finally on May 9, the commissioners decided to subdivide into four groups. They sent Terry to Forts Randall, Sully, and Rice to provide subsistence for the Indians along the Missouri River and to treat with the Indians at these forts. Augur was to proceed to Fort Bridger to negotiate with the Snakes, Bannocks, and other Indians along the Union Pacific Railroad line in Utah. Sherman and Tappan were to proceed to New Mexico Territory to conclude a treaty with the Navajos, while Harney and Sanborn were to remain at Fort Laramie to conclude a treaty with the Northern Sioux. Once this was achieved, Harney and Sanborn were to join Terry to resolve treaties at Forts Sully and Rice.[16]

At Fort Laramie Harney and Sanborn had little success in luring the Northern Sioux to the treaty table. Red Cloud and the Oglalas would not budge until the soldiers abandoned the Powder River forts. After three months of waiting, Sanborn and Harney finally gave up on the coming of the hostiles and joined Terry at Fort Rice.[17]

Before they arrived, Terry had visited several forts on the Missouri, handing out provisions to the hungry natives. Indians gathered in great numbers at Fort Rice, and Terry issued them "sufficient provisions to keep them good natured." The general seemed lonely and shut out from the world. He disliked the wait and routine of camp life. In a letter to his sister Fanny, he complained of nothing to write about: "One might as well attempt to discourse on a pan of dish-water as to say anything about our life here." Fanny, no doubt, would have enjoyed reading descriptions of the Indian throngs at Fort Rice, but her brother seemed depressed by the futility of the whole affair.[18]

1. General Alfred H. Terry *(Courtesy Minnesota Historical Society)*

2. Peace Commissioners: Alfred Terry, William Harney, William Sherman, Unidentified Sioux Woman, Nathaniel Taylor, Samuel Tappan, and Christopher Augur (*Courtesy National Archives*)

3. Peace Commission of 1867-1868 in Session at Fort Laramie, Wyoming   *(Courtesy National Archives)*

4. Red Cloud, a Hostile Sioux Warrior *(Courtesy State Historical Society North Dakota)*

5. Major General William S. Hancock *(Courtesy Minnesota Historical Society)*

FORT SNELLING.

6. Fort Snelling, Minnesota (*Courtesy Minnesota Historical Society*)

7. Fort Stevenson, 1867-1868, Winter Quarters, de Trobriand Painting
(Courtesy State Historical Society North Dakota)

8. Spotted Tail, a Friendly Sioux *(Courtesy State Historical Society North Dakota)*

9. General George Crook *(Courtesy Minnesota Historical Society)*

10. Dakota Infantry *(Courtesy State Historical Society North Dakota)*

Upon the arrival of Harney and Sanborn at Fort Rice, the three commissioners were successful in treatying with a large number of the Sioux. Father de Smet and his companions had traveled for days to reach Sitting Bull's camp at the mouth of Powder River. After several talks the Jesuit was successful in persuading the Hunkpapa chief to send a delegation to Fort Rice to participate in the council. The leader of Sitting Bull's representatives was Gall, who was also known as The-Man-Who-Goes-in-the-Middle. He was a respected warrior who hated the whites and who later distinguished himself at the Battle of the Little Bighorn. He was accompanied by Bull Owl, Running Antelope, and others.[19] Sanborn explained the treaty terms, and he promised presents if the Indians would sign the treaty. The commissioner explained that if they refused to sign, the war that would follow would destroy most of the Indians and those who were left would lose all of their land.[20] The natives responded by citing some of their grievances against the whites. Bull Owl demanded that the whites remove their forts and steamboats from the Missouri River area so that the buffalo would return.[21] It became apparent that what the Indians really wanted were the presents that the runners had promised in order to entice the Indians to come to council. Gall was more precise when he demanded twenty kegs of powder and ball. The Indians signed the treaty on July 2, 1868, after which it took an additional day to distribute the presents.[22] The commissioners had gained success at Fort Rice by coaxing the hostiles to sign. Bribery had won the day, but maintaining the peace was a long-range program that depended on an understanding and fair play on the part of the whites.

Once again the commissioners made the long journey back to civilization and gathered at the Fremont House in Chicago. The atmosphere in which these meetings were held was less than convivial. The commissioners were weary from travel, and no doubt most of their initial crusading spirit had waned. No longer did Terry and his associates feel that they could solve the Indian problem to the benefit of all concerned. Disillusionment and frustration hung over the men as they conferred in Chicago. Some, like Sherman, had felt all along that the objectives of the commission had been out of reach.[23] Terry, of course, realized the folly of negotiating with friendly Indians while the hostiles roamed at will. He had learned that it was a game where the commissioners bribed the Indians to behave themselves while whites took more and more of the natives' land.

The commissioners were also concerned about the inactivity of Congress on the Indian question. It had taken about a year for it to ratify the Medicine Lodge treaty, and the Indians had not yet received annuities. They feared the same would be true for the northern plains Indians. The army had abandoned the Powder River forts in August, and the Sioux had destroyed them, but Red Cloud still had not signed the treaty. The Indians around Fort Rice were restless, and Colonel David S. Stanley reported an attack on the fort by hostiles.[24] The entire procedure must have been frustrating to Terry. He and the commissioners struggled to have the councils and negotiate the treaties, only to suffer a disinterested Congress and an Indian Department that seemed crooked and greedy. Terry felt he now understood the true situation, and he was ready to make his move in Chicago where the commissioners would draw up their final recommendations.

For these sessions, which began on October 7, Terry, Taylor, Sherman, Sanborn, Harney, and Tappan were present. Augur joined the group later, but the civilian element truly missed the services of Henderson, who was still in Washington detained by the impeachment proceedings and trial of President Johnson. Grant attended the sessions in Chicago, and while he did not formally participate in the meetings, his presence would certainly stimulate a more aggressive role by the military. These first meetings started out pleasantly enough with reports from the four groups who had visited the Indians. Sherman and Tappan reported on the treaty they had gained in New Mexico, and Augur did the same for his treaty with the Shoshonis and Bannocks. Harney and Sanborn had experienced no success at Fort Laramie, but when they had joined Terry at Fort Rice, the three had gained treaties with both hostile and peaceful Sioux. The commissioners drew together these documents and others and included them in their report to President Johnson.[25]

During their next meeting, Sanborn was the first to take the initiative. He recommended that the government protect and clothe all reservation Indians and that the military force the hostiles to give up their nomadic ways and remove to the reservations. Then Congress would appoint two governors who would be responsible to the head of Indian affairs. These recommendations were discussed, but no action was taken at this time.

Terry, the ex-lawyer, had listened and learned long enough and was now ready to give the military commissioners some direction. He followed with five resolutions that represented his solution to the Indian problem as he perceived it. He recommended that the government "cease to recognize the Indian tribes as domestic dependent nations" except when existing treaties made this impossible. He thought that it was foolish for the United States to treat the Sioux nation the same as it would France or Spain in terms of treaty making. In this connection Terry also recommended that the practice of making treaties with Indian tribes be abolished but that existing treaties be respected unless the Indians violated such treaties, at which time the guilty Indians would be dealt with without reference to such treaty. Thus the strength of the tribal system would be weakened to the point where each individual Indian, like all white Americans, would be held personally responsible to the laws of the United States.

Terry also recommended that plains Indians no longer be allowed to roam and hunt outside their reservations. For those who resisted, the military would force them back to the reservations. The general concluded his program by recommending that control of all Indian affairs be transferred to the War Department. His stance was quite different from the commissioners' earlier recommendation that Indian affairs be put under a separate Indian bureau or department. Terry's resolutions created much discussion, but no direct action was taken at this time. None of these ideas necessarily originated with Terry, but his resolutions did indicate that the military would be much more aggressive in making up this report than it had been in drawing up the January 1868 commission report.

The following day Commissioner Taylor presented the civilian side of the controversy. He opened by recommending a seven-point resolution that had as its cornerstone a separate Indian Department with cabinet status. He called for the retention of capable and honest Indian agents and superintendents who would receive adequate salaries. He asked for faithful observance of treaties and modification only with the concurrence of both parties. He encouraged Indians to obey all laws of the United States and induced them to abandon their tribal organization. He felt that the government should provide clothing, food, and teachers to instruct in "the arts of civilization." Taylor concluded that the government would protect the reservation Indians while the War Department would have jurisdiction over the hostiles. The commissioners voted on the resolution with only Taylor and Tappan in support and Terry, Sherman, Harney, Sanborn, and Augur in opposition.

The military element seemed ready to assert itself. They no doubt agreed with much of what Taylor had resolved but took particular exception to his first point, which called for a separate Indian Department with cabinet status. This solution did not seem the answer to the military contingent because the doors of corruption would remain open, and when the Indians in a desperate situation broke from their reservations, the soldiers would have to do the dirty work of forcing their return to the reservations. The Indian Department would get the spoils, and the military would get war and the harassment of humanitarians.

At this point Terry returned to his original five-point resolution. Taylor was in a quandary. Attention returned to the transfer question, and Taylor offered an amendment in opposition to Terry's motion to which he attached lengthy remarks. Adoption of Terry's motion, he insisted, would necessitate the maintenance of a large standing army, which would bring chronic war with accompanying expenses of from $50 million to $150 million annually. Only higher taxes could cover this immense cost. Taylor went to extremes when he explained:

> I object, because our policy towards the Indian tribes is peace, and the proposed transfer is tantamount in my judgment to perpetual war. Everybody knows that the presence of troops with the avowed purpose of regulating affairs by force, the sound of the bugle, the drum, the fife, the glitter of military insignia and regulation arms, arouse feelings of hostility and beget sentiments of resistance and war even in the most civilized communities. How much more intense and bitter are the feelings of hostility naturally engendered in the bosoms of the free, wild savages, barbarians, and semi-civilized Indians by the presence of soldiers who they know are sent to force them into subjection and keep them so? To their ears the sound of the drum, the fife and the bugle, the tramp of cavalry and the boom of the morning and evening gun are the infallible signs of oppression and war and the very presence of armed and uniformed soldiers in their haunts and hunting grounds provokes and inflames the profoundest feelings of hostility and hate.[26]

Taylor continued his argument by pointing out that military control of the Indians was "inhuman and unchristian" because it would destroy a whole race by demoralization and disease. Indian domestic morals, he believed, would decline, and female chastity would yield to bribery or fear. Shameless concubinage would result among these "miserable creatures." One had only to inspect the hundreds of syphilitic half-breeds who loafed around Fort Laramie or any of the posts along the Missouri River for evidence, he maintained.

The commissioner continued by explaining that if the government desired extermination as a policy, then military control was the answer, but if they sought peace, Christianity, and civilization, then the civilian arm of the government should and must control Indian destiny. He pressed the point when he maintained that the conduct of Indian affairs was "incompatible with the nature and objects of the military department. One does not send his son to West Point if he wishes him to be educated in agriculture, mechanics, or the ministry." Taylor tried to clinch his argument by explaining that the Indians opposed transfer. He described how he had visited with thousands of Indians and found none who were willing to have the military control their destiny.

To the relief of most of the assembled, Taylor concluded his remarks. He reiterated his support for a separate Indian department as the commission had recommended in July 1867. He could not understand why there was a change in feeling unless this was a power grab on the part of the military. He correctly predicted that the commissioners would support transfer, but he vowed to continue the fight against transfer in Congress.

The military had its side of the issue, which Terry, Sherman, Augur, and others supported. One could make the argument in terms of economy and agree that one agency of the government could enforce Indian policy better than two. Military leaders suggested that if the Interior Department could do the job, then the army could be withdrawn from the Indian country. On the other hand, if the military was needed to protect railroad construction and frontier settlements, army officers could also serve as Indian agents and thus save the expense of the civilian agencies.[27]

Efficiency was another concern of the military. Army control of Indian affairs would put an end to the corruption and graft found in the Interior Department. As the commissioners explained, an army officer had his military reputation and commission at stake and was subject to trial by court-martial for any misconduct in office. This possibility alone would provide the strongest possible security for honesty in Indian affairs. By comparison, the civilian agent was only a temporary officer of the government and could easily escape trial and punishment for misconduct.[28]

Other arguments for transfer came in the form of statements about concern for justice to the Indians. This approach sometimes got lost in the shadow of Sherman's and Sheridan's militant statements, but generally military leaders did not desire to fight Indians except as a last resort. Terry had experienced the frustrating aspects of the treaty system with the Indians. In his experience treaties had been concluded with generally friendly Indians. The next step in the travesty was for congressional approval of treaties and subsequent legislation and appropriations to enforce the treaties. When this came months and even years later, the civilian Indian agent sometimes succumbed to the temptations of fraud, theft, and greed. No wonder the military felt they could do a better job.[29]

In a vote that followed, Terry's motion to recommend transfer passed six to one with only Taylor voting against it. Now Terry pressed his advantage and won his other four points.[30] Thus the military faction of the peace commission, with Terry as its spokesman, had managed to pull together their solution to the Indian problem. They had recommended that the government cease to recognize Indian tribes as independent nations and that as a step toward possible United States citizenship, each Indian was to be held responsible to the laws of the country. The military was to return hostile Indians to their reservations and not allow them to roam and hunt. The treaty system was to be brought to an end because it proved in the eyes of the soldiers an unrealistic tool in the solution of Indian problems. Finally the military had recommended the transfer of Indian affairs from the Department of the Interior to the War Department as the government agency best suited to deal with the native Americans.

In their last meeting, on October 10, the commissioners dealt with money matters, heard several statements by agents, signed various treaties, and adjourned for the last time.[31]

Before the commissioners returned to the routine of their respective posts, they received news from Fort Laramie that Red Cloud and his warriors had signed the treaty. The deed was accomplished, but few were convinced that peace on the plains would last.[32]

Now Terry could reflect on his more than fifteen months of service with the commission. No doubt he had mixed feelings about this experience. He had learned much of the plains Indians. He had heard the Indians complain of fraud among the Indian agents, and he concluded that the civilian arm of the government was not doing its job to the best interest of the Indians or the United States. He noted the poverty among the friendly Indians and the haughtiness of the hostiles. He concluded that the military branch of the government could best project honesty and firmness into the Indian situation. Terry supported the idea that Indians must be forced to stay on their reservations. Only trouble, usually caused by whites, occurred when the Indians strayed. By the same token, whites must not be allowed on Indian reservations unless in an official capacity. The Indians must settle down to agriculture since the buffalo and other game were fast disappearing. To Terry the Treaty of 1868 held out great hope for the solution to the Indian problem if it could be properly enforced.

These were hard lessons to learn, but at the time they seemed the best for both Indians and whites. Terry's stand on the Indian question did not represent a power grab on the part of the military but rather an honest effort to come to grips with the situation and resolve it in a manner that would be best for all involved. In his opinion there seemed to be more of a humanitarian element in the army and more of a spoilsman atmosphere in the Interior Department.[33] Terry, the humanitarian, proved his mettle in the next several years by trying to provide for the Indians of his department and by protecting their lands from the whites as called for in the Treaty of 1868.

NOTES

1. Indian Peace Commission, Special File 3A, vol. 1, Records of the Office of the Secretary of the Interior, RG48, NA, pp. 140-142.

2. Ibid., pp. 127-140.

3. George E. Hyde, *Spotted Tail's Folk: A History of the Brulé Sioux* (Norman: University of Oklahoma Press, 1961), pp. 125-126.

4. For the authorship of the report, see Henry E. Fritz, *The Movement for Indian Assimilation, 1860-1890* (Philadelphia: University of Pennsylvania Press, 1963), p. 64; Douglas C. Jones, *The Treaty of Medicine Lodge: The Story of the Great Treaty Council as Told by Eyewitnesses* (Norman: University of Oklahoma Press, 1966), p. 193; Report of Indian Peace Commissions, January 7, 1868, H. Ex. Doc. 1, 40 Cong., 3 sess., Serial 1366, p. 491.

5. For the discussion of the commission's report to the president, see Report of Indian Peace Commissioners, pp. 486-509.

6. Ibid., p. 503.

7. Ibid., p. 509; Laurence F. Schmeckebier, *The Office of Indian Affairs: Its History, Activities, and Organization* (Baltimore: The Johns Hopkins Press, 1927), pp. 53-54; George W. Manypenny, *Our Indian Wards* (1880; reprint ed., New York: Da Capo Press, 1972), pp. 203-204.

68   PACIFYING THE PLAINS

8. Report of Indian Peace Commissioners, p. 510.

9. Indian Peace Commission, vol. 2, Records of the Secretary of Interior, pp. 20-51.

10. Hyde, *Spotted Tail's Folk,* pp. 126-127.

11. Charles J. Kappler, ed. and comp., *Indian Affairs: Laws and Treaties* (1904; reprint ed., New York: Interland Publishing Inc., 1972), p. 998.

12. Ibid., pp. 999-1001.

13. Ibid., pp. 1001-1002.

14. Ibid., pp. 1002-1003.

15. James C. Olson, *Red Cloud and the Sioux Problem* (Lincoln: University of Nebraska Press, 1965), p. 75; Remi Nadeau, *Fort Laramie and the Sioux Indians* (Englewood Cliffs, N.J.: Prentice-Hall, 1967), pp. 242-243.

16. Robert G. Athearn, *William Tecumseh Sherman and the Settlement of the West* (Norman: University of Oklahoma Press, 1956), pp. 199-200.

17. Indian Peace Commission, vol. 2, p. 100; Charles Griffin Coutant, *The History of Wyoming* (Laramie: Chaplin, Spafford and Mathison, 1899), pp. 599-605.

18. Alfred Terry to Fanny, June 13, 1868, Terry Papers, Yale University.

19. Hiram M. Chittenden, and Alfred T. Richardson, eds., *Life, Letters, and Travels of Father de Smet* (1905; reprint ed., Arno Press, 1969), p. 92; Albert Antrei, "Father Pierre Jean de Smet," *Montana, The Magazine of Western History* 13 (April 1963): 41-42.

20. Indian Peace Commission, vol. 2, pp. 121-124.

21. Stanley Vestal, *New Sources of Indian History, 1850-1891* (Norman: University of Oklahoma Press, 1934), pp. 219-230.

22. Indian Peace Commission, vol. 2, pp. 125-138; Chittenden, *Life, Letters,* p. 921.

23. Athearn, *Sherman,* pp. 171-173.

24. Annual Report of Secretary of War, November 8, 1868, LS, AGO, RG94, NA.

25. For the Peace Commission deliberations, see Indian Peace Commission, vol. 2, pp. 170-194.

26. Ibid., pp. 187-188.

27. *Abstracts of Reports, Military Division of Missouri, Commanded by Sherman, Annual Report Secretary of War,* November 20, 1868, H. Ex. Doc. 1, 40 Cong., 3 sess., Serial 1367, pp. ix-xviii.

28. Ibid.

29. Ibid.

30. Indian Peace Commission, vol. 2, pp. 170-197.

31. Ibid., pp. 194-197.

32. George E. Hyde, *Red Cloud's Folk: A History of the Oglala Sioux Indians* (Norman: University of Oklahoma Press, 1957), pp. 165-167; Olson, *Red Cloud*, pp. 76-82.

33. See Richard N. Ellis, "The Humanitarian Soldiers," *Journal of Arizona History* (Summer 1969): 53-66; Richard N. Ellis, "The Humanitarian Generals," *The Western Historical Quarterly* 3 (April 1972): 169-178.

5 Reservations and Railroads, 1869-1873

The late 1860s and early 1870s were significant years in the decline of the Teton Sioux. The peace commissioners of 1867 and 1868 had gained a paper peace with the Sioux, and the treaties had been signed and ratified. The natives, however, gave little indication that they actually understood the meaning of the agreements or that they would adhere to them. To the Indians the councils represented social occasions where they received presents and food. Few of the young warriors had signed the treaties, and fewer planned to abide by them.

White men took the treaties seriously and endeavored to carry out or enforce the articles of the agreements. Paramount to them was the concentration of the Indians on the Great Sioux Reservation as called for by the Treaty of 1868. This meant that the Sioux must settle along the Missouri River where they might be provisioned at a minimal cost. The task of establishing the Sioux on permanent reservations became the job of the civilian and military arms of the government during the early 1870s. If the whites were successful in enforcing the treaty, the Sioux would witness the end of their nomadic life, which had centered on the horse and buffalo.

A second major challenge for the Sioux in Dakota during this time concerned the construction of a railroad across the northern plains. The Northern Pacific had been chartered in 1864, and by 1869 construction crews in Minnesota were working hard to push the road into Dakota and Montana. Engineer and surveyor groups worked well ahead of the construction gangs to plot the course of the rails. The army provided escort service for these surveyors as they explored the terrain of northern Dakota and Montana in search of suitable routes for the trains. The Indians of the northern plains understood the disruptive effect the railroads would have in their hunting lands and threatened a determined stand against these men who menaced their way of life. The army was equally resolved to protect these railroad employees just as they had done for those whites who earlier had traveled along the Minnesota roads and Missouri River route to Montana.

General Terry did not command the Department of Dakota in the first years of the 1870s. He was replaced on May 18, 1869, and reported to his new assignment in Georgia. He was to be part of the Reconstruction army and served as commander in the Department of the South. His knowledge of law and his earlier experiences in Virginia shortly after the war would help him in dealing with another large minority group, the blacks.

While in the South Terry received a pleasant expression of his professional worth from his superiors. A vacancy occurred in the major general rank when George C. Meade died on November 6, 1872. President Grant was free to nominate anyone for the position, and he decided to pass up more senior brigadier generals like Irvin McDowell, Philip St. George Cooke, John Pope, and Oliver Howard in favor of Terry. General-in-chief of the Army Sherman agreed that Terry was the best man for the job, but appealed to the president that McDowell's reputation would be greatly damaged. Grant decided to adhere to the seniority practice and promoted McDowell. Had it been in time of war, the president conceded, he would have awarded the position to Terry.[1]

Terry's replacement in the Department of Dakota was Major General Winfield Scott Hancock, who had won wide recognition during the Civil War as one of the best corps commanders in the Army of the Potomac. After the war, the tall, handsome officer had commanded the Department of the Missouri, but he had performed poorly in the campaign he led against the Cheyennes in 1867. The next year he headed the Reconstruction effort in the Department of Texas, and the following year he moved to Dakota.[2]

It became his task to continue the work that Terry had started in establishing the reservation system and in forcing the Indians to remain at their agencies. Indeed President Grant had grappled with this very question and tried to put the whole Indian question in proper perspective in 1869 when he drew up his widely celebrated peace policy, a comprehensive plan that dealt with all phases of the problem. The president tried to draw from the experiences of the past and also to add bold, imaginative direction to his policy. The major thrust of the plan was to place all Indians on reservations where they might receive the benefits of the white man's civilization.[3]

The idea of Indian reservations certainly was not new, but Grant's means of implementing this idea were. Much criticism had been leveled at the corruption and inexperience of many previous Indian agents. The president wanted to obtain competent, upright, faithful, and moral people to serve the natives. Religious people, like Quakers, might best fill these positions. They could easily distribute food and supplies and also set up schools and churches. Who better to teach the ideas of American culture, citizenship, and Christianity than these dedicated missionaries, he thought.[4]

Grant and his advisers felt that it was paramount to gather the natives on reservations where they might be better served. Here they could learn agricultural techniques and crafts, as well as cultural and moral lessons. The president clearly indicated that Indians who continued to live the nomadic life of the hunter or who determined to make depredations and outrages on white frontier settlements would receive severe punishment. Put another way, civilians would teach the natives on the reservations, and the army would deal with those off the reservations. In the long run, "humanity and kindness would replace barbarity and cruelty."[5]

Theoretically Grant's policy made sense to many white Americans. It was a more humane and realistic course of action than the government's feed-them-in-the-winter and fight-them-in-the-summer approach. The government had tried a type of reservation system before, but Grant's policy was different. Previously the government had placed natives on small reservations, which were gradually surrounded by white settlers until the Indians were crowded out and forced to settle elsewhere. The new policy called for several large permanent reservations where the more civilized natives would mix with the less civilized ones and influence them toward progress and humanity.[6]

As a result of the 1868 treaty, Sherman had divided the Great Plains into two districts coinciding with the two large Indian reservations that had been established (map 4). Brigadier General William B. Hazen became superintendent in the southern plains and Brigadier General William S. Harney the superintendent in the Great Sioux Reservation in Dakota. The superintendent's main function was to oversee the feeding and handling of the Indians. He required that army officers be present when agents distributed annuities, and in this way an effort was made to eliminate corruption and to ensure the natives the supplies the commissioners had promised.[7]

The Teton Sioux were centered at five agencies, most of them located on the Missouri River. The northernmost agency was Grand River, where

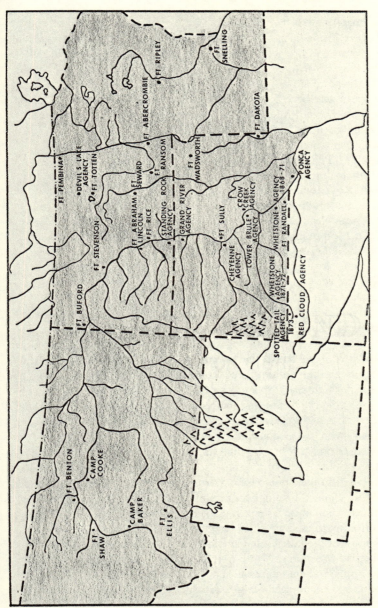

Map 4 THE DEPARTMENT OF DAKOTA, 1869-1873

approximately seven thousand Blackfeet, Yanktonais, Hunkpapas, and others were located. All of these natives seemed peaceful except the Hunkpapas. To the south was Cheyenne River Agency, where five thousand Miniconjous, Sans Arcs, and Two Kettles resided, but who longed for the days of the hunt and were reluctant to try their hand at farming. Farther to the south was located Crow Creek, whose twenty-four hundred Lower Yanktonais, Lower Brulés, and Two Kettles lived in peace and practiced limited agriculture.[8]

Two other tribes, the Brulés and the Oglalas, lived to the southwest on the North Platte River near Fort Laramie, Wyoming Territory. They liked it there, but the whites applied pressure on them to remove to the Missouri. Red Cloud and most of the Oglalas resisted the pressure but finally consented to move near the headwaters of the White River in northwestern Nebraska in 1873. Spotted Tail and the Brulés were persuaded in 1868 to migrate to Whetstone Agency north of Fort Randall on the Missouri. They stayed there until 1871 when they moved two hundred miles to the west along the White River. They remained there one year and then moved farther up that stream and located in northwestern Nebraska near the Oglalas in 1873.[9]

General Hancock's job was to station officers at the agencies and one or two companies of soldiers nearby to protect the whites who worked there. He was also responsible for supervising the distribution of annuities. This was part of the policy that maintained the civilians in power on the reservations and the military in control when Indians left the agencies.[10]

The major military problem centered on the hostiles, the Indians who clung to the old life of hunting and roaming. These natives, most of them from the tribes of the Teton Sioux, were those who were dissatisfied with the Indians who had assumed treaty relations with the United States. They were bound together by their hatred of the whites and the white man's way of life. Most of the time the malcontents lived in bands under various chiefs in the Yellowstone, Powder, and Bighorn river valleys. Occasionally they joined together for ceremonies and to war on the Crows or the whites. When united, these Indians were under the influence of Sitting Bull, a Hunkpapa medicine man, who seemed to have great authority among most of the hostile elements. Periodically some of the hostiles returned to the Missouri or White river agencies to trade their fur skins for supplies, guns, and ammunition. They also collected their annuities from the agents and encouraged the peaceful Indians to stop farming and to

join the hostiles for the summer buffalo hunt.[11] These actions of the natives were frustrating to military and civilian officials, but no immediate
solution was in the offing.

There were other Indians in the Department of Dakota with whom
Terry and Hancock experienced more success in their civilizing efforts.
About two thousand Yankton Sioux and fewer than one thousand Poncas
lived in southeastern Dakota on reservations. They were peaceful natives
toward white Americans and even had served as scouts for the United
States in actions against their brethren. The Poncas were better farmers
than the less industrious Yanktons, but neither were very successful in
their agricultural pursuits. The soldiers at Fort Randall were available
to police the natives, but there was little trouble.[12]

In northeastern Dakota bands of the Sisseton and Wahpeton Sioux
lived at Lake Traverse and Devils Lake. The twenty-two hundred Indians
lived in peace and farmed as best they could. Under the system practiced
there, the Indians were paid in goods and supplies according to the work
they performed. Only the aged, infirm, and sick received food and clothing from the government without work on their part. This agrarian experi-
ment worked well, and the agents recommended that the system be spread
to other agencies. Four schools with 123 students were in operation, and
the agents reported that the parents seemed concerned that their children
receive a good education.[13]

The Arikaras, Gros Ventres, and Mandans lived in northwestern Dakota
and northeastern Montana and numbered twenty-two hundred. Fort
Berthold Agency served them, but these Indians had a difficult existence.
A short growing season and periodic invasions by thousands of grasshoppers thwarted their efforts at farming. The commissioner of Indian
affairs recommended that they be moved to Indian Territory in the
southern plains where their farming might be more successful. The soldiers
of the area described the natives as "good Indians," who had served as
scouts with the army on several military expeditions against the Sioux.[14]

A number of Indians lived in Montana, but the most numerous were
the Blackfeet, Bloods, and Piegans who lived at an agency on the Teton
River in northwestern Montana. These seventy-five hundred natives did
not farm but subsisted on the game they could kill and government provisions they could collect. They were not peaceful and harassed the
whites of western Montana until about 1870.

North of the Blackfeet on the Milk River lived a mixed collection of about sixty-five hundred Gros Ventres, Assiniboines, River Crows, Sioux, Northern Cheyennes, and Arapahos. These natives were generally peaceful and lived off the chase and the government. Most of the Sioux at the Milk River Agency had participated in the Minnesota outbreak in 1862 and had fled to northern Montana. They had put their feuds with the Crows behind them and lived in peace with their former enemies. The Cheyennes and Arapahos spent much of their time south of the Yellowstone hunting and roaming with the hostiles. About three thousand Mountain Crows lived south of the Yellowstone River and completed the list of major Indian peoples in Montana.[15]

Estimating numbers of natives was a difficult task even for the most experienced, but knowledgeable Indian experts placed the number of Indians in Dakota at twenty-eight thousand, the number of friendly Indians in Montana at twenty-two thousand, and the number of hostiles at eight thousand. The hostiles' numbers decreased or increased dramatically depending on whether it was annuity time at the agencies or hunting time on the plains.[16]

The churchmen who administered to this vast congregation were drawn primarily from three religious groups: Methodist missionaries served as agents in the Montana agencies; Catholic priests labored among the Sioux and other tribes of northern Dakota at the Grand River and Devils Lake agencies; and Episcopalians worked with the Sioux of southern Dakota in the Missouri and White River agencies.[17] These missionaries in the northern plains, though inexperienced, had the advantage over the former agents of continuous employment at the agencies rather than being replaced every four years or sooner because of an administration change in Washington. Many of the missionaries did fine work among the Indians, especially Episcopal Bishop Henry B. Whipple, who worked with whites to develop fair Indian policies, and Jesuit Pierre J. de Smet who traveled among the hostiles and became a legend among the whites and Indians because of his unceasing efforts to help the natives and to bring peace to the Sioux.

Government officials found several problems with Grant's peace policy. Sometimes annuities were paid in cash, and unscrupulous frontier traders and agents could easily take advantage of this situation. It was best to pay annuities in goods and supplies, or the Indians might receive nothing.[18] The major problem with Grant's policy was the inability of officials to keep whites away from the agencies and to keep Indians on the reservations. One purpose of the reservation was to isolate the Indians from the white man's vices, but this was difficult to accomplish. Many Indians hated the reservations and desired to be left to enjoy the freedom of roaming and hunting on the plains. Article XI of the Treaty of 1868 granted the Sioux hunting rights off their reservations until the lack of game could no longer justify the chase. Until the buffalo were annihilated, Indians would not settle down to permanent homes, Christianity, farming, or the white man's education.[19]

Officials were also concerned about the question of sovereignty and law among the natives. Since America's inception, it had treated the Indians as sovereign nations, much like foreign states. Terry felt that having sixty-five Indian nations within the United States was a farce. Instead he realized that they must be viewed as wards of the government. The absence of the white man's law among the Indians was also felt to be a regrettable oversight. The first condition of life and property, argued Commissioner of Indian Affairs Edward P. Smith, was the protection of life and property through the administration of law. Indian crimes must be defined by United States law and made punishable before American courts.[20]

Officials in the Interior Department also criticized the army for using Indians as scouts and auxiliaries against the hostiles, a practice that tended to intensify and perpetuate intertribal feuds. Many raids by the Sioux on the Arikaras or Crows were the result of some recent service the friendly Indians had rendered for the whites. The army needed these allies, however, in their efforts to follow up Sioux raids in unfamiliar country.[21]

During one stretch of nine months in 1872-1873, the Sioux attacked Fort Abraham Lincoln, a new fort on the Missouri, on five occasions.[22] The army had its hands full maintaining and developing its fort system, protecting the civilian agents at the agencies, and supervising the annuity distributions. The military did not plan expeditions at this time to remove the hostiles forcibly to their reservations. Instead they counted on the annihilation of the buffalo and the westward surge of white settlers to force the hostiles to return to their agencies.[23]

In 1873 Red Cloud and his Oglala followers were persuaded to give up their Wyoming lands in return for a reservation near the headwaters of the White River in northwestern Nebraska. This was accomplished after Red Cloud and several chiefs visited Washington where they were assured they could still hunt in the North Platte area.[24] Thus progress was made in getting many natives to reservations assigned to them, but to the regret of most whites, the agricultural program was not working well. Indians were reluctant to farm, and the poor soil of Dakota did not help their enthusiasm for the project. The great dryness of the summers and intense cold of the winters thwarted the Indian desire to farm. Only with irrigation, concluded the secretary of the interior, could the Sioux of Dakota experience success in agriculture.[25]

In western Montana the army faced problems with the Blackfeet Indians as well as the Sioux. The Gallatin Valley was a favorite target area for the Indians to raid because there was scattered population and thus horses were there for the taking. In order to protect the mining town of Diamond City and the farmers of the Gallatin Valley, a new post, Camp Baker, was established in the area in 1869, and troops were moved from Camp Cooke to occupy it. Camp Cooke, which was located in a region where few Indians roamed and fewer white people lived, was abandoned the following year.[26]

In 1870 matters came to a head with the Blackfeet in Montana. In late 1869 marauding Indians had killed two white men near Fort Benton. In retaliation, four Indians were captured shortly afterward and executed, though only two of the dead natives were guilty of the murders. After this incident Indians attacked a government wagon train, but no one was killed. Still later, in a family dispute, William Clarke was killed by his Piegan brother-in-law. The Indians also stole a number of horses in the vicinity and sought refuge near the Yellowstone. There were other horse-stealing incidents in the area, and it became clear that the whites expected an end to these activities. They were frightened and demanded action by the military.[27]

Hancock was ready to take the offensive when four companies of the Second Cavalry were transferred to Fort Ellis in the summer of 1869. This was the first time cavalry had been available for use in the Department of Dakota. Hancock planned a winter campaign to punish the Piegans who had caused trouble for the previous three years but who were always able to escape across the border into Canada out of the reach of United States soldiers.

The cavalry left Fort Ellis on January 6 under the command of Major Eugene M. Baker. At Fort Shaw they added a mounted company of infantry and another infantry company to guard the supply train. From there they marched north to the Marias River, and on the morning of January 23, they attacked a Piegan village. Indians were killed in their tents or shot as they ran half-clothed from their dwellings to fight the soldiers. The surprise was complete, and the Piegans suffered terribly; of 173 killed, 120 were warriors and 53 were women and children. An additional 140 women and children were captured, but they had to be released because some of them were suffering from smallpox and presented a danger to the soldiers. The Piegans lost their pony herd of 314 and also their village of forty-four lodges, which the American troops destroyed. Baker returned to Fort Shaw on January 29, completing a six hundred mile march in the coldest of winter weather.[28]

The victory over the Piegans received a mixed reaction from the nation. Public officials were distressed that women and children had been killed in the attack and grieved that the Indians were so weakened from small-pox that it was difficult for them to resist the white soldiers. Eastern humanitarians compared this attack with that horrible defeat of the Cheyennes in 1864 called Chivington's massacre. Much public sentiment was against Baker's effort and the military treatment of the Indians.[29]

Colonel de Trobriand and General Hancock supported Baker's conduct of the expedition. The colonel was pleased that the Blackfeet had been taught a lesson and predicted little trouble with them in the future. He excused Baker for releasing the women and children captives in below-zero weather because of the smallpox and the lack of provisions with which to feed them. It was no small consolation to the Piegans that Congress rushed smallpox vaccine to them. Hancock, too, was sorry over the death of so many women and children. He explained that there were necessarily accidental killings in such a raid because soldiers fired their guns into the tents without knowledge of who was inside. The dim light of the early morning attack explained other deaths, and he also pointed out that Indian women were excellent fighters and many times fought beside the men. Hancock concluded that no women were killed except those inside the tents and used Father Imoda, a priest who had lived with the Piegans for seventeen years and knew all the Indians killed in the battle by name, as his source of information.[30]

Military men, government officials, and westerners applauded Baker's attack on the Piegan village as a victory of civilization over the barbarians who had ravaged the farmers of western Montana.[31] But easterners were just as sure that the attack was uncalled for, especially on the ill, innocent victims of the Baker pillage.

Terry must have read the Atlanta newspapers with heightened interest about his old post in Dakota. Had he been in command there, the Baker incident might not have taken place. The general was keenly interested in the transfer question, which was before the Congress at this time. Legislation in support of transfer had passed the House and needed only Senate and presidential approval to become law. Terry, ever cognizant of political maneuvering in Washington, might not have been so rash as to order the attack on the Piegans when legislation that he had so strongly supported in the peace commission discussions of 1868 was pending. That the attack was made and that the transfer bill suffered defeat in 1871 was something that Terry could not change.[32]

Once the Piegan question was solved, the military had to face the ever-present problem of hostiles in Montana. The Crows and Sioux seemed constantly at war with each other, and this took some of the pressure off the Montana army. But the hostiles raided into the Gallatin Valley in 1871, stealing hundreds of horses, while the whites were unable to stop them.[33] Some hope lay in the anticipated coming of the Northern Pacific Railroad and the settling effect it would eventually have on the Indians. Officials speculated that its route would pass through the heart of Sitting Bull's hostile country and cause great commotion among these natives. Earlier settlement patterns suggested that thousands of whites would come in the wake of the train and that the hostiles would be outnumbered and overwhelmed. The only course of action left for the natives would be to retreat to other wilderness areas if any were left or to settle peacefully on their reservations and to accept the stultifying and subservient life of agency Indians.

The Northern Pacific Railroad was chartered by Congress in 1864 and received a land grant of twenty sections per mile in states and forty sections per mile in the territories. It did not, however, obtain mileage loans from the government and later had financial difficulties. In 1866 General Montgomery C. Meigs, quartermaster general of the United States Army, promised Northern Pacific officials that the army would annually need transportation for fifteen hundred men and 15,330,000 pounds of military stores to supply an estimated fifteen military posts along the railroad line. Each fort would have an average force of 140 foot soldiers and 70 cavalry. This would be a sizable contract for the company, but it was not a sufficient basis to fund the construction.[34]

It did not become feasible to build the road until 1869, when Jay Cooke and Company agreed to fund the construction. In that year the company had other problems, mainly with the army. Few soldiers were available to escort the railroad surveyors because they were guarding the Minnesota road and Missouri waterway with the small number of soldiers in the department.[35]

Thus it was not until 1870 that construction on the railroad began in Minnesota. Even then the operation was slowed by labor troubles. Hancock had to send a company of infantry from Fort Ripley to Brainerd to suppress a riot. They arrested twelve troublemakers in early November, and the construction workers were free to push to the west.[36] By 1873, the Northern Pacific reached from St. Paul to Brainerd in the north, west to the town of Moorhead on the Red River, and to Bismarck, Dakota Territory, on the east bank of the Missouri.[37]

The role of the army in performing escort duty for the railroad surveyors in 1871, 1872, and 1873 was a major chapter in the history of the growing dominance of the Dakota army over the declining Sioux. Sherman had grown to appreciate the advantage the army would enjoy on the frontier by having the railroad pass through the area. The Northern Pacific would transport troops and stores rapidly across the plains; before, it took slow wagon trains drawn by oxen, which were dependent upon grass for food, months to reach the West. He further realized that the Indian problem could be extinguished when the trains crossed their hunting lands and brought permanent white settlers to scattered areas on the plains. With this realization and the added pressures put on the government by Jay Cooke and other wealthy businessmen, the army became quite cooperative in the matter of furnishing escorts for railroad engineers.[38]

The surveyors had to work well ahead of the construction gangs. While the laborers worked across Minnesota and eastern Dakota, the surveyors headed into western Dakota and Montana to select a suitable course for the Northern Pacific. Jay Cooke paved the way by writing Vice-President Schuyler Colfax for a personal favor, which involved directing Hancock to gather eight hundred to one thousand men in the department for escort duty for the Northern Pacific. Cooke maintained that if the surveying could be completed, he would put the road under contract and complete it to the Pacific Ocean by the middle of Grant's second term in 1875.[39]

Hancock was able to spare six companies of infantry for escort duty in 1871, although both he and Sherman agreed that the force should ideally include eight companies of cavalry, plus three or four infantry companies. The cavalry was simply not available, as Hancock explained to J. Gregory

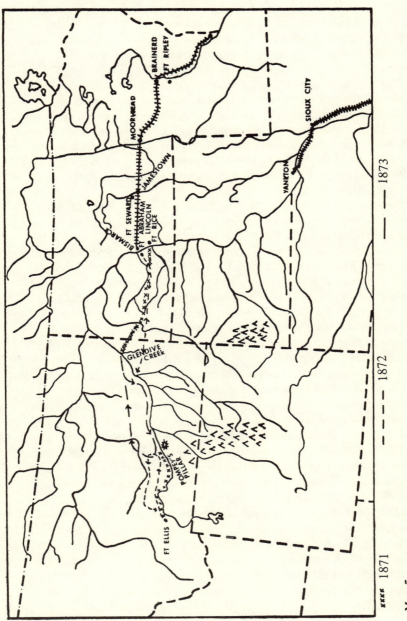

Map 5

THE MILITARY ESCORTS, 1871, 1872, and 1873

Smith, president of the Northern Pacific. Only four companies had been assigned to the department, and Smith could certainly understand Hancock's concern for the wise deployment of these troops.[40]

When final preparations were made in the Department of Dakota, Hancock found that he had available more than the promised six companies. He eventually sent out two detachments of men, one from Fort Rice and the other from Fort Ellis (map 5). The first left the Missouri River fort on September 9, 1871, with about 450 soldiers under the command of Major J. N. C. Whistler and included an additional 150 railroad and quartermaster employees. The expedition left with sixty days of provisions for the men and forage for the animals. They traveled through the Badlands of western Dakota where grass was sparse or burned off by the hostile Sioux who vowed to fight the railroad builders. The expedition continued its march into eastern Montana, stopping at Glendive Creek on the Yellowstone. Their return trip was made without incident.[41]

The second detachment left Fort Ellis in Montana on September 16, with Captain Edward Ball commanding two companies of the Second Cavalry and explored along the Yellowstone eastward for about 140 miles. They met no hostiles but found signs of Indians in many places. Because of an early snowfall the members of the expedition suffered terribly, and when they returned to Fort Ellis, twenty-three were reported frostbitten.[42] Their exploration was generally successful, and in addition they captured some illegal traders. They conducted other shorter escorts, but much remained to be accomplished during the next year.[43]

The Indians displayed greater hostility to the 1872 surveys, but the army was equally determined to complete these escorts. Hancock planned for two expeditions during the summer—one from Fort Rice under Colonel David Stanley and the other from Fort Ellis commanded by Major Baker (map 5). Stanley was to move his men eastward to the mouth of the Powder River about 240 miles distant, while Baker was to march westward to the Powder about 310 miles away. The two were to rendezvous and then return to their respective bases.[44]

Stanley left first on July 26 with a command consisting of about six hundred infantry and including two Gatling guns and one brass twelve-pound cannon. The hostiles, true to their word, harassed the troops on numerous occasions. Twice the men had to circle their 150 wagons, drive the cattle herd inside the circle for protection, and fight the attacking Sioux. Most of the time the hostiles simply followed the column and picked off stragglers. It was mainly the Hunkpapas who gave Stanley's troops so much concern. Chiefs Gall and Sitting Bull made their presence known to the soldiers and vowed to exterminate the entire force. The Hunkpapas fell significantly short of this goal, but they did kill two soldiers and Stanley's servant while he was out hunting.[45]

The results of the expedition were pleasing to the railroad engineers, but Colonel Stanley was disturbed. He was amazed that the Indians had so many guns and of such recent issue. The colonel implored Hancock to clamp down on the traders within the department who were selling Winchester rifles and ammunition to the Indians in unlimited quantities. Stanley personally ordered the commanding officers of posts and stations in his Middle District to take possession of all arms and ammunition that traders possessed and allow them to be sold only to friendly Indians in small quantities.[46]

Major Baker headed the second column of about four hundred foot and mounted soldiers that left Fort Ellis on July 27. They marched north of the Yellowstone River where they found Indians in large numbers. A combined force of about five hundred Sioux, Cheyennes, and Arapahos attacked them at Pryor's Fork 148 miles from Fort Ellis. In the lengthy battle that ensued, four soldiers were killed. It was reported that one Indian was killed and ten severely and perhaps mortally wounded. The expedition moved off toward the Powder River the next day, but when it reached Pompey's Pillar about twenty-four miles distant, the Northern Pacific engineers persuaded Baker that the command was not strong enough to fight the Indians and convinced him that a return to Fort Ellis would be a prudent move. Although they had failed to meet Stanley's column at the mouth of the Powder, Baker's command explored the Musselshell River valley on their return trip to Fort Ellis.[47]

As a result of the railroad surveys of 1872, military and Northern Pacific officials were convinced that the hostiles' vow to stop the railroad construction was no idle threat. Sheridan prepared to meet the Indian challenge by ordering additional troops to the Department of Dakota. Since Terry and Hancock had requested cavalry for several years and because they felt the need of the horse soldiers in the northern plains, Sheridan ordered the Seventh Cavalry from the Southeast to report to Dakota in the spring of 1873. Terry also was ordered back to the northern plains from his Reconstruction duties in Georgia. His orders were dated December 3, 1872, but he did not arrive in Dakota until May 9, 1873.[48]

Hancock had done an adequate job filling in for Terry during the four years from 1869 to 1872. He had continued Terry's program of guarding the Minnesota roads and the Missouri River route to the Montana settlements. He had provided military escorts for the railroad engineers in 1871 and 1872, but he had not had sufficient force in his department to defeat the hostiles. His only policy recommendation, that of removing the friendly Indians to the east bank of the Missouri River for their own protection from the hostiles, had not been implemented by Sheridan. Now he was removed to serve in the East, and Terry returned to his old spot in St. Paul.[49]

The general arrived in Dakota in time to help plan for the summer expedition of 1873, which would escort the railroad engineers once again (map 5). With the arrival of the Seventh Cavalry, Terry had sufficient strength to protect the Northern Pacific officials and to punish the hostiles if they were in the mood to fight. Again, Terry placed Colonel Stanley in overall command of the expedition, since it would originate from the Middle District, which he commanded. Two thousand men, including ten companies of the Seventh Cavalry under the command of Lieutenant Colonel George A. Custer, 275 wagons, and 2,321 animals made up the expedition. Three riverboats loaded with provisions also steamed to Glendive Creek on the Yellowstone, where a temporary supply camp was established.[50]

The column moved through western Dakota to the supply camp and from there along the north bank of the Yellowstone to Pompey's Pillar. They had several serious encounters with Sitting Bull's hostiles, but the army was strong enough to scatter the Indians and to continue the survey of the proposed railroad route. The abrasive Custer seemed to forget who was in command of the expedition, but Stanley, who had a drinking problem, sobered up long enough to exert his authority. From Pompey's Pillar they moved north to Musselshell River and eastward back to Glendive Creek. The expedition returned to Fort Rice by September 21, about three months after it had begun.[51]

The expedition of 1873 had been a success from the viewpoint of the Northern Pacific engineers. They had located a definite route from the mouth of the Heart River, where Bismarck was located, to the mouth of Glendive Creek on the Yellowstone, a distance of 205 miles. In conjunction with previous surveys and that of 1873, the engineers now had a continuous line surveyed from Lake Superior to Puget Sound. Soon the railroad would serve as a broad highway for settlers into the northern plains.[52]

For the military the expedition had been only a partial success. The hostiles had not stopped the surveys and indeed had fled from the powerful force. In addition, the soldiers had located several key spots where forts might be built in the future. The army, however, had desired a military victory over the hostiles, which might in turn impress upon the Indians how senseless it was to protest the coming of the railroad and perhaps might even induce them to return to their reservations permanently and give up their nomadic ways.[53]

Other problems continued to plague the department commander, even though the Northern Pacific railroad surveys had to take top priority. Illegal woodcutters and traders were a constant source of annoyance. The trade in guns and ammunition with the Indians was also difficult to stop, and soldiers spent many hours trying to stifle the traders.[54]

Terry was away from St. Paul for a short time in 1873 to serve as chairman of a board of officers to select a suitable rifle for the army. After careful deliberation, they chose the Springfield breechloading system as the best, and it was the one that the army used until 1893. Terry also spent much time traveling from post to post conducting court-martial trials. The general, uncovering another concern, was dumbfounded when he read in the *New York Times* that soldiers had forced Indian women into concubinage at Fort Wadsworth. Terry brushed this accusation aside by explaining that Indians did not distinguish between a female servant and a wife, which he felt was the basis of the newspaper article.[55]

The construction of new forts and abandonment of old ones had been held to a minimum in the Department of Dakota during the period 1869-1873. In the Montana District Camp Baker was built, and Fort Benton, an old fur company post, was put into use in 1869. Camp Cooke, located on an ill-chosen spot and of little use, was abandoned in 1870. In the Middle District, the coming of the Northern Pacific necessitated the construction of two new posts. Fort Seward was built in 1872 on the west bank of the James River at the crossing point of the Northern Pacific. It replaced Fort Ransom, which had outlived its use as a sentinel of the Minnesota road. In that same year Fort Abraham Lincoln was constructed on the west bank of the Missouri River north of Fort Rice. Its purpose was to protect the citizens of Bismarck, a new town built at the point where the Northern Pacific crossed the Missouri River. Within two years Fort Abraham Lincoln was enlarged and became the most complete army post on the plains and a model for all others.[56] Another post, Fort Pembina, was built in the northeast corner of the territory to guard the town there and to watch over the northern boundary with Canada.[57] In the South Eastern District, Fort Dakota, located in the southeast corner of the territory, was abandoned because farmers had filled up that part of the territory, and the Indians in the area had been peaceful for many years.

With the completion of the Northern Pacific to Bismarck in 1873, that town took on new significance as a steamboat port on the Missouri. The same was true for Yankton, when in the same year the Dakota Southern Railroad completed its line to that Missouri River port city. No longer would St. Louis dominate the trade on the upper Missouri, and until railroad construction pushed farther west, Bismarck and Yankton were in an enviable position to control this trade. Their position remained unchallenged for the next six years as the financial panic of 1873 and the failure of Jay Cooke and Company halted railroad construction in this area.[58]

The soldiers of Dakota had accomplished most of the goals set for them by Sherman, Sheridan, Hancock, and Terry in the early 1870s. They had secured the routes to Montana and protected the railroad construction workers while they completed the line to Bismarck. Also the soldiers had successfully escorted the Northern Pacific engineers, so that they might survey the trans-Missouri region to determine the future route of the railroad.

Conflict with the Indians was a growing concern. The Blackfeet had been punished and peace was restored in western Montana. The military had felt the wrath of eastern humanitarians, but they came to expect this after major victories over the Indians. Many agencies had been established on the Missouri and White rivers, and thousands of Sioux lived there in peace. Only the hostiles roamed western Dakota and eastern Montana and made trouble for the whites. A major battle with Sitting Bull's warriors had not taken place, but the time was coming for a showdown.

In the meantime, the two agents most responsible for breaking up the Sioux way of life, the reservations and railroads, had gained a firm hold in the northern plains. The hostiles were determined not to relinquish any more of their prized hunting grounds to the whites and prepared to fight the coming of the railroad into the Yellowstone valley with all their resources. Instead, with the financial depression of the mid-1870s, the Indians found that the whites turned their attention from the projected railroad construction to the Sioux treasure house in the Black Hills.

NOTES

1. Sherman to Pres. Grover Cleveland, April 8, 1885, and Grant to Cleveland, June 13, 1885, Terry Papers, Yale University Library.

2. Glen Tucker, *Hancock the Superb* (Indianapolis: Bobbs-Merrill Co., 1960).

3. *Report of Secretary of Interior Columbus Delano,* October 31, 1873, H. Ex. Doc. 1, 43 Cong., 1 sess., Serial 1601, pp. iii-iv. See also Loring B. Priest, *Uncle Sam's Stepchildren: The Reformation of United States Indian Policy, 1865-1887* (1942; reprint ed., New York: Octagon Books, 1969), pp. 28-41; Robert M. Utley, "Celebrated Peace Policy of General Grant," *North Dakota History* 20 (July 1953): 121-143.

4. *Delano Report,* October 31, 1873, pp. iii-iv.

5. Ibid.

6. *Report of Secretary of Interior Jacob D. Cox,* 1869, H. Ex. Doc. 1, 41 Cong., 2 sess., Serial 1414, pp. vii-viii.

7. *Report of Secretary of Interior Zachariah Chandler,* October 31, 1875, H. Ex. Doc. 1, 44 Cong., 1 sess., Serial 1680, p. x.

8. *Acting Secretary of Interior B. R. Cowen to Speaker of the House,* January 10, 1873, H. Ex. Doc. 96, 42 Cong., 3 sess., Serial 1566, pp. 9-10.

9. Ibid.; George E. Hyde, *Spotted Tail's Folk: A History of the Brulé Sioux* (Norman: University of Oklahoma Press, 1961), pp. 172-186.

10. *Annual Report of Sherman,* November 1, 1868, H. Ex. Doc. 1, 40 Cong., 3 sess., Serial 1367, pp. 1-2, 7-8.

11. *Acting Secretary of Interior Cowen to Speaker of the House,* January 10, 1873, H. Ex. Doc. 96, 42 Cong., 3 sess., Serial 1566, pp. 4-8.

12. *Annual Report of Comm. of Indian Affairs Walker,* November 1, 1872, H. Ex. Doc. 1, 42 Cong., 3 sess., Serial 1560, pp. 432-435.

13. Ibid., p. 433.

14. Ibid., p. 435.

15. Ibid., pp. 435-437.

16. Ibid., pp. 432-436.

17. *Annual Report of Comm. of Indian Affairs Walker,* November 1, 1872, pp. v-viii.

18. *Report of Secretary of Interior Delano,* October 31, 1873, pp. v-viii.

19. Ibid.

20. *Report of Comm. of Indian Affairs Smith,* November 1, 1873, H. Ex. Doc. 1, 43 Cong., 1 sess., Serial 1601, pp. 371-373; Priest, *Uncle Sam's Stepchildren,* pp. 96-97.

21. *Report of Secretary of Interior Delano,* October 31, 1873, pp. vii-viii.

22. Annual Report, HQ Fort Lincoln to AAG, Department of Dakota, September 23, 1873, LR, AGO, RG94, NA.

23. *Annual Report of Comm. of Indian Affairs Walker,* November 1, 1872, p. 397.

24. Ibid.; *Annual Report of Comm. of Indian Affairs Edward P. Smith,* November 1, 1874, H. Ex. Doc. 1, 43 Cong., 2 sess., Serial 1639, p. 355.

25. *Annual Report of Secretary of Interior,* November 1, 1872, H. Ex. Doc. 1, 42 Cong., 3 sess., Serial 1560, p. 6.

26. *Report of Comm. of Indian Affairs,* 1869, H. Ex. Doc. 1, 41 Cong., 2 sess., Serial 1414, pp. 447-50.

27. Annual Report of Colonel de Trobriand to AAG, Department of Dakota, September 9, 1869, LS, AGO.

28. Annual Report of Major Baker to AAG, Department of Dakota, February 18, 1870, LS, AGO. See R. J. Ege, *"Tell Baker to Strike Them Hard!" Incident on the Marias, 23 January 1870* (Bellevue, Nebr.: Old Army Press, 1970), the best book on this topic.

29. Ege, *Strike Them Hard,* pp. viii, 59-64.

30. Annual Report of De Trobriand to AAG, Department of Dakota, February 18, 1870, LR, AGO; Annual Report of Hancock, November 1, 1870, LR, AGO; *Annual Report of E. S. Parker, Comm. of Indian Affairs,* October 31, 1870, H. Ex. Doc. 1, 41 Cong., 3 sess., Serial 1449, pp. 467-468.

31. Ibid.

32. See Priest, *Uncle Sam's Stepchildren,* pp. 15-27.

33. *Annual Report of F. D. Pease, Crow Agency, to Comm. of Indian Affairs,* September 28, 1873, H. Ex. Doc. 1, 43 Cong., 1 sess., Serial 1601, p. 616; Annual Report of Hancock, October 23, 1871, LR, AGO.

34. *Meigs to Senate,* November 30, 1866, S. Ex. Doc. 3, 39 Cong., 2 sess., Serial 1276, p. 8.

35. *Annual Report of Secretary of Interior Cox,* 1869, H. Ex. Doc. 1, 40 Cong., 3 sess., Serial 1366, p. xv.

36. Annual Report of Hancock, December 31, 1870, LR, AGO.

37. Robert E. Riegel, *The Story of Western Railroads, From 1852 Through the Reign of the Giants* (Lincoln: University of Nebraska Press, 1967), pp. 120-128.

38. Annual Report of Sherman, 1867, and Cooke to William D. Whipple, AAG, June 21, 1871, LR, AGO.

39. Cooke to Colfax, April 13, 1871, LR, AGO.

40. Hancock to Smith, June 28, 1871, LS, AGO.

41. Annual Report of Hancock, October 23, 1871.

42. Ibid.; William H. Goetzmann, *Exploration and Empire* (New York: Alfred A. Knopf, 1966), p. 412.

43. Annual Report of Stanley, October 28, 1872, LR, AGO; Annual Report of Hancock, October 3, 1872, LR, AGO; *Annual Report of Comm. of Indian Affairs Walker,* November 1, 1872, pp. 480-481.

44. Ibid.

45. Ibid.

46. Annual Report of Stanley, August 25, 1872, LR, AGO.

47. Baker Report, August 15, 1872, in Annual Report, 1872, LR, AGO; Annual Report of Hancock, October 3, 1872.

48. Annual Report of Terry, October 13, 1873, LR, AGO.

49. Annual Report of Hancock, October 20, 1869, LR, AGO.

50. Annual Report of Terry, October 13, 1873, LR, AGO.

51. Ibid.

52. *Annual Report of Comm. of Indian Affairs Walker,* November 1, 1872, Annual Report of Secretary of Interior, 1873, H. Ex. Doc. 1, 43 Cong., 1 sess., Serial 1601, p. xxv.

53. Mark H. Brown, *The Plainsmen of the Yellowstone: A History of the Yellowstone Basin* (New York: G. P. Putnam's Sons, 1961), p. 203.

54. *Bozeman* [Montana] *Courier,* July 7, 1875; Lt. Col. George L. Andrews to Terry, February 5, 1869, LS, Records of the U.S. Army Continental Commands, 1821-1920, RG393, NA.

55. Terry to Bishop Whipple, February, 1869, LS, Records of the U.S. Army Continental Commands.

56. Annual Report of Sheridan, October 12, 1872, and Sheridan to Sherman, May 1, 1874, LR, AGO.

57. Annual Report of Hancock, November 1, 1870.

58. Herbert S. Schell, *History of South Dakota* (Lincoln: University of Nebraska Press, 1961), pp. 113-115; William E. Lass, *A History of Steamboating on the Upper Missouri* (Lincoln: University of Nebraska Press, 1962), pp. 56, 87.

6 The Black Hills Problem

General Terry had learned of the significance of the Black Hills since his arrival in the northern plains in 1866. Located in the southwestern corner of Dakota Territory, the hills were a lush garden spot surrounded by flat and arid plains. To travelers the Black Hills were an oasis, a place to find cool, pure water, abundant game, radiant flowers, and ample timber. To farmers the rich soil gave promise of successful agricultural productivity. To miners the hills held mystery. Prospectors had heard stories of great mineral wealth stored in rich veins of ore in the hills. On occasion they had seen samples of gold dust supposedly taken from this area. If the rumors were true, almost anyone could counter the financial depression that gripped the nation in 1873 with hard work and luck in the gold diggings of the Black Hills.

To these white Americans the Black Hills also represented a problem: the land belonged to the Indians, who were reluctant to part with the valuable area. To the Indians, and particularly to the Teton Sioux, the Black Hills were an earthly paradise where they could gather herbs used for medical purposes, hunt wild game and fruit, and cut poles for their tepees. Here also resided their gods. Although the Sioux did not live in the hills for extended periods of time, they cherished the area as much as they did the plains where the bison roamed.

To General Terry the Black Hills at first represented a blessing more than a problem. The hills were located in the Department of Dakota and under his military jurisdiction. In serving on the Indian Peace Commission of 1867-1868 and in helping to draw up the Treaty of 1868, Terry had come to realize the importance of civilizing the Indians. To most white Americans this meant that the natives must adapt to agriculture. Terry believed that much of the land where the Sioux lived in the arid plains was not suitable for farming. The Black Hills, a potential agricultural bonanza, represented a partial solution to the Indian problem in Dakota. Keeping this land in the hands of the Indians and away from the whites, however, proved to be Terry's problem.

One of the architects of the Treaty of 1868, Terry worked hard to uphold it. He tried to do what was best for the Sioux, but in doing so, the general must have undergone some kind of a personal crisis. He battled for everything he believed to be legal, humane, and Christian. In the end his position was undercut by his superior, General Sheridan, and the treaty was violated. A realist, Sheridan saw the opportunity to slice away the Indians' sanctuary and to open up thousands of acres of rich land to white Americans. In his mind this was a much more effective way to conquer the Indians than on the field of battle.

For the Sioux the loss of the Black Hills would be catastrophic. It would prove once again that whites would break a treaty whenever it would benefit them. With a diminishing land base and an influx of white settlers, the Sioux would find it increasingly difficult to remain a nomadic, hunter culture as an island in a white sea of settlers.

White men had visited the Black Hills long before Terry came to the northern plains. The first recorded in history were François and Joseph de la Verendrye, Frenchmen from Canada, who visited the hills in 1742 while seeking a route to the Pacific. Many other French Canadian and American explorers and fur traders passed through the hills in succeeding years. Miners in small numbers penetrated the hills during the period from 1804 to 1865, but little came of their exploits except persistent rumors that the Black Hills held extensive goldfields. Miners were discouraged from coming to the hills because of the existence of proven mines in other locations in the United States and because of the hostility of the Sioux.[1]

Military and scientific expeditions penetrated the hills during the 1850s and 1860s. In 1855 General William Harney and his command, including a geologist, Dr. Ferdinand V. Hayden, journeyed through the northern part of the hills on their way to Fort Pierre. Two years later Dr. Hayden accompanied the scientific expedition led by Lieutenant Gouverneur K. Warren into the southern part of the Hills. Although Warren's command penetrated only a short distance into the hills, he reported finding gold. In 1859 Captain William F. Reynolds led an expedition that traveled through the northern hills. Some of his men found traces of gold there, but the information was not made public until eight years later.

In 1865 three army expeditions touched the fringes of the hills. None of the military movements had to do specifically with the Black Hills, but the hills were located along routes that were increasingly being used by white men. Prior to this time the main western trails had bypassed the hills. The Oregon and California overland trails passed to the south, and the Missouri River route to Montana passed to the east and the north.

During the later 1860s and early 1870s white men continued to explore and to speculate about the Black Hills. Dr. Hayden privately explored the region in 1866, and his report of the discovery of precious metals set off a serious epidemic of gold fever among the civilians of the area. Terry forcefully turned back groups of miners who had designs on the hills. Soldiers deserted their ranks in order to prospect for gold, but the threat of a Sioux war and Terry's efforts stymied the flow of whites into the Black Hills for the time being.[2]

Thus by 1874 the whites had penetrated the hills, but no systematic exploration had taken place. Rumors persisted of gold, which most wanted to believe, but with little actual knowledge of the existence of gold in paying quantities, the Black Hills remained a mystery.

Two tribes of Teton Sioux, the Oglalas and the Hunkpapas, guarded the hills from white encroachments with particular zeal. Their war leaders, Gall of the Hunkpapas and Red Cloud and Crazy Horse of the Oglalas, were determined to retain the land. Another Sioux rallying point was Sitting Bull, the Hunkpapa medicine man, who held the respect of many of the hostiles. To his camp, usually located in Montana, a number of recalcitrant Sioux warriors made their way to sulk over white encroachments and revel in freedom away from the reservations.

Many whites chose to ignore Indian claims to the Black Hills and demanded government action to return the hostiles to their reservations. In 1873 the legislatures of Minnesota and Dakota both sent memorials to the United States Senate requesting a thorough exploration of the Black Hills. The politicians felt that the Treaty of 1868 was contrary to the desires of the American people, who wished to open the rich and underdeveloped region to white civilization rather than leave the control of the Black Hills "to an ignorant and barbarous race." Drawing from the reports of explorers and scientists, they concluded that the region abounded in precious metals, iron, coal, salt, timber, and petroleum. John Colter, the famous trapper and explorer of the early nineteenth century, even reported virgin coalfields that burned out of control in the Dakota wilderness. These were resources that were desperately needed to develop the northern plains.[3]

Concern over the Black Hills spread to the Interior and War departments. General Sheridan, the commander of the Missouri Division, had contemplated the establishment of a military post in the Black Hills since 1871 in order to thwart the Sioux who raided south of the hills into Nebraska and Wyoming, part of the military Department of the Platte. In his annual report for 1873 Sheridan recommended the establishment of such a fort located in the heart of the Sioux country where the army could threaten the villages and livestock of the hostiles. President Grant showed sufficient interest to meet with Secretary of War William W. Belknap, General of the Army Sherman, Secretary of the Interior Columbus Delano, and Sheridan in the fall of 1873 to discuss this matter. During this meeting Sheridan received authority to investigate the feasibility of carrying out a reconnaissance of the Black Hills in order to find a suitable location for a fort from which the army might better control the restless Indians.[4]

Government interest in the hills at this time was primarily military in nature. Few whites had attempted the dangerous journey into the Black Hills. Threats of vicious reprisal on the part of the Sioux and army enforcement of the Treaty of 1868 made it unlikely that whites would pose an immediate problem in the hills. The military was concerned with Indian raids into Wyoming, Nebraska, and Dakota that were initiated by the hostiles who lived in western Dakota. In their view a fort located near the hills would go a long way toward establishing white authority in the northern plains.

Sheridan thought first of Fort Laramie as the best place from which to initiate the reconnaissance because it was located about one hundred miles from the Black Hills. But the general was concerned about the hostile temper of the Indians around Fort Laramie, and after visits there during the fall and winter of 1873, he concluded that the Wyoming post was not the best choice for an embarkation point for the expedition.[5]

His attention next turned to the Department of Dakota and Fort Abraham Lincoln in particular. Although this post was located on the west bank of the Missouri River about three hundred miles from the Black Hills, it was still the best site under the circumstances.[6] This was the headquarters of the Seventh Cavalry regiment, which was commanded by Sheridan's old friend, Lieutenant Colonel George A. Custer. The aggressive colonel asked permission to lead the expedition to the Black Hills, and Sheridan visited Fort Abraham Lincoln in the spring of 1874 and found that Custer had secured two Indian guides who testified that there

was a good route from the fort to the hills.[7] Sheridan was convinced that
Fort Abraham Lincoln was the best choice under the circumstances and
speculated that the troops should leave by mid-June for a sixty-day excur-
sion. He needed only confirmation of his plans from Interior and War
department officials before he could order Terry to organize the expedition within his department.

Enthusiasm for the proposed expedition declined within the Department of Interior when it received communications from the frontier.
Bishop William H. Hare, an Episcopal missionary and chairman of a commission sent by Secretary of Interior Delano to visit the Sioux in 1873
and 1874, argued against a military expedition. He and his fellow commissioners felt that a special effort should be made to conciliate the
Sioux so that they would not raid into Nebraska during the winter.[8]
Instead of a military expedition, the commissioners recommended that
an agency be established near the Black Hills where the northern Sioux
might draw rations. Bishop Hare predicted that if the proposed expedition were carried out, a war that would involve several thousand Sioux
warriors would result. He was concerned for the lives of the numerous
Episcopal missionaries who worked among the Sioux, and he predicted
that a number of undesirables seeking gold and timber would invade the
Black Hills if the military were allowed to publicize the value of the area.
In addition Bishop Hare was anxious that the United States not tarnish
its national honor by violating the Treaty of 1868.[9]

Terry was also concerned whether the Black Hills expedition would be
a violation of the Treaty of 1868. In an "endorsement" of the expedition,
the general elaborated on a number of items pertinent to the Custer movement. The proposed expedition, he maintained, would not break Indian
rights because the government had always held the right to send exploring
parties into unceded Indian territories. In the case of the Custer expedition, the route would be both within and outside the Sioux reservation
established in 1868. In article II of the treaty, he explained, the United
States had agreed not to allow whites on the reservation except officers,
agents, and other employees of the government authorized to discharge
their duties there. Terry found it difficult to believe that anyone would
question that the army should be allowed on reservation land as officers
of the government. As a member of the commission that drew up the
treaty, he felt sure that all the treaty commissioners held this same inter-
pretation.[10]

He explained further that in practice three military posts had already been established on Sioux reservation land since the signing of the treaty and that Congress had appropriated thirty thousand dollars for the construction of two more such posts within the Sioux reserve. Terry found it hard to understand the Interior Department's new-found reluctance concerning the presence of the military on reservations when they were there for the express purpose of protecting Indian agents and other reservation employees. The Indian Bureau had even requested a military escort for Bishop Hare and his commission when they visited the Sioux in 1874.[11]

Turning to article XI of the Treaty of 1868, Terry was again able to support the legality of the Black Hills expedition. In that passage the Indians agreed not to object to the "construction of railroads, wagon roads, mail stations, or other works of utility or necessity which may be ordered or permitted by the laws of the United States." Terry maintained that the right to construct roads also carried with it the right to make surveys and explorations, which was basically the purpose of the Custer expedition.[12]

Terry also argued from a common-sense point of view when he speculated that the intent of the treaty was certainly not one of establishing a sovereign nation within the United States. The Sioux reservation, almost as extensive in size as the largest state east of the Mississippi River and two-thirds as large as the combined area of six New England states, could not possibly be set aside as a foreign territory. The government must be allowed to exercise its power in all parts of the nation, whether it be on an Indian reservation or in Washington, D.C.[13]

Terry took exception to one comment that Bishop Hare made in a telegram to Secretary Delano concerning the proposed Black Hills expedition. Hare, anxious over military objectives for the expedition, proclaimed that "we are the Marauders in this case."[14] The general politely but firmly reminded the bishop that a marauder is one "who roves in quest of booty or plunder." This did not describe the purpose of the expedition in Terry's view. The military did not seek gold, timber, or arable land in sending the soldiers to the Black Hills.[15] Terry recognized the fact that two or three newspaper correspondents, a photographer, and two scientists would accompany the expedition. He attributed the correspondents and photographer to Custer's well-known proclivity for public exposure. The scientists were Professor Newton H. Winchell, the state geologist of Minnesota, and George B. Grinnell of Terry's alma mater, Yale College, who was sent at the request of Professor Othneil C. Marsh to study the paleontology of the region.[16]

Terry's concluding argument in favor of the Black Hills reconnaissance was that the expedition was not a military movement. It was true that the military force to be used was the largest and best equipped that had ever been used in the northern plains, but the purpose of such a large force was to prevent hostilities. The Sioux, he explained, seemed ever ready to attack small parties but had never attacked large bodies of men. Thus the expedition was peaceful in nature and basically sought routes of communication between the posts on the Missouri River and those of the northwestern section of the Department of the Platte. In the event of trouble with the hostile Sioux, cooperation and communication between the two departments was imperative.[17]

Although many questioned the motivation behind the expedition, Terry was convinced that the purpose of the Black Hills expedition was exploration. The Sioux had concerned the commander for years, and there seemed little reason to believe that they would change. It became extremely important to locate a site for a post in or near the Black Hills and to explore the area in order to locate the best possible routes and lines of communication. If in the future the hostiles carried out attacks on the sparsely settled Dakota frontier or the more promising Nebraska settlements, the white settlers of the area and the friendly Indians of the Red Cloud and Spotted Tail agencies could look for efficient military protection. If rich soil that gave promise of agricultural success was discovered in the area, hostile natives could be introduced to farming with a favorable chance for success. In either light Terry supported the Black Hills expedition as a better means for determining his course of action.[18]

Others saw the motivation for the Black Hills expedition in another light. Newspaper editors and town boomers in Dakota were convinced that desire for wealth and exploitation of the Sioux lands were the purposes of Custer's expedition. A Sioux City reporter explained:

This movement will be the wedge which will open the coveted country. Even if there be no gold worth delving for in the Black Hills, it is known positively that there is pine timber and coal in almost inexhaustible supplies, and the presence of these valuable articles of themselves is sufficient cause for the throwing open to civilization of the coveted region.[19]

While Dakota newspapermen saw the opening of the Black Hills to white civilization as their salvation from the general economic depression of the times, others sympathized with the native Americans. In St. Paul, Terry's headquarters, the editor of the *Daily Dispatch* bemoaned the fact that Custer would take newspaper reporters on the expedition only if they would submit to his inspection of all communications addressed to the public. He concluded that little of truth would result and that one could expect

> glowing descriptions of the march and bivouac, graphic pictures of prairie and stream and forest, splendid eulogies on the brilliant achievements and dash of the General and warm commendations on the patience, endurance and stubborn courage of the troops. The resistance of the miserable savages will be represented in the darkest colors and the nation called upon to exterminate a race with the impudence to defend their homes and rights.[20]

Certainly Terry was aware of this dimension of the expedition and realized that if gold was discovered, whites would desire the land. This was not new to Terry, however, for it had been known for some time that gold was to be found in the Black Hills. In the past the army had been able to keep most prospectors out, and the Sioux had killed a few trespassers while defending their sacred hills.[21] The general believed that Custer's expedition would not change this situation and that the benefits he would enjoy in the way of expanded geographical knowledge of the area would more than outweigh any negative results of the expedition.

The Interior Department reluctantly agreed to the reconnaissance, and the War Department instructed Terry to begin preparations for the expedition. Fort Abraham Lincoln would be the embarkation point with six companies of the Seventh Cavalry from Fort Rice, all under Colonel Custer, serving as the backbone of the expedition. In order to guard the wagon trains, Custer requested two companies of infantry, which Terry dispatched from Grand River Agency and Fort Pembina. It was to be an imposing force of about one thousand men, two thousand animals, and one hundred and ten wagons.[22]

Terry ordered Custer to be ready to leave on or about June 20, but complications slowed his departure. The general was determined that Custer be equipped with the best arms available. He had sent requisitions

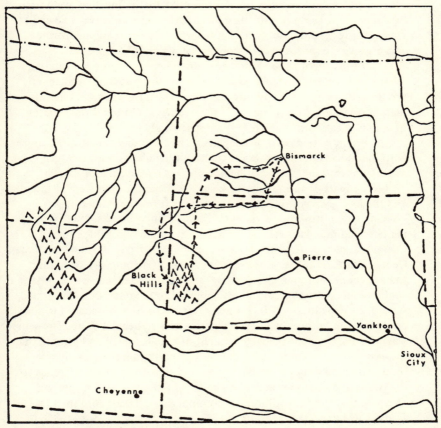

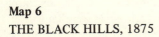 Custer's Route 1874

Map 6
THE BLACK HILLS, 1875

for new pistols and carbines for the Seventh Cavalry, but they were slow
in coming.[23] It was not until June 30 that the arms were available and
issued. Custer could now claim that his was "the best equipped, armed,
and organized expedition ever seen on the plains."[24]

Terry's instructions to Custer gave him much leeway in determining
his routes (map 6). The colonel was to locate the best route available to
the Belle Fourche River and into the Black Hills. He was to obtain information regarding "the character of the country and the possible routes
of communication through it." Terry specifically required that Custer
return within sixty days of his departure, but if at any time trouble arose
with the Indians that the soldiers could not handle, he was to return to
Fort Abraham Lincoln even if he had not yet reached the Black Hills.[25]

Terry's fears of an Indian attack against the expedition were ill founded,
and the journey went smoothly. It is true that for the soldiers it was a
grueling trip, but when the Seventh Cavalry band played some rollicking
marches and popular tunes of the day, it did seem like a fine time.[26]
Custer was busy writing his reports and hunting grizzly bear and antelope.
George Bird Grinnell, one of Professor Marsh's paleontologists, found
some specimens of prehistoric animal and marine life, and several prospectors found traces of gold. Terry reported to Sheridan that Custer had
started the expedition on July 1 and returned to Fort Abraham Lincoln
on August 30, within the sixty-day period he had been allowed. The general
was encouraged about the large amount of data gathered and pleased that
the expedition encountered no hostile Indians during their nearly one
thousand mile journey.[27] It is not clear if Terry was making reference to
the traces of gold discovered when he wired Sheridan, who in turn wired
Sherman that "the expedition has accomplished all and more than I
[Terry] had expected from it."[28]

Sheridan, in his annual report to Sherman, did mention Custer's gold
discovery near Harney's Peak in the Black Hills but concluded that no
reliable information was available on its abundance. He felt that Custer
had not had sufficient time to make a thorough investigation of the quantity
of gold in the area and concluded that the color of gold could be found
almost anywhere in the western territories. Actually Sheridan seemed
more enthusiastic about the prospects of finding gold in paying quantities
in the area west of the Black Hills between the Powder and Bighorn rivers.
He speculated that the Black Hills were more significant from a military
standpoint for controlling the hostile Sioux and for timber and rich soil.[29]

More to the point were Custer's reports, one dated August 2 and the
other August 15. The first brought word of the discovery of gold. Evidently Custer had hired two miners, Horatio N. Ross and William McKay,
at his own expense. At midday on July 30, the expedition reached the
area around Harney's Peak. Custer and an escort climbed the mountain
and enjoyed the view of the hills. Soldiers not so lucky to participate in
the mountain climb enjoyed a spirited game of baseball, and the officers
relaxed over a champagne dinner in Custer's absence. With all of this excitement, Ross and McKay were little noticed as they panned for gold in
nearby French Creek. The miners discovered traces of gold but were disappointed in the sparsity of their find. The next day camp was moved
three miles away for better grazing, and again the miners were busy. This
time their efforts were better rewarded, and Custer could report that gold
had been discovered in paying quantities. His first report, delivered to
Fort Laramie by scout Charlie Reynolds, however, made little of the gold
discovery. Custer realized that the newspaper men in his expedition would
report the discovery and felt he must also, but he emphasized that until
further investigations could be made, no conclusions could or should be
reached about the extent of gold in the Black Hills. Most of the colonel's
dispatch dealt with glowing reports on the breathtaking extent of flowers,
rich soil, and abundance of wooded lands.[30]

In his August 15 report from Bear Butte camp, Custer reiterated his
previous statements on the general desirability of the Black Hills and the
discovery of gold. He found the grazing land excellent and maintained
that his beef cattle herd was in better condition now than it had been
upon leaving Fort Abraham Lincoln six hundred miles before. He further
commented on the numerous deer and elk he had seen and the rich soil,
which would provide excellent land for wheat farming. In describing the
terrain for military use, he made the point that fairly easy travel and communications could be maintained through the Black Hills. Most previous
exploring parties, he explained, had explored only the outer hills, which
proved too rugged and confusing in layout. The interior, however, was filled
with easy routes and numerous parks. This information was of particular
interest to Terry and made the expedition worthwhile as far as the department commander was concerned. On the question of gold, Custer again
urged caution but explained that gold was found at every site on which
they searched for the precious metal. He reported gold at the "grass
roots" on one occasion and explained that men with no mining experience

were finding it in paying quantities.[31] Terry must have wondered at the sincerity of Custer's words of caution when he used such language as "gold at the grass roots" and "gold in paying quantities."

Knowledgeable people on the expedition interpreted Custer's words of caution and newspaper reports that circulated during this same time as reckless and misleading. Captain William Ludlow, chief engineer of the Corps of Engineers for the Department of Dakota, had much to say concerning the expedition. He concurred with Custer's reports on the rich soil, abundant wildlife, impressive forests, and general desirability of the area. He explained how Indians cherished the region as a hunting ground and asylum. He further stated that the Indians planned to settle the area permanently when all the buffalo were killed and that they would not tolerate white occupation of the hills. Ludlow recommended that the best possible use to be made of the region was that of a permanent reservation for the Sioux "where they could be taught occupations of a pastoral character which of all the semicivilized means of subsistence would be most natural and easy for them, and result in relieving the United States Government of the burden of their support."[32] Terry expressed his hearty concurrence with Ludlow's opinions when he forwarded the engineer's report to division headquarters in Chicago.[33]

Others who accompanied Custer on the expedition were equally convinced that the reports lacked validity. Luther North, who officially traveled as Grinnell's assistant, felt strongly that the gold discovery reports by Custer and the newspaper men were exaggerated.[34] Professor Winchell claimed he never saw any gold and hinted that there might not have been any at all.[35] Frederick Dent Grant (son of the president), who joined the expedition as an assistant to Custer, was another who claimed not to have actually seen any gold in the Black Hills. He wrote in his journal that he did not "believe that any gold was found at all."[36] Secretary of Interior Delano repeated Custer's reports about great mineral wealth in the Black Hills but felt that "subsequent information establishes the fact that no evidence of valuable mineral deposits were furnished."[37]

If the official reports were generally skeptical about the presence of gold in paying quantities in the Black Hills, the newspaper coverage was just the opposite. Newspapers from the surrounding areas were particularly enthusiastic about Custer's expedition. The *Yankton Press and Dakotaian* filled its pages with details on routes to the Black Hills, mileage costs, and other pertinent information for potential miners.[38] The *Bismarck*

Tribune reported rich discoveries of silver and gold in the Black Hills and predicted economic prosperity for the area.[39] If the newspaper editors could help bring about a rush to the Black Hills, it would mean a great deal in terms of the development of the northern plains. Bismarck, Sioux City, Yankton, Cheyenne, and Sidney were potential supply and transportation centers. Merchants would become rich, and farmers would operate in a more desirable market. The Northern Pacific Railroad, whose construction was stymied at Bismarck because of the depression, perhaps could now build its tracks farther to the west to serve a new and developing section of the nation. The newspaper writers went through a period of booming the Black Hills in an effort to stimulate a gold rush, and at the same time they sang the merits of their particular town as the best embarkation point from which to reach the Black Hills.[40]

The Custer expedition had caused quite a stir. Terry was pleased to have the geographical information derived from the expedition and felt more able to cope with Sioux hostilities if any should occur. But he maintained that the Black Hills area should serve as a grazing and farming area for the Sioux. This was the humane way to treat the natives and a means to introduce them to civilization. In the long run it would also be best for all concerned if a peaceful and honorable solution could be found.

Custer viewed the Black Hills question from a different point of view. He felt that Indians made little practical use of the hills and concluded that the future of the area lay primarily in agriculture and stock raising. The colonel desired not so much the influx of transient miners but rather the permanent settlement of the area by white farmers and stockmen.[41] The *Yankton Press and Dakotaian* expressed this same view when the editor reported that he felt that Custer had faith in Dakota and "desires to promote its development."[42] Elizabeth Custer rounded out this picture of her husband as a harbinger of civilization to the northern plains:

> I wish I could give you an idea of the earnestness of General
> Custer in everything that pertained to Dakota. He felt that it
> was such a privilege to get the detail to be assigned to duty in
> the new country. Even when we were shut off from all the
> world at Fort Abraham Lincoln he delighted in the making of
> that wonderful Dakota. The pictures that he drew of the future
> we sometimes protested, but nothing moved him—and how
> right he was![43]

Sheridan stood somewhere between Terry's and Custer's viewpoints. He appreciated the importance of obtaining information that would be useful in case military movements in the Black Hills region were necessitated by Indian depredations. He also felt that the Sioux should retain the Black Hills for the time being, but the general believed that eventually the region must fall to white control. Sheridan had chosen Custer to lead the expedition and generally respected his approach to the Black Hills question. Sheridan, the division commander and Terry's superior officer, and Sherman, the commander of the army, both felt that the Indians must be defeated and white settlement encouraged in the region. Terry's minority stand had little chance of success in the face of this opposition, but he tenaciously fought for a legal and moral solution to the Black Hills question. In the meantime he used his energy to help keep whites out of the Black Hills.

All three military men seemed to agree that the army could prevent trespassers from coming into the Black Hills. Sheridan was confident that the infantry and cavalry would not allow a repetition of the California gold rush in the Black Hills. He promised to perform his duties in keeping the whites out of the hills until the government might gain concessions from the Sioux. He felt that if the towns from which the miners started were so remote that it was impossible for the army to stop them there, the next move was for the army to occupy the two or three gaps in the Black Hills to prevent trespassing. Sheridan, Terry, and General George Crook, commander of the Department of the Platte, soon would have the opportunity to put this plan into effect.[44]

Terry had reason for concern even before Custer returned from the Black Hills. He heard rumors of a party that was being organized in Bismarck and immediately sent a telegram on August 27 to the acting commanding officer at nearby Fort Abraham Lincoln with orders to notify any such parties that they would not be permitted to leave for the hills unless authorized by the secretary of the interior.[45] On that same day Terry received correspondence from Detroit, Michigan, inquiring about possible action the military might take if a party from that city passed through the area on the way to the hills. Terry replied that any unauthorized party would be driven back by United States soldiers if the Sioux did not destroy them first. He explained that the Treaty of 1868 forbade miners in the Sioux reservation, that this treaty was the law of the land, and that he intended to enforce it.[46]

Sheridan sent specific orders to Terry and Crook when he learned that parties were organizing in Yankton and Sioux City for the purpose of going into the Black Hills. The generals were authorized to use force, to burn wagon trains, to arrest the leaders of such groups, and to confine them at the nearest military post. If the parties reached the hills before they could be stopped, the generals were instructed to send cavalry to bring the trespassers out. Sheridan concluded that should Congress extinguish the treaty rights of the Indians to the Black Hills, he would give "cordial support to the settlement of the Black Hills."[47]

This last statement must have bothered Terry somewhat, because he felt that the Treaty of 1868 was the final word concerning the Sioux reserve. Terry made this point when he notified the commanding officers of the various posts in the department to "rejoin the utmost vigilance in regards to parties of miners attempting to go into the Black Hills. You will spare no efforts to prevent such movements," he added.[48] As 1874 came to a close, most waited out the cold winter to see if Congress would initiate action to take the Black Hills from the Sioux or if the vigilance of the military would wane and thus clear the way for a rush of miners into the hills in the spring. It was clear that Terry would maintain the Treaty of 1868 as best he could, but higher authority might change the whole outlook in Dakota.

Although valid reports about activity in the Black Hills were scarce during the early months of 1875, the Dakota newspapers endeavored to keep interest alive by publishing stories of successful mining operations in the hills. Reports from the Gordon party indicated that an industrious man could make twenty-five dollars a day easily. There was "plenty for everybody."[49] Another report said that Russell's group entered the heart of the hills and that since they had stayed the whole time, they must be doing well.[50]

Terry heard these rumors and expressed his concern to Sheridan that miners in greater numbers awaited only the spring thaw before they journeyed to the hills. He appealed to Sheridan:

It is of the greatest importance that any attempts to defy the law and to trample on the rights secured to the Sioux by the Treaty of 1868 should be met in the most vigorous manner *at the very outset.* If during the coming season the Hills can be absolutely closed to intruders those who would be influ-

enced by no other consideration will become convinced that
to attempt to enter them is a fruitless undertaking and here
after they will give us little trouble.[51]

Terry concluded by pointing out that Fort Sully, near the conflux of the
Missouri and Cheyenne rivers, could be utilized as a supply depot for
troops operating in the Black Hills and warned that he would need a much
larger mounted force than what he now had if the Sioux attacked in the
spring.[52]

Terry also prepared his strategy for stopping the miners. He would
utilize troops from Fort Randall located in southern Dakota Territory in
patroling the Niobrara River line from its mouth to the Black Hills. They
would intercept miners coming from Sioux City, Yankton, and Sidney.
Cavalry from Fort Sully would march along the Missouri River to discourage miners from Pierre and other points to the east.[53] If Crook in the
Department of the Platte would take similar actions, the miners could be
stopped.

By mid-March the government seemed to be reconsidering its policy
for the Black Hills, and Terry was concerned. President Grant proclaimed
that all expeditions headed for the Black Hills must be prevented from
reaching their destination while the government took steps toward extin-
guishing the Indian title and opening the country to white Americans.
He warned that only proper means would be used with the Indians and
that if these failed, those already in the hills must be expelled.[54] Terry
immediately wrote for clarification, expressing bewilderment that miners
in the Black Hills would be allowed to remain while negotiations with the
Indians proceeded. He closed by saying, "I earnestly hope that it is not
so for in the first place these people have openly and imprudently defied
the law and in the second place I think it will be almost impossible to keep
others out if they are allowed to remain."[55]

Two weeks later Terry received news that the miners were to be removed, and he happily relayed the word to Custer at Fort Abraham
Lincoln that they must be expelled as soon as the weather permitted.[56]
There were plenty of intruders because prospectors continued to send
word from the Black Hills that gold was there in abundance. Miners also
disclosed that there was a ready market for water pumps and mining tools.
Western newspapermen published these stories and many others in order
to bring new population, capital, and prosperity to their region.[57]

During April and May the weather improved to the extent that Terry feared a full-scale rush on the hills by thousands of people. He encouraged officials in Sioux City to publish in newspapers that he would use the whole military force of his department to prevent an invasion of the Black Hills by unauthorized parties and to expel the people already there.[58]

Terry's persistence began to pay off by mid-May when he received reports that miners were being apprehended. The Andrews-Wharton party, consisting of forty-two men, six wagons, and twenty-two horses, was escorted 170 miles back to Fort Randall near Yankton, where they were released on the promise that they would never again enter the Black Hills illegally.[59] A week later Terry heard of the capture of the Gordon party on its way to the Black Hills.[60] Newspaper accounts described how the party was interrupted from its breakfast by the quick arrival of two companies of cavalry. The miners were ordered to form a line so that their names might be noted. While this was taking place the soldiers trained a Gatling gun on the unsuspecting miners. Next the soldiers destroyed the miners' wagons and supplies, although it appears that some revolvers, boots, stores, money, and clothing were stolen by the soldiers. The cavalrymen also helped themselves to the breakfast that the miners had just prepared. It was a long journey for the half-dressed miners to march back to Fort Randall. They would think twice before making another illegal trip to the Black Hills. Terry ordered a full investigation of the affair, but little evidence against the soldiers seems to have been uncovered.[61]

The general continued to move his troops into areas where he suspected miners might be organizing for a trip to the Black Hills. Rumors of parties leaving from Montana to avoid the vigilance of the Dakota troops persisted, and Terry alerted the commanding officer at Fort Ellis to stop miners bound for the Black Hills.[62] Many times miners eluded the military and made their way to the hills despite the army's efforts. To combat this Terry sent Captain Frederick Benteen with his cavalry to sweep through the Black Hills to round up the miners and escort them back to Fort Randall.[63]

In August the situation got out of hand. Sources from General Crook's Department of the Platte reported that approximately twelve hundred miners were in the Black Hills scattered along different creeks.[64] Terry, no doubt, felt that most of these trespassers had filtered through Crook's lines in Nebraska and Wyoming. Terry had Captain Benteen in the hills and was aware that Crook had been directed to send troops there from Fort Robinson. Terry was not aware that Sheridan had authorized Crook to go to the hills in person to establish his headquarters near French Creek and to assume command. Crook proceeded to the hills and in a proclamation on July 29, he suggested that the miners organize and draft resolutions that would ensure them the land claims that they had discovered and worked. In this way, Crook explained, they would not lose the benefit of their labor when the lands were opened up.[65]

Terry had lost control of the situation. He was furious that Crook would issue proclamations in derogation of his authority as department commander, proclamations that in substance countermanded the orders he had given to his own troops employed in removing miners in his own department. "It will be a new thing in the history of law and of governments," Terry wrote, "if men who have audaciously and flagrantly violated the law can by their very crime acquire vested rights, as against those who obey the law."[66] It seemed that more and more Sheridan was turning the Black Hills problem over to Crook. Perhaps the division commander felt that Crook shared his feelings more by his show of understanding for the miners or perhaps Crook's department was more strategically located along the main routes that miners were using to reach the Black Hills and thus in a better position to handle the situation. Terry could sense that white settlement and development of the hills had taken priority over concern for law and Indian rights.

Other events taking place during the summer of 1875 had bearing on the Black Hills question. In order to set rumors at rest concerning the presence of gold in paying quantities in the hills, Walter P. Jenney of the New York School of Mines led a scientific expedition into the Black Hills. Authorized by the secretary of the interior, Jenney was charged with obtaining accurate information on the mineral deposits in the hills. Escorted by cavalry from the Department of the Platte, Jenney also took a number of scientists and miners on the four-month trip. They made a thorough investigation of the hills region and concluded in their seventy-two page report that gold could be found in paying quantities in the Hills but that it would take mining companies with sophisticated machinery to extract the gold.[67] The newspapermen covering the Jenney expedition simply reported that rich discoveries of gold had been located in the French Creek and Custer's Gulch area.[68]

It seemed impossible to keep the thousands of gold-hungry Americans out of the Black Hills region. The army could deal with a few hundred miners by watching their embarkation points and stopping parties before they reached the hills, and army units could patrol the routes into the hills and make an occasional sweep through the region to rout out miners;

but when the miners numbered several thousand rather than a few hundred, the military was unable to enforce the Treaty of 1868.

More important, perhaps, was the will of the commanding officers. Terry was adamant in his stand to protect Indian rights and to expel the whites from the Sioux reservation, but his superior officer, General Sheridan, and his fellow department commander, General Crook, were less enthusiastic in this endeavor. Sheridan especially saw the diminution of Sioux lands and the civilization of the Indians as the proper policy. In his annual report for 1875 he estimated the Sioux population at roughly twenty-five thousand, and figuring the acreage of their reservation, he guessed that each Indian head of a family had about ten thousand acres of unimproved land. By comparison each white farmer through the Homestead Act could acquire only 160 acres of land. On this land he built a house, put up fences, tilled the ground, and paid taxes. The white farmer worked to better his lot while the idle Indian lived as a pauper with the compliments of the government. Sheridan concluded that "there is true humanity in making the reservations reasonably small by dividing them into tracts for the heads of families, making labor gradually compulsory, and even compelling children to go to school."[69]

Terry saw humanity in another light. He believed the Indians must be allowed to retain the land. But the division commander had won the day. Sheridan, a realist, knew that there was little the undermanned army could do to stop the ore-hungry miners from flocking onto the Indian lands. Terry, somewhat idealistic and naive, fought to keep the trespassers off the reservation. His efforts had been significant at first, but when Sheridan and Crook adapted a more lenient policy concerning the miners, Terry was helpless to counter the flood of white settlers that advanced into the Black Hills. Many of the Sioux sulked at their agencies, and the more militant moved from their reservation to camps in Montana. For whites who demanded that Indians live on reservation lands and for Indians who were equally determined to retain their freedom of movement, an eventual showdown loomed in the future.

NOTES

1. For Black Hills background, see Watson Parker, *Gold in the Black Hills* (Norman: University of Oklahoma Press, 1966), pp. 6-23. See also James D. McLaird, and Lesta V. Turcher, "Exploring the Black Hills, 1855-1875: Reports of the Government Expeditions," *South Dakota History* 3 (Fall 1973): 359-389.

2. Roderick Peattie, ed., *The Black Hills* (New York: Vanguard Press, 1952), p. 71.

3. *Memorial of the Legislative Assembly of Minnesota Territory,* January 24, 1873, S. Mis. Doc. 26, 40 Cong., 2 sess., Serial 1319, pp. 1-2; *Memorial of the Legislative Assembly of Dakota Territory,* January 24, 1873, S. Mis. Doc. 45, 42 Cong., 3 sess., Serial 1546, pp. 1-2.

4. Annual Report of Sheridan, October 1, 1874, LR, AGO, RG94, NA.

5. Ibid.

6. Ibid.

7. General Edward S. Godfrey, "Custer's Last Battle," n.d., p. 10, Edward S. Godfrey Papers, LC, Washington, D.C.

8. Hare's fellow commissioners were S. D. Hinman, C. C. Cox, and R. B. Lines.

9. Hare to Grant, June 9, 1874, and Delano to Belknap, June 9, 1874, LR, AGO, RG94; *Report of the Sioux Commission, William H. Hare, Chairman,* November 28, 1874, H. Ex. Doc. 1, 43 Cong., 2 sess., Serial 1639, pp. 397-407.

10. Fourth Endorsement, Terry to Sheridan, July 27, 1874, LR, AGO.

11. Ibid.

12. Ibid.

13. Ibid.

14. Delano to Hare, June 9, 1874, LR, AGO.

15. Fourth Endorsement, Terry to Sheridan, July 27, 1874.

16. Donald Jackson, *Custer's Gold: The United States Cavalry Expedition of 1874* (New Haven: Yale University Press, 1966), pp. 48-58.

17. Fourth Endorsement, Terry to Sheridan, July 27, 1874.

18. Ibid.; Special Orders No. 117 by Order of General Terry, June 8, 1874, Sheridan to Whipple, May 25, 1874, LR, AGO.

19. *Sioux City Journal,* n.d.

20. *St. Paul Daily Dispatch,* July 2, 1874.

21. *Yankton Press and Dakotaian,* April 10, 1872.

22. Special Orders No. 117.

23. Terry to Sheridan, May 30, 1874, LS, Records of the U.S. Army Continental Commands, RG393, NA.

24. Ibid., July 2, 1874, LS, Records of the U.S. Army Continental Commands.

25. Special Orders No. 117.

26. See "Journal of Private Theodore Ewert" in Jackson, *Custer's Gold,* pp. 26-45.

27. Annual Report of Terry, September 9, 1874, LR, AGO.

28. Sheridan to Sherman, September 1, 1874, LR, AGO.

29. Sheridan to Whipple, October 1, 1874, LR, AGO.

30. Custer to Terry, August 2, 1874, LR, AGO.

31. Ibid., August 15, 1874, LR, AGO.

32. Ludlow Report of Black Hill's Expedition, 1874, LR, AGO.

33. Terry to Sheridan, May 10, 1874, LR, AGO.

34. Donald F. Danker, ed., *Man of the Plains: Recollections of Luther North, 1856-1882* (Lincoln: University of Nebraska Press, 1961), pp. 307-308.

35. Jackson, *Custer's Gold,* p. 108. On one occasion Grant claimed that gold was imported to make it look as if the precious metal was discovered in the Black Hills. On another occasion he admitted that gold was discovered in the Black Hills. Grant had a drinking problem. For a summary on him, see Herbert Krause and Gary Olson, *Prelude to Glory: A Newspaper Accounting of Custer's 1874 Expedition to the Black Hills* (Sioux Falls: Brevet Press, 1974), p. 237.

36. Ibid., pp. 109-110.

37. *Report of the Secretary of Interior,* 1874, H. Ex. Doc. 1, 43 Cong., 2 sess., Serial 1639, p. xi-xv.

38. *Yankton Press and Dakotaian,* August 27, 1874.

39. *Bismarck Tribune,* August 19, 1874, quoted in Jackson, *Custer's Gold,* p. 69.

40. Parker, *Gold in the Black Hills,* pp. 38-52; Jane Conard, "Charles Collins: The Sioux City Promotion of the Black Hills," *South Dakota History* 3 (Spring 1972): 131-171.

41. J. S. Radabaugh, "Custer Explores the Black Hills, 1874," *Military Affairs* 26 (1962): 162-170.

42. *Yankton Press and Dakotaian,* July 9, 1874.

43. W. M. Wemett, "Custer's Expedition to the Black Hills in 1874," *North Dakota Historical Quarterly* 6 (July 1932): 292-301. For more of Custer's promotion of Dakota, see Marvin Kroeker, "Deceit about the Garden: Hazen, Custer and the Arid Lands Controversy," *North Dakota Quarterly* 38 (Summer 1970): 5-21.

44. Sheridan to Sherman, March 1, 1875, in *Yankton Press and Dakotaian,* April 1, 1875.

45. Terry to Capt. Joseph S. Poland, August 27, 1874, LS, Records of the U.S. Army Continental Commands.

46. Terry to John W. Clark, August 29, 1874, LS, Records of the U.S. Army Continental Commands.

47. Sheridan to Terry, September 3, 1874, LR, AGO.

48. Terry to Commanding Officers of Posts, December 23, 1874, LS, Records of the U.S. Army Continental Commands.

49. *Yankton Press and Dakotaian,* March 4, 1875. H. W. Bingham, a

Sioux agent, claimed that Gordon received a thousand dollars from the citizens of Sioux City to stir up excitement in the Black Hills. "Note and Documents," *North Dakota Historical Quarterly* 6 (July 1932): 306-307.

50. *Yankton Press and Dakotaian,* January 28, 1875.

51. Terry to Sheridan, March 9, 1875, LS, Records of the U.S. Army Continental Commands.

52. Ibid.

53. Terry to Sheridan, November 12, 1875, LR, AGO.

54. Grant to Sheridan, March 17, 1875, LR, AGO.

55. Terry to Sherman, March 17, 1875, LS, Records of the U.S. Army Continental Commands.

56. Terry to Custer, April 7, 1875, LS, Records of the U.S. Army Continental Commands.

57. *Yankton Press and Dakotaian,* March 18, 1875.

58. Terry to Sherman, March 17, 1875, and Terry to Capt. C. W. Foster, April 10, 1875, LS, Records of the U.S. Army Continental Commands.

59. Terry to Sheridan, May 14, 1875, and Terry to Commanding Officer Fort Randall, May 14, 1875, LS, Records of the U.S. Army Continental Commands.

60. Terry to Sheridan, May 22, 1875, LS, Records of the U.S. Army Continental Commands.

61. Terry to Commanding Officer Fort Randall, May 30, 1875, LS, Records of the U.S. Army Continental Commands; *Yankton Press and Dakotaian,* June 10, 1875.

62. Terry to Commanding Officer Fort Ellis, June 20, 1875, LS, Records of the U.S. Army Continental Commands.

63. Terry to Commanding Officer Fort Randall, July 8, 1875, LS, Records of the U.S. Army Continental Commands.

64. Crook to Terry, August 5, 1875, LR, AGO.

65. Jackson, *Custer's Gold,* pp. 114-115; Peattie, *Black Hills,* pp. 95-96.

66. Terry to Sheridan, August 6, 1875, LS, Records of the U.S. Army Continental Commands; Annual Report of Terry, November 12, 1875, LR, AGO.

67. *Mineral Wealth, Climate and Rain Fall and Natural Resources, the Jenney Report on the Black Hills,* S. Ex. Doc. 51, 44 Cong., 1 sess., Serial 1664; *Annual Report of Edward P. Smith, Commissioner of Indian Affairs,* November 1, 1875, H. Ex. Doc. 1, 44 Cong., 1 sess., Serial 1680, pp. 538, 683-85.

68. *Yankton Press and Dakotaian,* July 8, 1875.

69. Annual Report of Sheridan, November 23, 1875, LR, AGO.

7 The Road to War, 1875-1876

The middle years of the 1870s were a turning point for the Indians and the whites of the northern plains. The Black Hills problem remained unsolved as thousands of whites poured into the new mining centers of Custer City and Deadwood. The government needed a legal clarification of the hills situation, and it also desired to address itself to the broader question of defining the proper place for the hostiles within the northern plains.

General Terry realized the significance of these questions. He was sympathetic to the Sioux determination to maintain the Black Hills, but he had little patience with the hostiles who roamed in Montana. They must be forced back to their agencies if peace and security were to be restored in Dakota. If the Tetons acquiesced in these matters, their most prized reservation land would fall to the whites, and their symbolic Montana stronghold of freedom and the old way of life would signal the decline of the Sioux.

The problem of the moment was the Black Hills question, and the government made an effort to solve that by inviting prominent Sioux chiefs to Washington to discuss the matter. Red Cloud had actually requested a hearing before the president at an earlier time, and now his solicitation was granted. The Oglala chief even persuaded Spotted Tail to accompany him. The delegation numbered nineteen, with Red Cloud bringing twelve chiefs from Red Cloud Agency and Spotted Tail bringing five others with him from his agency. The first session in Washington was held in the Indian office on May 18, 1875. It quickly became apparent that a misunderstanding had occurred over the purpose of the Washington trip and the proposed meetings with the president. Although Red Cloud knew of the government's interest in the Black Hills, he maintained that he had come to consult on the topic of the Red Cloud agent, J. J. Saville. The Oglala chief had grievances over food allocations and corruption at the agency, which he hoped to talk over with Grant. The president, however, as well as Secretary Columbus Delano and Indian Commissioner Edward P. Smith, hoped to persuade the Sioux to relinquish their hunting rights in Nebraska and Kansas and to gain concessions for white Americans in the Black Hills. Specifically, they wanted to pave the way for a future commission, which they planned to send to the Sioux during the summer in order to obtain mining rights in the Hills or outright purchase.[1]

After about three weeks of haggling, the Sioux and the whites had made little progress. Red Cloud had not been able to make his case stand up against agent Saville, but the chief had thwarted the efforts of the whites to gain the hills. The two sides argued so much over the hunting rights question that the hills were all but forgotten. Delano had promised the Sioux twenty-five thousand dollars for their hunting rights in Kansas and Nebraska, and since the buffalo had all but disappeared in this area, the Sioux were interested in the money. The Indians asked for at least forty thousand dollars, and Delano promised he would do all that he could to gain this for them. The Sioux proposed to return home in order to determine what their people wanted to do, but Delano and his aides persuaded them otherwise. On June 23, the Sioux agreed to sell their hunting rights in Kansas and Nebraska for twenty-five thousand dollars to be paid in cows, horses, harnesses, and wagons.[2]

Little else could be accomplished during the Washington visit. The Indians argued among themselves, and Red Cloud alienated most of the officials with whom he had dealings. The natives were extremely disappointed that Grant would not spend more time with them, but he wanted Delano and Smith to handle the whole situation. The government officials could do no more about the disastrous Washington visit, but they did take solace in the hope that a commission would be allowed to go to Nebraska to negotiate with the Sioux for mining rights or purchase of the Black Hills.[3]

Their hopes were realized when Grant directed that such a commission be appointed by the secretary of the interior. Delano selected the names by June 18, 1875, and planned a "grand council" for some point on the Missouri River for late July.[4] The newly chosen commission was an inexperienced group except for Terry, Samuel D. Hinman, an Episcopal missionary, and George P. Beauvais, a western trader from St. Louis who had dealt with the Sioux for many years. Delano selected Senator William B.

Allison of Iowa, a friend of President Grant, to serve as chairman, but the senator had little practical experience with Indians. The other members of the commission—Abram Comingo of Independence, Missouri, W. H. Ashby of Beatrice, Nebraska, and Albert G. Lawrence of Providence, Rhode Island—lacked qualifications for this type of job. John S. Collins, post trader at Fort Laramie, served as secretary.[5]

Delano instructed the commissioners to gain cession of the Black Hills and the relinquishment of Indian rights to the Bighorn Mountains area in Wyoming. This would leave the Sioux with the area in the middle known as the Powder River region. The secretary explained in his letter of instructions that approximately thirty-five thousand Sioux lived at six agencies—Santee, Crow Creek, Cheyenne River, Standing Rock, Red Cloud, and Spotted Tail—and that another three thousand to five thousand nonreservation Sioux roamed the Black Hills country. He requested that the commissioners visit the six agencies and inform the Indians of the government's wishes and announce that a grand council was to be held in late July at Fort Sully on the Missouri River. Hinman, Comingo, and Ashby visited the Indian agencies and explained the nature of their visit to the various bands of Sioux. They related that many of the articles of the 1868 treaty that provided subsistence goods had lapsed since the agreed-upon four-year period had ended in 1872. They commented that the government was now paying $1.2 million to $1.5 million per year for their subsistence, which it was not required by treaty to pay. The commissioners hinted that this might be withdrawn if the Indians did not relinquish the Black Hills and Bighorn country.[6]

After these preliminary meetings with the Indians, the three commissioners journeyed to Omaha to meet with the other commissioners for an organizational conference. Terry found it impossible to join the commissioners there because he first had to meet with Secretary of War Belknap, who had planned to visit Terry at Bismarck on the way to Yellowstone Park.[7] The commissioners met in Omaha on August 26 and agreed to have the grand council with the Sioux at Red Cloud Agency in northwestern Nebraska rather than at Fort Sully on the Missouri River as they had hoped. This concession was necessary in order to obtain greater participation in the council on the part of Red Cloud's people.

The commissioners reached Red Cloud Agency on September 4, and Terry joined them ten days later. The general found a rather disgruntled collection of commissioners and Indians still arguing over the site for the grand council. Red Cloud insisted that the council be held at his agency, while Spotted Tail adamantly announced that it would be held at Chadron Creek about twenty-five miles distant from each agency. It was not until September 17 that they agreed to hold the council almost eight miles east of Red Cloud Agency on an open plain, which was not satisfactory for anyone.[8]

With this decision reached, Commissioner Allison called the opening of the grand council on September 20. Terry, the other six commissioners, and representatives of the Brulés, Oglalas, Miniconjous, Hunkpapas, Blackfeet, Two Kettles, Sans Arcs, Lower Brulés, Yanktons, Santees, Northern Cheyennes, and Arapahos were all present. Allison began the council with a brief statement of the government's object in holding the meeting. He explained the white man's need for at least the mining rights in the Black Hills plus the Bighorn Mountain region, which he told the startled Indians had little value to the natives. Allison vaguely promised that in return for these rights, the Indians would receive a fair return from the government. He emphasized that the government had helped the Indians with liberal sums of money well beyond the treaty stipulations of 1868 and that with their cooperation in this matter, they would continue to receive federal aid.[9]

The Indians would not come to an immediate decision and asked for time to consider the government's proposition. The natives seemed divided on the matter. The majority was willing to part with the Black Hills for an extremely large sum of money. The younger, more resolute minority was opposed to relinquishing the area at all. It was in a divided and ugly frame of mind that the Indians gathered for the second meeting of the grand council on September 23.[10]

No formal business actually took place at this meeting, but the outcome of the council was sealed at this time. Spotted Tail warned that there could be trouble and advised the commissioners to hold the meeting where only about twenty chiefs would be present, rather than an open meeting where thousands of Indians might attend. The commissioners, who were guarded by two troops of cavalry and a large force of friendly Brulé warriors brought along by the cautious Spotted Tail, decided to have an open meeting. The government negotiators seated themselves in the shade of a canopy and awaited Indian spokesmen to step forward. Instead, a commotion broke out, and a large force of Sioux warriors painted for combat rode up and circled the commissioners before retiring to form a line facing the whites. Other warrior bands repeated this per-

formance until a huge number of mounted Indians had gathered. Before
Red Cloud could open the discussions, an Oglala by the name of Little
Big Man caused a stir and rode forward and shouted he had come to kill
the whites. Friendly Indians under Young-Man-Afraid-of-His-Horse and
the white cavalry intercepted the Oglala while Terry quickly gathered
the dumbfounded commissioners into their wagons and led a speedy retreat to nearby Fort Robinson.[11]

The commissioners had witnessed either an example of the extremes
to which Red Cloud would go to stall or breakup the talks, or they had
come very close to losing their lives at the hands of the angry young
warriors who did not want to give up the Black Hills. It was a frightening
experience for Terry and his associates and left a lasting impression upon
them. After several informal sessions among themselves, the commissioners
decided to try once again to negotiate with the Indians. This time they
took Spotted Tail's advice and on September 26 asked twenty leading
chiefs to meet with them away from the masses of their fellow Indians.
During the next three days, the talks took place and the commissioners
were made to realize fully the enormousness of the Indian demands for
the Black Hills.[12]

One Indian chief after another explained his position to the commissioners. Red Cloud claimed that six nations had passed before him and that
he was part of the seventh. He closed by demanding that the whites must
take care of the next seven generations of his people. Red Dog rather un-
realistically suggested that the whites take only that part of the hills
where there was gold and leave the rest for the Indians. Little Bear put
it best when he asked what the whites would do if someone came into
their house and took all of the gold in it. The Black Hills, he explained,
was the Indian house of gold. Spotted Tail seemed to understand the
concept of gaining interest on money and prescribed as the best solution
that the whites award the Indians a large sum of money, which the
Indians would draw interest upon. Crow Feather likened the hills to his
head and described how he would be headless if the land were taken by
the whites.[13]

The various Indians presented their views in different ways, but they
all came out the same way. They were extremely reluctant to part with
the Black Hills and placed a value on the region that money could hardly
buy. Yet they were faced with the reality that the more powerful whites
were going to take the area regardless of how the Indians felt.[14]

At the meeting on September 28, Spotted Tail requested the commissioners to state in writing the amount they were willing to pay for the hills and the manner by which they would pay. That evening the whites drew up their "final proposition." In its final form the whites gave the Indians a choice of two proposals. One called for the purchase of mining, grazing, and farming rights in the Black Hills region defined as that area between the north and south forks of the Cheyenne River and west to the 104th meridian. In return for this lease, the whites would pay four hundred thousand dollars annually. Of this, a hundred thousand dollars or more would be expended on "objects beneficial for their civilization," and the remainder would be used to purchase subsistence goods. The United States could terminate this agreement upon a two-year notice, with all private property reverting to the Sioux. The alternate proposal was for the outright sale of the hills for $6 million to be paid in fifteen equal, annual installments.[15]

Other articles in the proposition called for three routes to the Black Hills through the Sioux reserve, purchase possibilities of the Bighorn country, which the commissioners did not push because they felt it was a waste of time under the present conditions, and provisions for the customary distribution of presents to the Indians. The commissioners made it clear (and one can see Terry's guiding hand here) that the chiefs must obtain approval by three-fourths of the adult Sioux males as stipulated in the Treaty of 1868. In the same manner, the commissioners must gain approval of Congress and the president to make the agreement binding.[16]

The chiefs retired to contemplate the matter. Neither the leasing nor the outright sale of the Black Hills appealed to them. If they leased the region, they knew they would never get the whites to leave. On the other hand, the whites were already there, and they probably would never leave, so why not get as much money as they could, they reasoned. This made sense, but the commissioners had offered only four hundred thousand dollars per year under either plan. This figure seemed low because the government claimed to be spending on an average of $2 million per year for subsistence for the Sioux.[17]

The grand council ended on the evening of September 29, with the Indians reaching no decision. Spotted Tail and the other chiefs could only promise to bring the proposition to their people. They did request that two or three prominent chiefs from each tribe be selected to return to Washington to continue the negotiations. On this note the conference ended, with little or nothing gained. Terry was impressed by the futility of continuing the negotiations because both sides seemed at loggerheads.

On the other hand he had gained personally from the sessions, if only to broaden his knowledge of the Sioux. In 1867 and 1868 when he had served on the peace commission, he had seen primarily the peaceful Sioux. Now he had firsthand knowledge of the wrath of the hostiles.[18]

The commissioners were quite open in admitting their failure to reach an agreement with the Sioux. In their report to the Interior Department they cited five reasons for failure. Uppermost was the belief that the Indians placed such a high value on the hills that no sum of money could adequately compensate them. Terry and his companions could also recommend not dealing with the Indians in grand council when a large number of Indians were in attendance. The absence of large quantities of presents for the Indians was unusual in that by this means treaties had been successfully concluded in the past. The Indians also believed that giving up the Black Hills was only a first step in the white man's plan of eventually taking the entire reservation from the Sioux. Finally the commissioners regretted the influence that non-Indians had on the Sioux. These people always seemed to benefit financially by preserving an atmosphere of distrust and unrest between the Indians and the whites.[19]

The commissioners unanimously concluded their report with the general recommendation that Congress must take the initiative and legally settle the question, and then notify the Sioux of their decision. They philosophized that force must be used in the beginning in order to achieve the end product of civilization. They further recommended that if the Indians protested or refused to give their consent to congressional action, the government must withhold all support not specifically called for in the Treaty of 1868.[20]

While Terry must have been reluctant to support these provisions, he could favor other commission recommendations in trying to keep with the spirit of the 1868 treaty. Education was to be compulsory for Indians between the ages of six and sixteen and offered at places away from adult Indians. The natives were expected to labor for their subsistence just as whites did and would be encouraged to seek private ownership of land. Thus the Indians were to become civilized and self-supporting as quickly as possible. The commissioners also recommended that the Sioux living in northwestern Nebraska at Red Cloud and Spotted Tail agencies be removed to the Sioux reservation onto lands suitable for farming and closer to transportation facilities so that provisions might be furnished at a lower cost. These supplies, the commissioners pointed out, must be issued under the "direct supervision of officers of the Army," and detailed reports were to be published annually. Finally, the commissioners stressed the need to abolish the agency system as it then functioned on the Sioux reserve and reorganize the whole system in order to provide adequate salaries for the government agents to ensure honesty and competency.[21]

General Terry's hopes for settling the Black Hills question were shattered by the failure of the Allison commission. He had lost control of the hills when thousands of miners had made their way to the mountains and the military had been unable to cope with the large influx. The presence of the military in the hills tended to scare the Indians more than it did the miners, and as a result the miners were generally not harassed by the Sioux. Since most of the miners approached the hills from the south, General Crook with headquarters in Omaha had gained primary responsibility for stopping them. His disposition was friendlier to the miners, and although Terry had struggled to maintain this region for the Sioux, the miners were there to stay. Serving on the Allison commission, Terry seemed to face up to the reality of white occupation of the hills and sought a revision of the Treaty of 1868 that would be more in tune with the events of the day. What seemed best in his judgment was for the Sioux to accept the loss of the Black Hills and seek to receive the largest compensation that was possible.

The Black Hills question passed out of Terry's hands with the failure of the Allison commission. In early November President Grant, Secretary Belknap, Generals Sherman and Crook, and Secretary of the Interior Zachariah Chandler met in conference in Washington and agreed upon a new policy for the Black Hills. As a result the government moved to a position of neutrality concerning the miners and their efforts to enter the hills. The gold seekers could go at their own risk, and the army would not molest them. Crook reported that miners were coming from all directions and that it would be impossible to keep them out.[22] Now restless souls cut loose by the panic of 1873 were free to try their hand in the Dakota goldfields. The Sioux could accept the loss of the Black Hills or they could stir up trouble in the northern plains, but it seemed unlikely that they could ever call the cherished Black Hills their property again.

Terry found the new unofficial policy hard to accept and although it was a lost cause, he continued his hard line against the miners in his department. When questioned by news reporters as late as mid-March 1876, he maintained that the orders he received during the past summer had not been officially modified or withdrawn and that he fully intended to enforce them even if he had to resort to force. He further explained to the newspapermen that "there was no question as to the explicitness or sacredness of the original treaty stipulations by our government with the said Sioux tribes as to utterly prohibit the molestation of that region in any manner by the whites."[23]

While Terry continued to talk of upholding treaties and laws, others contemplated harsh retribution against the hostile Sioux. Interestingly enough, this talk emanated from the offices of the Interior Department. One supporter of this stance was E. C. Watkins, an Indian inspector who reported to the commissioner of Indian affairs on November 9, 1875, on his recent investigation of the hostile Sioux. At first the inspector explained that "wild and hostile" bands of Sioux under Sitting Bull and other chiefs roamed over western Dakota and eastern Montana and camped in the rich valleys of the Yellowstone River area between the Bighorn and Little Missouri rivers. He described the area as a hunting "paradise," and because of the abundance of game the hostiles rarely had need of government subsistence. Instead they laughed at the white man who had failed to subjugate them and scorned "the idea of white civilization." The hostile Sioux, he reported, were rich in horses and robes and extremely well armed, each warrior carrying a pistol and a breech-loading rifle in addition to his bow and arrows. From their central location, Watkins related, the hostiles attacked their neighbors, the Arickarees, Mandans, Gros Ventres, Assiniboines, Blackfeet, Piegans, Crows, and Sioux, as well as white frontiersmen.[24]

In his report the Indian inspector pointed out that these hostiles numbered but a "few hundred warriors," and he recommended a winter campaign led by an experienced officer and one thousand men as ample to defeat the hostiles. He emphasized that the United States had done everything possible to civilize these Indians and to induce them to respect its authority, but they remained "as uncivilized and savage" as during the time of Lewis and Clark. Watkins warned of the danger that young men from friendly tribes would fall under the influence of the hostiles and join them in their plundering and killing. The result would be chaos among the peaceful tribes who suffered the injurious effects of repeated attacks and the loss of their young men. The peaceful Indians would never learn to farm while the hostiles were free to undermine the efforts of white humanitarians. Watkins concluded that the "*only* policy worthy an enlightened, Christian nation" was to fight a winter campaign and "*whip* them into subjection. They richly merit the punishment for their incessant warfare on friendly tribes, their continuous thieving, and their numerous murders of white settlers and their families, or white men wherever found unarmed." The battle was to be fought in the name of "civilization and the common cause of humanity."[25]

The Watkins report put matters in perspective for government officials. The hostile bands of Sioux had been an almost continuous problem for military and civilian authorities during the 1870s, and now Watkins had made a specific proposal that called for action. Interior Secretary Chandler was also under pressure from War Secretary Belknap to force the hostiles to remove to a reservation. On December 3 Chandler made his move; he ordered the commissioner of Indian affairs to notify the hostiles that they must remove to their assigned reservations by January 31, 1876. If they refused, he ordered that they be reported to the War Department and that a military force be sent to force compliance.[26] This order meant that the hostiles had about two months to move from their winter quarters to their reservation. It was an extremely demanding order and one that the hostiles would find difficult to comply with even if they so desired. It was almost as if the civilians in the government had concluded that they could not negotiate or lure the hostiles back to the agencies and under the pretext of the ultimatum they could turn the problem over to the military for a speedy settlement.

On December 6, the commissioner instructed the agents at Red Cloud, Spotted Tail, Lower Brulé, Crow Creek, Cheyenne River, Standing Rock, Devils Lake, and Fort Peck agencies to send runners to the hostile camps to make known the government demands. The orders were also communicated to the reservation Indians so that they might inform their relatives if they could reach them. It is a matter of conjecture whether all the hostile camps received notification of the government ultimatum or, indeed, if the government actually expected the hostiles to comply.[27]

The War Department, anticipating noncompliance on the part of the hostiles and the need to use force on these Indians, made preparations for a winter campaign. General Sheridan contacted Terry and Crook, the department commanders who would be involved in planning any military movements needed. Terry agreed that the hostiles in Montana (map 7) needed to be taught a lesson. He replied to Sheridan's query that his scouts believed that Sitting Bull's camp was located near the mouth of the Little Missouri River and well within the reach of troops from Fort Abraham Lincoln in normal winter weather. The general advised that he had five well-mounted

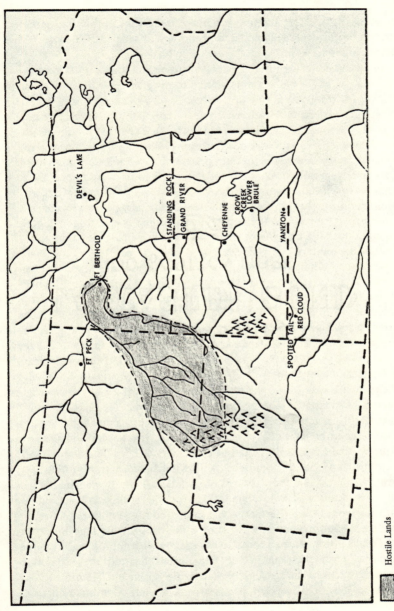

Hostile Lands

Map 7
INDIAN LANDS AND AGENCIES, 1875-1876

companies at that fort and two at nearby Fort Rice and thus had sufficient strength to make a quick and decisive movement against the hostiles if he were so ordered.

Terry was concerned that the movement be conducted with secrecy and rapidity. If the Indians were alerted to his plans, it would be extremely difficult for troops to follow the hostiles for any distance if they decided to flee. The general said nothing of the contemplated military operation to any of his men. To avoid suspicion he decided to order scouts from Fort Stevenson, a fort to the north, to try to locate Sitting Bull's camp. Because the troops at Fort Stevenson were infantry and thus not capable of a winter campaign against the hostiles, Sitting Bull would not become suspicious even if he learned of the scouting activity.[28] Crook was less specific in his reply and simply indicated a willingness to undertake any action necessary to force the hostiles back to their reservations.[29] Sheridan was anxious that a decision be made soon because he needed time to conduct the military operations before winter abated.[30]

While the military made their plans, Indian agents kept the commissioner abreast of activities at the agencies. Many reported that the hostiles had learned of the government demand, sometimes from Indian runners and sometimes from relatives. Most government officials in the Indian Office correctly concluded that a majority of the hostiles learned of the ultimatum during December 1875 and January 1876 and that they realized that they would have to fight the soldiers if they did not return to their agencies by January 31.[31]

The hostile reaction to the ultimatum received mixed reports. One agent guessed that a large number of these "wild and lawless Indians" would come to the agency. Others learned that many Indians planned to return to the reservation later in the winter or early spring. Several Indian agents predicted that the Indians would not return by the deadline and requested an extension of the time period. The Fort Berthold agent reported that Sitting Bull and "about 500 lodges of lawless ruffians" were near his agency and advised that they were a bad influence on his agency Indians and hoped that they would leave. Farther to the south about one hundred miles from Red Cloud Agency, it was rumored that Crazy Horse and Black Twin, two Oglala chiefs, were en route to the agency with approximately three thousand to four thousand people. Other agents heard that the Sioux declined to return to the agencies until after the spring buffalo hunt when they would visit the agency to trade their robes and skins and perhaps discuss the future location of their home. Rumors were numerous, but no one could tell the hostiles' intentions at this time.[32]

During January, Terry received intelligence concerning the location of the hostiles. Lieutenant Colonel Dan Huston, Jr., at Fort Stevenson reported that Sitting Bull's band had moved in the direction of the Yellowstone River to the west.[33] Major James Brisbin, commanding at Fort Ellis, Montana Territory, revealed that a large body of Sioux had been spotted in the Bighorn River area where they had killed six white trappers and wounded eight. Terry ordered Brisbin to rescue the remaining nineteen men, a task accomplished in late February and early March. Brisbin's scouts reported that the Sioux were camped to the south on Rosebud Creek.[34]

Although the hostiles' intentions were not known, it seemed obvious that they did not intend to come to the reservations as the government had ordered. On February 1, 1876, Interior Secretary Chandler wrote to Secretary of War Belknap, explaining that Sitting Bull and his people had evidently refused to obey the directions of the Indian commissioner and chose rather to continue to hunt and roam on nonreservation land. Chandler turned the problem of the hostiles over to the War Department "for such action on the part of the Army as you may deem proper under the circumstances."[35]

Sheridan had been waiting for this moment, for he saw in it a chance to end the Sioux problem. In the past a winter campaign with converging columns directed at the heart of the Indians' winter camp region had helped to settle the Southern Cheyenne and Arapaho question and had accomplished the removal of most of the natives to their reservations. Sheridan saw no reason why the same strategy would not work in the northern plains against the hostile Sioux. With this in mind he planned to bring General Crook from Fort Fetterman located in east central Wyoming, Colonel John Gibbon from Fort Ellis in southwestern Montana, and General Terry from Fort Abraham Lincoln. The columns would converge on the Indians, whose numbers were estimated at two hundred warriors with Crazy Horse and seventy warriors with Sitting Bull.[36]

Crook's men were first to start, leaving Fort Fetterman on March 1 with 883 men. Colonel Joseph J. Reynolds of the Third Cavalry actually commanded the expedition, and Crook merely accompanied it as an observer in order to determine by personal experience if winter campaigns on the northern plains were feasible. Reynolds and his men scouted the Tongue and Rosebud rivers but found no Indians. Next they crossed eastward to the Powder River and on the morning of March 17, they found the camp of Crazy Horse. The soldiers forced the Sioux to retreat and then destroyed the village. In the camp the soldiers had discovered a large storehouse of arms, ammunition, and supplies, which were probably obtained at Red Cloud and Spotted Tail agencies. The soldiers were able to capture most of the Indian herd of horses but lost it the next morning when the warriors attacked the unsuspecting soldiers. Because of the severity of the weather, Reynolds deemed it prudent to return to the relative warmth of Fort Fetterman. The expedition had been a partial success, but the failure to maintain the horse herd was a severe blow. Crook was also able to draw some conclusions about the practicality of winter campaigns. It had snowed every day but one on the campaign, and temperatures had reached well below freezing, the mercury actually congealing in the thermometer on several occasions. Crook concluded that a summer campaign with all its disadvantages was more desirable than suffering the winter season in the northern plains.[37]

Colonel Gibbon's column from Montana ran into cold weather also but not so many Indians as did Reynolds. They left Fort Shaw on March 17 and marched to Fort Ellis where other detachments joined them to bolster their number to 453 men. They suffered from frostbite and snow blindness but continued their march along the Yellowstone River. They explored the Rosebud and Bighorn rivers but found no Indians. On April 21, Gibbon received a dispatch from Terry informing him that Crook would not be ready to take to the field again until the middle of May and also that because of late snows in Dakota, he would not leave until May either. Terry ordered Gibbon to remain at makeshift Fort Pease at the mouth of the Bighorn on the Yellowstone River because he was in hostile territory with no support. Terry feared that the Indians might combine and overwhelm Gibbon before he or Crook arrived. Gibbon made camp at Fort Pease although he did send scouting parties up the Bighorn and Little Bighorn rivers. The hostiles had not yet arrived in this area in any force.[38]

Terry, no doubt, was disappointed that he could not get his column away for the winter campaign, but his men suffered frostbite as they gathered at Fort Abraham Lincoln. He concluded that the snow was too deep and that Sitting Bull had moved too far to the west to be reached by the Dakota column in the winter.[39] The general awaited the spring thaw and anticipated a military movement that would force the trouble-some hostiles to their reservations. It was not to be a campaign against the Sioux but a military movement aimed only at the hostiles, representing about 10 percent of the Sioux nation.

Government officials had used all of their weapons of diplomacy but to no avail. The Allison commission had failed to negotiate a treaty for the Black Hills, and the Sioux had made it clear that they did not want to relinquish their sacred lands at any price. Terry could not blame the Indians and only wished his soldiers were powerful enough to expel the white miners who were flooding into the region by the thousands. Next the whites had ordered the hostiles out of the Bighorn region, but instead of complying with the government demands, hundreds of Sioux had left their reservations along the Missouri to join their relatives and friends in the hostiles' camps and await the coming of the soldiers. The time for negotiation had passed, and the soldiers prepared to settle the problem with the hostiles on the battlefield. An abortive winter campaign by the soldiers left the stage set for a summer expedition that the military hoped would be their last against the Sioux.

NOTES

1. Payments did not begin until 1876. *Report of Commissioner of Indian Affairs Edward P. Smith,* November 1, 1875, H. Ex. Doc. 1, 44 Cong., 1 sess., Serial 1680, pp. 506-509.

2. Ibid.

3. For a good discussion of Red Cloud's visit to Washington, see James C. Olson, *Red Cloud and the Sioux Problem* (Lincoln: University of Nebraska Press, 1965), pp. 175-189.

4. Report of the Secretary of the Interior, *Report of the Commission Appointed to Treat with Sioux Indians for the Relinquishment of the Black Hills,* June 18, 1875, H. Ex. Doc. 1, 44 Cong., 1 sess., Serial 1680, pp. 686-687 (hereafter cited as *Allison Report*).

5. Ibid., pp. 687-688; Olson, *Red Cloud,* pp. 201-202. Two other men, Bishop E. R. Ames of Baltimore, Maryland, and Chicago Judge F. W. Palmer were appointed but refused to serve on the commission.

6. *Allison Report,* pp. 686-688.

7. Terry to Allison, August 27, 1875, LS, Records of the U.S. Army Continental Commands, 1821-1920, RG393, NA.

8. Terry to Gen. G. D. Ruggles, September 8, 1875, LS, Records

of the U.S. Army Continental Commands; *Yankton Press and Dakotaian,* September 23, 1875; Allison Report, pp. 688-689.

9. *Allison Report,* pp. 688-689.

10. Ibid.

11. George E. Hyde, *Spotted Tail's Folk: A History of the Brulé Sioux* (Norman: University of Oklahoma Press, 1961), pp. 212-214. The commissioners in their official report mentioned only that a serious outbreak was avoided by the quick action of Young-Man-Afraid-of-His-Horse. *Allison Report,* p. 689.

12. *Allison Report,* pp. 689-692.

13. Ibid.

14. Ibid.

15. Ibid., pp. 692-693.

16. Ibid.

17. The cost of subsistence for the Sioux by fiscal year follows: $1.9 million for 1870-1871, 1871-1872, and 1872-1873; $2.4 million for 1873-1874; $2 million for 1874-1875; and $1.7 million for 1875-1876. The figures are from ibid., p. 689.

18. Ibid.

19. Ibid., pp. 696-701.

20. Ibid.

21. Ibid., pp. 696-702.

22. *Yankton Press and Dakotaian,* November 11, 1875.

23. Ibid., March 18, 1876.

24. Watkins to Smith, November 9, 1875, in *Military Expedition Against the Sioux Indians,* H. Ex. Doc. 184, 44 Cong., 1 sess., Serial 1691, pp. 8-9.

25. Ibid.

26. Chandler to Belknap, December 3, 1875, in *Military Expedition,* p. 10.

27. Smith to Chandler, January 21, 1876, in *Military Expedition,* pp. 12-13.

28. Terry to Sheridan, December 28, 1875, in *Military Expedition,* p. 15.

29. Crook to Sheridan, December 22, 1875, in *Military Expedition,* p. 16.

30. Sheridan to Sherman, January 3, 1876, in *Military Expedition,* pp. 11-12.

31. Burke to Smith, December 31, 1875, Smith to Chandler, January 21, 1876, Bingham to Smith, January 24, 1876, in *Military Expedition,* pp. 12-13, 17, 18-19.

32. Burke to Smith, January 31, 1876, Darling to Smith, January 15, 24, 1876, Hasting to Smith, January 28, 1876, Bingham to Smith, February 12, 1876, in *Military Expedition,* pp. 19, 22-26.

33. Huston to Terry, January 15, 1876, in *Military Expedition,* p. 45.

34. Brisbin to Terry, March 21, 1876, in *Military Expedition,* pp. 50-51.

35. Chandler to Belknap, February 1, 1876, in *Military Expedition,* pp. 17-18.

36. Whipple to Sherman, March 25, 1876, in *Military Expedition,* p. 52; Annual Report of Sheridan, November 25, 1876, LR, AGO, RG94, NA.

37. Annual Report of Sheridan, November 25, 1876, LR, AGO, RG94, NA. For the best account, see J. W. Vaughn, *The Reynolds Campaign on Powder River* (Norman: University of Oklahoma Press, 1961).

38. Annual Report of Sheridan; Edgar I. Stewart, *Custer's Luck* (Norman: University of Oklahoma Press, 1955), pp. 97-119. For detailed coverage, see James H. Bradley, *The March of the Montana Column: A Prelude to the Custer Disaster* (Norman: University of Oklahoma Press, 1961).

39. Annual Report of Sheridan.

8 The Summer Expedition

For the previous twenty-five years the United States government had tried to negotiate with the hostile Sioux. Those efforts had failed for the most part because the hostiles did not want to make treaties with the whites. From their point of view, they had little to gain and would lose their land and freedom if the white man got his way. Because the whites had the advantage of a much larger population and superior technology, the Indians could do little but stall for time and appeal to the white man's sense of justice. This sense of justice in the 1870s centered on the concentration of Indians on reservations where they might be taught the ways of the white man.

The summer expedition of 1876 was important if the government planned to strengthen its Indian reservation program. Hundreds of formerly hostile Indians had settled down to live a quiet and sometimes productive life on the reservations. Others, however, left the agencies and roamed and hunted in Wyoming and Montana territories. The government could not allow the Indians this alternative and still expect to civilize and Christianize these people. Once the government pronounced its ultimatum and the hostiles failed to return to their agencies by February 1, the army was called into action. The much-heralded winter campaign had proven a frigid farce. There was little left for the military but to sit out the rest of the season and await the spring thaw, when the problem of the hostiles would be the first order of business.

General Terry approved of the plans for the summer expedition, and he felt that the hostiles must be forced to adhere to the reservation policy. These Indians could not be allowed to continue to threaten white settlements and disregard government orders. In the long run it would be best for the Sioux if they learned the white man's way because isolated land and buffalo were becoming scarce. This approach was consistent with

Terry's feelings that Indians must be dealt with in a legal and humane way. The general became upset with whites when they broke treaties as in the case of the Black Hills question. He also could side against the Indians when they left the reservations. To round them up and force their return to the agencies could only speed up the day when all Indians could enjoy the benefits of white civilization.

The hostiles had rejected the white ways and preferred to live in the old manner as long as possible. The warriors could hope only to escape the soldiers or inflict defeat on them in order to gain a few more months or years of freedom.

In the past the department commanders had allowed their top subordinates to lead expeditions into hostile territory. General Crook had placed Colonel Joseph Reynolds in command of the recent winter campaign from the Department of the Platte, and Terry had done the same with Custer's expedition of 1874 and the winter campaign of 1876 with Colonel Gibbon in charge of the Montana column. Terry had chosen Custer to head the Dakota column for the expedition against the hostiles in 1876, but events that transpired during the winter changed his thinking.[1]

Custer and his wife, Libbie, had spent part of the winter of 1875-1876 in the East at the time when a House committee under the chairmanship of Hester Clymer had begun to uncover some of the wrongdoings of Secretary of War William Belknap and Orvil Grant, the president's brother. The secretary and other War Department officials were suspected of selling Indian agency traderships, and the Clymer committee intended to gather all available information. Custer, rash and politically naive, maintained that he was well informed on the subject of corruption at the agencies and offered his services. The Clymer committee took him at his word and ordered him to Washington to testify.[2]

Custer was willing to appear before the committee, but he did not want this to interfere with the military operation that he was to lead in the spring. Terry had scheduled the expedition against the hostiles for a time shortly after the spring thaw and no later than mid-April. Custer testified on March 29 and April 4 and implicated both Secretary Belknap and Orvil Grant on hearsay evidence. He expected to return to the northern plains after he had given his testimony, but he was detained in the East by the Belknap impeachment proceedings, which began on April 17.[3]

Custer was anxious to return to Fort Abraham Lincoln and the organization of the expedition, but officials in Washington had other plans for him.

He sought support from Sherman, Sheridan, and Terry to intercede in his behalf with the impeachment managers to allow his removal from the East. He wrote to his wife that he heard often from Terry by telegraph, that a mutual good feeling existed between the two soldiers, and that Terry was anxious for him to return to Dakota.[4]

Because of Custer's troubles in Washington, events took a turn on April 28. Sheridan telegraphed Terry that instructions from the president through the secretary of war and general of the army had reached him and that someone other than Custer was to lead the expedition. Terry replied immediately with the names of two other colonels, but Sheridan was not satisfied. The next day Sheridan sent a dispatch explaining that for the "greatest success" of the expedition he wanted Terry to command the expedition.[5]

Custer, no doubt, had angered the president by presenting his circumstantial evidence against his brother at the Clymer hearings, and either Grant sought revenge or simply felt that Custer was not the best choice to lead the expedition. His administration was under much criticism because of blundering bureaucrats, and he could not afford to have the military expedition against the hostiles be unsuccessful. Custer had already been court-martialed once in 1868 when he had abandoned his command while on an expedition against Indians. Grant could not afford another such fiasco at this time. After Custer's return to Dakota, Grant stood firm in his decision not to allow the colonel to accompany his men on the expedition.[6]

Custer, depressed but still fighting, appeared before Terry with "tears in his eyes" and begged for aid. The kindly general helped Custer draw up a letter to the president in which the colonel respectfully but earnestly requested that as senior officer of the regiment that would march against the hostiles, he be spared the humiliation of seeing his men meet the enemy and he not share in the dangers.[7] Terry forwarded the dispatch and added a note that he felt Custer's services would be valuable to the regiment. Sheridan, in his turn, forwarded the telegram to Sherman. In it he expressed his sorrow that Custer did not show his interest in the expedition by staying at Fort Abraham Lincoln to organize his regiment for action rather than go east and become involved in a political question. Sheridan, somewhat embarrassed that he had requested executive clemency for Custer in 1868 so that the colonel might accompany his troops on that occasion, hoped that the officer would not discredit his profession in 1876.[8]

President Grant succumbed to Terry's wishes, and by May 8, it became clear that Custer could go on the expedition as commander of the Seventh Cavalry but that Terry would remain in overall command of the expedition against the hostiles. Sheridan advised Custer "to be prudent, not to take along any newspaper men who always work mischief, and to abstain from any personalities in the future."[9]

Now that Custer had been reprimanded and the command question had been cleared up, the military could outline their strategy. Sheridan planned to use converging columns to the area where the Indians were thought to have set up their camp. Crook was to march his approximately 800 troops from Fort Fetterman in Wyoming toward the Powder River-Bighorn River region. Gibbon was to continue his watch along the Yellowstone River with his estimated 450 men, and Terry was to move his command of about 925 soldiers from Fort Abraham Lincoln toward this same area. Unless these columns made physical contact with each other, it would be difficult to coordinate their movements. Terry knew of Gibbon's movement because he had given him his initial orders, and he planned for the two columns to link together along the Yellowstone River. Terry was less informed about Crook's troop deployment and knew it would be difficult to communicate with him.

Another problem that Terry contemplated was that of determining the location and the number of the hostiles. Numerous reports filtered into his office, but no clearcut picture materialized. From scouting reports Terry determined that the hostiles had left the Little Missouri River area and had moved west to the area between the Powder and Bighorn rivers. He could never be certain of their number, but on May 14, three days before the expedition left, Terry telegraphed Sheridan that he estimated their strength at fifteen hundred lodges and that the Indians were reported confident and ready to make a determined fight. If there were two to three warriors per lodge, the hostiles could field a force of from three thousand to forty-five hundred warriors. Terry could not be sure about their number, but he did expect a sizable force intent on making a stand against the army he commanded.[10]

The general and his staff arrived at Fort Abraham Lincoln on May 10, formally assumed command of the column on May 14, and embarked on the expedition the morning of May 17.[11] (See map 8.) Although many had been involved in frontier scouting activities and had encountered an occasional brush with Indians, few had been faced with the wrath of hundreds of warriors gathered in one place awaiting the arrival of the

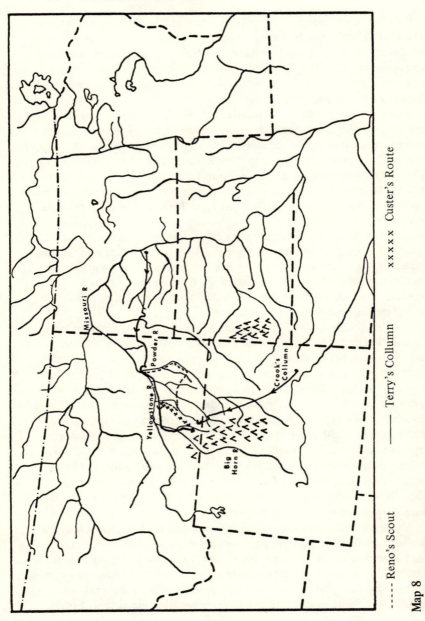

----- Reno's Scout   ——— Terry's Collumn   x x x x x Custer's Route

Map 8

THE SUMMER EXPEDITION OF 1876

military. Custer's only real experience had been in 1869 along the Washita River on the southern plains where he had surprise attacked a village of over one hundred Cheyennes in winter quarters. Indians usually did not fight when thousands of combatants were involved, preferring hit-and-run tactics where the element of surprise could be utilized. Terry's lack of experience in Indian-type guerrilla warfare, however, was not to be a factor in the battle just ahead.

The Dakota column that left Fort Abraham Lincoln was made up of all twelve companies of the Seventh Cavalry, three companies of infantry, forty Arikara scouts, twenty infantrymen to operate the three Gatling guns, and a train of 150 wagons. A cattle herd, which would supply fresh meat, extra horses, and about two hundred packers, teamsters, and herders completed the assembly.

The usual routine of camp life on the expedition began with reveille at 3:00 A.M. and included the march that commenced at 5:00 A.M. and setting up camp by mid-afternoon around 3:00 P.M. It was a rigorous experience for the forty-nine year old Terry but one to which he became accustomed. The general and his close friend and brother-in-law, Captain Robert P. Hughes, who served as his aide, spent much of their time writing letters and reports. Terry kept a field notebook in which he jotted down weather conditions, daily mileage figures, and times for starting and stopping the march. More revealing were the letters he sent to his four sisters, Polly, Betsey, Fanny, and Caddy (who was married to Captain Hughes), all of whom lived in St. Paul.[12]

The first night out of Fort Abraham Lincoln, Terry wrote from his camp on the east bank of the Heart River about thirteen miles from the fort. He was concerned that the march was so slow but realized that the wagons were overloaded with grain. With the animals eating twelve thousand pounds of grain a day, the wagons would soon be lightened enough to make faster marches. Hughes was busy during the march getting the wagons to close ranks and moving them to camp as soon as possible. Terry was quite tired at the end of the march and settled down to a good meal and warming fire.[13]

May 18 was spent in crossing the Heart River, an expanse of two hundred feet of mud and water. Terry found the view of his men building a corduroy road across the mud a picturesque sight. It took thirty to fifty of the men stripped to their pants and those rolled above their knees, pulling on ropes attached to the wagons, to move the stubborn wagons across the river. After covering about eleven miles and witnessing a vivid lightning storm, Terry made camp near the Sweet Briar River. He had a warm fire in his tent and ate a meal of roast beef, mashed potato, warm biscuit, and raw onions that were "beyond praise." Terry and his companion, Hughes, were feeling better now, and the general found his old powers of endurance returning.[14]

The next day was spent in avoiding swollen streams and marching on muddy terrain. After traveling twelve and a half miles, Terry decided to make camp. Just as his men had erected his tent, a violent storm of rain and one-inch hailstones came down, and all the men crowded into Terry's tent. It proved to be a short storm, and the "furious drying wind" that followed helped the uncomfortable men. Terry slept warm under his buffalo robes that night. May 20 proved to be another day of muddy travel. Terry was disappointed in their progress so far and felt they should be fifty-six miles from the fort rather than the forty-six miles they had actually covered. The rain and heavy wagons had slowed them considerably.[15]

May 21 was a gloomy, rainy day, but the column moved out early in the morning. The men bridged the Little Muddy stream, and by noon they were warmed by the sun. The country that the column passed through was better now, and Terry was pleased to find green valleys and gentle slopes, which facilitated his movement. He rode with the advanced guard on this occasion and liked it so well that he decided to continue the practice. By doing this it allowed him to reach camp earlier in the day and gave him time to write reports and rest while the wagons came up several hours later. The next day was bright and clear, and the column covered fifteen miles. They camped on the headwaters of the Knife River only seven miles from Young Men's Buttes. The following day the column moved to the grassy area around the buttes and rested for the remainder of the day.[16] The men lived in a relaxed atmosphere because there was little fear of Indian trouble until they reached the Little Missouri River.

Terry pushed the column hard during the next three days, covering nineteen, twenty, and thirteen miles respectively. On May 27, the general had unkind words about Custer's scouting ability. The colonel served as guide and undertook to lead the column through a pass in the mountains that he had traveled before. He got lost, however, and although the soldiers marched eighteen miles during the day, they wasted nine miles in searching for the pass. The column had penetrated the badlands, which

Terry described as "desolate, picturesque, naked hills of mud, clay, and partially formed stone." They were made of fantastic forms ranging from dull gray to almost fiery red. On May 28 the soldiers covered eight miles and built eight bridges; the following day they traveled six miles and constructed five more bridges before reaching the Little Missouri River for their camp.[17]

May 30 was a day of rest for some of the men but not for the bridge builders and the cavalry. Some men built a bridge across the Little Missouri River and worked on the road beyond. Custer took four companies of his regiment to the south looking for an Indian trail, but without success. Terry wrote to his sisters of his plans, explaining that he expected to break camp the next morning and to travel two or three marches west before he sent out reconnaissance parties in search of an Indian trail. If they found none, he wrote, the column would move to the Yellowstone River to resupply, although he still had sixteen or seventeen days of supplies left. Terry was disappointed that he found no sign of Indians on the Little Missouri and feared that they had scattered. He concluded that it would "be a most mortifying and perhaps imperious result to me" if he could not find any Indians. He could only hope that they were farther to the west and that he would find them and force them back to their agencies.[18]

Terry delighted his sisters with descriptions of the countryside. The land was destitute of trees, but the soil and grass were very good. He described the "profusion of beautiful flowers" that they traveled through and promised to bring home some seeds or roots of rose-colored flowers he found but could not identify. He also portrayed the men around him with their flaking, pealing, red noses and jet-black beards. Terry had praise for the cook who prepared antelope, venison, and beef to his taste.[19]

The soldiers crossed the Little Missouri on May 31 and covered about eleven miles. Again Terry had occasion to mention Custer in his field notebook. The impetuous colonel seems to have taken command of the wagon train or, as Terry put it, Custer was "playing wagon master." Later the general noted that Custer left the column to make a scout "without any authority whatever." Terry perhaps reflected in his tent that night as the rain fell that Custer had cut loose from Stanley's column in 1873 and there had been trouble over that. The general contemplated a get-tough policy with Custer and decided to use subordinate officers in place of the colonel to command reconnaissance parties, hoping that this subtle action might have the effect of putting the officer in his place.

About midnight the rain shower turned to snow, and the next morning the soldiers awoke to three inches of snow. The snow continued to fall all day, but at least the kegs for water were filled with fresh liquid. The men remained in camp for the next two days rather than trudge through the snow and mud that lay ahead.[20] Most of the soldiers played poker and cribbage. First Lieutenant Edward S. Godfrey of the Seventh Cavalry noted in his diary that he finished his *Harper's Monthly* for May, and most of the men had a good rest.[21] During this time Terry and Hughes had their tents pitched facing each other. The two officers used the front tent as a sitting room and the rear one as their bedroom. A Sibley stove in the front tent kept both tents warm. Their black cook served them a leg of Rocky Mountain sheep, bread, canned vegetables, and dried apple pie that night. Terry was impatient with the slow progress of the column but thought it better to go slow and give the animals proper rest so that they would be fit if Indians were sighted.

On June 3 the column resumed the march, and during the morning they came into contact with scouts from Colonel Gibbon's Montana column. Excitement grew when Terry learned that Gibbon was on the north side of the Yellowstone River and that the Indians were in great number opposite him and down the Rosebud. The colonel could not cross the river with his men since he had no river steamer and thus was not able to attack the hostiles. Terry marched his men twenty-five miles to Beaver Creek and made camp. While there he changed his plan and sent dispatches to Gibbon telling him to remain opposite the Rosebud while the Dakota column pushed on to the Powder River. During the next three days the column marched eighteen, twenty, and eighteen miles and searched out the headwaters of Beaver, Cabin, and O'Fallon's creeks. There were signs of small numbers of Indians but nothing of significance.[22]

By June 8 the Dakota column made camp at the mouth of the Powder River. Here they made contact with the steamer *Far West*, but to Terry's regret, he learned from some of Gibbon's men aboard the steamer that they had not received the general's latest orders, and thus the Montana column had moved east along the north bank of the Yellowstone in the direction of Terry's column. The next morning Terry took the steamer and reached Gibbon's camp thirty-five miles west of his own camp. The two officers talked on board the ship and agreed that Gibbon should return to his old position opposite Rosebud Creek on the north side of the Yel-

11. Sitting Bull, a Hostile Sioux Warrior and Medicine Man *(Courtesy State Historical Society of North Dakota)*

12. Colonel John Gibbon *(Courtesy National Archives—Brady Collection)*

13. Lieutenant Colonel George A. Custer *(Courtesy State Historical Society North Dakota)*

14. Captain Edward S. Godfrey *(Courtesy State Historical Society North Dakota)*

15. Major Marcus A. Reno *(Courtesy National Archives−Brady Collection)*

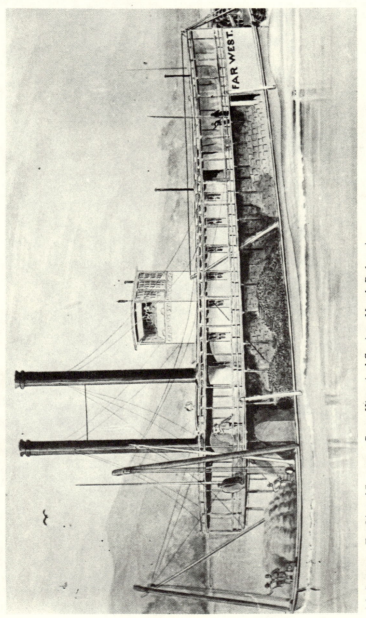

16. Steamer *Far West* (Courtesy State Historical Society North Dakota)

17. Fort Buford 15th Infantry Band (*Courtesy State Historical Society North Dakota*)

18. General Nelson A. Miles *(Courtesy Montana Historical Society)*

19. Gall, a Hostile Sioux Warrior *(Courtesy State Historical Society North Dakota)*

20. Fifth Infantry in Buffalo Coats—Fort Keogh, Montana   *(Courtesy Custer Battlefield National Monument)*

lowstone. It had taken Terry eight and a half hours against the current to reach Gibbon's camp, but only one and three-quarters hours to return to his Powder River camp.[23]

On June 10 Terry sent Major Marcus Reno with six companies of the Seventh Cavalry to explore the valley of the Little Powder to its mouth and then to cross west to Mizpah Creek, Pumpkin Creek, and Tongue River before he returned to the Yellowstone River. He instructed the major not to cross to the Rosebud but to follow the Tongue back to the Yellowstone where the rest of the soldiers would be waiting. Reno evidently carried out the first part of these instructions and explored the various creeks assigned to him. Terry thought that Reno might locate General Crook and the Platte column to the south, but he did not. Crook was in the area and attacked the camp of Crazy Horse on June 17, but little of significance occurred except that the Platte column withdrew to the south to resupply and thus removed itself from the area where the big battle was to take place. It is possible that at the time of Crook's battle on the Rosebud, Reno's scout was fewer than forty miles away from the scene of the engagement.[24]

If Reno found no Indians, Terry planned to explore the Rosebud and fully expected to find the Indians that Gibbon's men had spotted opposite them on the Yellowstone. His plan of attack was to make a double movement with one-fourth of the force going up the Tongue close to its headwaters, then crossing to the headwaters of the Rosebud and descending the stream to meet the larger force, which would work its way up the Rosebud. In between the two forces, he expected to locate the large hostile camp and to defeat the Indians in battle.[25]

Reno had discovered a large Indian trail on the Tongue and had followed it for about a day and a half or about forty miles over to the Rosebud. They found deserted village sites along the way and estimated by the number of campfires that there were 350 lodges and that the Indians had camped there about three weeks ago.[26] Reno had nearly exhausted his ten days of supplies and decided to return to the Yellowstone.

Terry and his men had bided their time with camp routine, short scouting excursions, which uncovered no Indians, and moving the camp to the mouth of the Tongue River. Terry skillfully used the river steamer on some of these scouting trips and got his supplies in position by prudent use of the *Far West*. Lieutenant Godfrey speculated in his diary why Custer had not been sent in command of the scout. Perhaps Terry in his own way was trying to tell Custer to follow military procedure rather than to go his own individual way. If so, his warning fell on deaf ears.[27]

Terry received the anxiously awaited dispatches from Reno on June 19, and he was disturbed by what he read. The major informed Terry that he had been on the Rosebud and was now at the mouth of that stream. He had found the Indian trail and camp sites, and he awaited further orders. Terry was furious that Reno had knowingly disobeyed orders by going to the Rosebud and sent Hughes to determine the reason. Reno had no good reason other than that he hoped to attack and to defeat the hostiles before they could escape.[28] Terry, of course, had the same objective in mind but desired to get his entire force into position in order to prevent escape before he attacked. Custer was upset with Reno for just the opposite reason. He, no doubt, would have followed the trail until he found the Indians and attacked them. Terry was in an uncomfortable position: the two top field commanders of his best fighting unit were unreliable. Custer had been court-martialed once, threatened on another occasion, and was in difficulty with President Grant at the time. Reno, it was rumored, had a drinking problem, and now he was a prime candidate for court-martial. Terry must have been frustrated and concerned as he pondered the leadership question of the Seventh Cavalry. Now that a battle with the Sioux seemed imminent, he reluctantly concluded that his best choice was to go with Custer, the more experienced Indian fighter.[29]

Reno did bring back information that was helpful to the commander even if he had disobeyed orders. Terry now had a good idea of the location of the Indian camp. Reno's intelligence, added to that already obtained from some of Gibbon's Indian scouts, pointed conclusively to the valley of the Little Bighorn as the location of the Indian camp. The general still could follow his basic strategy of trapping the hostiles between his two columns if he could maneuver his men into position before the Indians escaped.

Terry spent the next three days in moving his men and supplies along the Yellowstone River to the mouth of the Rosebud.[30] Grant Marsh, who captained the *Far West* and played such a key role in supplying and transporting the troops, described Terry as the "dominating figure" on the expedition:

Quiet and undemonstrative, he sat hour after hour at his
desk in the cabin, poring over maps and papers, consulting

with the officers who came and went, working with an energy
which seemed tireless upon the innumerable problems of the
campaign he was conducting. The calm eyes which looked
forth from his strong, bearded face inspired in the observer a
sense of confidence and security. His brain seemed one capable
of grasping so firmly every phase of the situation, of guarding so
carefully against every danger, that his plans could not miscarry.
The military impulses of his nature were tempered and strengthened
by the legal acumen derived from his years of practice at the bar.
. . . He was a man whose words were not many, but, once spoken,
they were remembered. When he praised, the praise was merited;
when he censured, it was for grave cause. Though he was not one
whose characteristics suggested the ideal Indian fighter, he wove
a plan of campaign against the savage foe in his front which was
almost faultless in conception.[31]

The evening of June 21, Terry met on board the *Far West* with other
members of his staff to make final preparations for the campaign against
the hostiles. Gibbon, Custer, and Major James Brisbin of the Second Cavalry
gathered in the ship's cabin. Terry had a map of the country and with pins
stuck through the paper and into the table he traced the route he thought
Custer should take. The general was nearsighted and asked Brisbin to mark
Custer's line of march with a blue pencil. It was clear that Terry wanted
Custer to follow the Rosebud, locate the Indian trail, and follow it until
it was obvious in which direction the trail led. If the trail pointed toward
the Little Bighorn, as Terry was positive it would, Custer was not to follow
it but to continue south to the headwaters of the Tongue. Then he was
to turn westward toward the Little Bighorn.[32]

The general was concerned that the hostiles might retreat to the south,
and Custer's column was to cut off their avenue of escape. He ordered
this route also to allow Gibbon the extra day he would need to march
his slow-moving infantry to the mouth of the Little Bighorn from the
north. In addition Terry ordered Custer to examine the upper part of
Tullock's Creek, locate any Indians there, and send word by a scout of
the results of the exploration. Gibbon's column would explore the lower
portion of Tullock's Creek; if they found no Indians, this would eliminate
one further place where the Indians were not to be found. The careful
general was concerned with every detail in his effort to locate and defeat
the hostiles.[33]

Terry's plan was well drawn and might have succeeded if it had been followed. The only real avenue of escape from the area for the hostiles was to the south into the Bighorn Mountains. Once the Indians had gained this position, they could scatter and hide, and the army would be helpless to force their return to the reservations. The hostiles' enemy, the Crow, lived to the west and blocked that escape route, and Gibbon's column sealed off the north.[34]

Much has been written concerning whether Custer disobeyed Terry's orders. Certain points seem clear. The hostiles were aware of the presence of troops on the Yellowstone, and Terry knew he must cut off their escape route. Custer was sent to accomplish this and also to attack the Indian camp when he came upon it. Terry realized that it would be next to impossible for the two columns to act in concert because they did not know the exact location of the enemy camp. But he did hope to bring both columns into action and to entrap the hostiles between the two forces. This did not mean that the columns would attack the village simultaneously but that they would attack the hostiles when they came into contact with them.

Custer was not wrong in attacking the village once he had determined its location, but he was guilty of not following his instructions to the point where he could act in concert with Gibbon's column. Custer did not examine Tullock's Creek nor did he send a scout to report to Gibbon's column. He did not go to the headwaters of the Tongue, instead following the Indian trail straight to the Little Bighorn. His hasty marches allowed his column to reach the Little Bighorn a day and a half before Gibbon's column could reach the mouth of the Little Bighorn. Once in the valley, Custer had little choice but to attack the village.

Custer's actions were deliberate. Shortly after he had been reinstated in the summer expedition, he had told Colonel William Ludlow, chief engineer of the Department of Dakota, that he would cut loose from Terry and gain all the glory for defeating the hostiles.[35] On other occasions he had claimed that the Seventh Cavalry could "whip all the Indians in the northwest."[36] Custer had ordered that an unusually large amount of salt be taken with his column in case the soldiers had to live on horse meat during their long chase of the hostiles. Terry and his staff did not believe that the Indians would make a stand but would scatter when they realized the size of Terry's force. If the hostiles escaped, the expedition would be a failure, and the military would have to send another force the following summer. Custer was not going to allow the enemy to escape and was prepared to follow them back to their agencies if necessary.[37]

Terry had couched his orders in somewhat general terms, which gave Custer the leeway he needed to go his own separate way. The general had pointed out that it was impossible to give any definite instructions and that he had too much respect for Custer's ability to impose precise orders on him that might hamper his "action when nearly in contact with the enemy."[38] This was not an unusual type of comment to use in field orders because commanders could not anticipate the location of Indian villages or the actions of the hostiles.[39]

Terry believed that he must be in position at the mouth of the Little Bighorn by June 26 and that Custer should be ready at the other end so they could begin their closing movement with the first to locate the Indian village to begin the battle. After Terry reviewed the troops, Custer's men moved out of camp at noon on June 22. They traveled rapidly in marches of twelve miles on that day, thirty-five miles the next day, and on June 24, forty-five miles and after a rest ten miles farther. After a rest but without unsaddling, Custer marched his exhausted men twenty-three miles to the battlefield on June 25.[40]

Terry's column also made good time. They parted with Custer's command at the mouth of the Rosebud on June 21 and marched seventeen miles along a route south of the Yellowstone. That night it rained and hailed. The next day the soldiers marched over muddy terrain for twenty-two miles toward the mouth of the Bighorn River. The cavalry marched ahead of the infantry and Gatling guns, and Terry and his staff followed in the *Far West.* On June 23, the column reached old Fort Pease, opposite the Bighorn on the Yellowstone, after another twenty-two mile hike.

The following day Gibbon ordered a detachment of Indian scouts out to scout Tullock's Creek and to seek a crossing point on that stream. While the scouts were out, Terry arrived with the *Far West,* and Gibbon's column was transported from the north to the south bank of the Yellowstone. It took four trips for the boat to transport the cavalry, infantry, and artillery. Gibbon became ill at this time and was left on board the *Far West.* Brisbin reported that the colonel was suffering from "Hyatic Colic of the Stomach and bowels." The Indian scouts returned that evening and reported finding no hostiles, but they had seen buffalo, one of which was wounded by an arrow. They located a good crossing point of Tullock's Creek, and Terry planned his advance for the next day.[41]

June 25 was the date of Custer's battle, but for Terry it was a day of hard marching in order to be in position at the mouth of the Little Bighorn. The march commenced at 5:30 A.M. and followed over rough terrain. The absence of water in these badlands made the march difficult for the men, who had emptied their canteens of the alkali water they had in them. The infantry struggled until 6:30 P.M. when they made camp in the valley of the Bighorn. They had seen smoke in the direction of the Little Bighorn, and all believed that the hostile village would be found there the next day. Officers allowed no fires in camp, and the exhausted infantry rested after a grueling twenty-three mile hike.[42]

Terry was determined to push on with the cavalry to get as close to the Little Bighorn as he could. He left orders with the infantry commanders to break camp at 4:00 A.M., and then he moved off toward the Little Bighorn. The cavalry rode through unfamiliar lands without the benefit of knowledgeable scouts. As rain fell and it grew dark, there was danger that the detachment would break up into fragments and become lost. At one time the column rode out to a precipice with nothing but the Bighorn River 150 feet below. Confused and lost, Terry placed the command in the hands of an old Crow scout who claimed to have roamed the lands as a boy fifty years before. To the relief of all, he led the soldiers to a valley where they made camp by midnight. Most went to sleep that night knowing that they would meet the hostiles the next day.[43]

On the morning of June 26, Terry sent scouts out to locate the hostile camp while the main body of the cavalry awaited the arrival of the infantry. Lieutenant James Bradley and his Crow scouts left camp at 4:00 A.M. and shortly after came upon an Indian trail. Suspecting that they were made by a Sioux scout, the Crows followed them. The Indians crossed the Bighorn and were spotted by Bradley and the Crows. To their surprise the army detachment discovered that the Indians were really three Crow scouts who had been with Custer's column. Through smoke signals from across the river they told of the great disaster that had befallen Custer and his men.

Bradley quickly rode back to tell Terry the news. The cavalry had been joined by the infantry at about 10:00 A.M. and had pushed to within two miles of Bradley's encounter with the three Crows. He related the news to the startled officers, but many did not take Bradley seriously. Terry believed the story and hastened to push on toward the Indian village. The column advanced in fighting order, the Gatling gun battery and three companies of cavalry on one side of the pack mules and the other half behind. In the lead rode General Terry and Colonel Gibbon, now recovered from his illness. Two scouting detachments rode ahead of the column on either side determining the route and searching for the hostile camp. The infantry marched thirty miles before Terry decided to make camp around 9:00 P.M. The men were exhausted but they had reached the Little Big-horn on June 26, the day they had planned to be there. They had not yet fought the hostiles but were sure to do so the next day.[44]

Terry broke camp the next morning about 7:30 A.M. and marched four miles to the Indian camp. There they found ample supplies of lodge poles and camp utensils, indicating that the hostiles had hurriedly broken camp during the night.[45] While the soldiers rummaged through the aban-doned Indian camp, Lieutenant Bradley had been exploring the nearby hills with a mounted infantry detachment. In a voice trembling with emo-tion, he reported to Terry that he had counted the dead, naked bodies of 197 soldiers and had made an identification of a body he presumed was Custer's. The immensity of the disaster settled over the men, and the worst of their fears became reality.

Over half of Custer's command was still not accounted for, and Terry ordered his men to continue up the river bank until they were found. Two or three miles farther the Montana column reached a high bluff, and at about 11:00 A.M. they discovered the remainder of the Seventh Cavalry, over three hundred men. Lieutenant Godfrey best described the moving scene that followed:

> The grave countenance of the General [Terry] awed the men to silence. The officers assembled to meet their guests. There was scarcely a dry eye; hardly a word was spoken, but quivering lips and hearty grasping of hands gave token of thankfulness for the relief and grief for the misfortune.[46]

June 27 was a grim day for Terry. He sorted through the various bits of information he had in order to draw up an official report to forward to Sheridan. He related to the division commander that Custer had located the Indian village, divided his forces, and had met disaster. Reno had been sent with three companies to attack the village from the south. Reno's men had crossed the Little Bighorn and charged the camp, dismounted and fought on foot, retreated to a wooded area on the banks of the river, and finally recrossed the stream and sought refuge on the high bluffs on the right bank. Custer with five companies had attempted to enter the village three miles below where he and his men met their fate. Captain Frederick Benteen with three companies had been sent by Custer to explore some hills to the south and later joined Reno on the bluffs as did the supply train. There they were found the next day by the Montana column.

Terry estimated the total number of soldiers killed at over three hundred and listed the wounded at fifty-one. He reported the escape of the Indians and calculated their number of warriors at not fewer than twenty-five hundred. The size of the Indian village, he estimated, was about three miles in length and one mile in width. In this initial report, Terry had simply outlined the course of the battle, took full responsibility for the defeat, and expressed his feelings of the terrible loss that they had suffered.[47]

On July 2, five days later, Terry wrote a confidential letter to his commanding officer describing Custer's conduct and disregard for orders and in general putting Sheridan "more fully in possession of the facts of the late operations." Terry outlined his plan of attack, and drawing upon information furnished by surviving officers of the Seventh, he showed how Custer had disregarded his orders and marched his men to an early confrontation with the Indians. Unfortunately Terry's confidential report reached Sheridan before the earlier dispatch and became part of the official documentation of the battle. Terry had tried to take the responsibility for the defeat rather than harm the reputation of a dead soldier, but to no avail.

The general reflected on the recent battle and might have had second thoughts about his ability as commander, but his lack of experience had not been a key factor. He had moved his column of over nine hundred men through mud and snow and across numerous streams and rivers. He had correctly located the hostile camp, and he had planned a campaign that stood a good chance of success if his subordinates had carried out their instructions.[48] Terry might be faulted because he did not go in command of the Seventh Cavalry himself. He had experienced problems with both Colonel Custer and Major Reno, the top commanders of the Seventh Cavalry, and he might have kept them in harness by his presence.

Custer supporters usually blamed Reno, not Terry, for the failure at the Little Bighorn. The major's lack of aggressiveness in his attack on the Indian village was an important factor, but in retrospect it seems to have been a saving grace for most of his men. The hostiles were in too great a number for Reno's 150 men to have survived a charge into the large village.[49] It is true that the major acted badly on the bluff later in the day, and only the timely arrival of Captain Benteen saved that situation. Terry has stood above the controversy in most cases. His gentlemanly conduct and his support of Custer in the Grant question were factors in his support, and his willingness to shoulder the blame for the failure of the battle has removed him as a target of the Custer supporters. Instead more vulnerable persons like Reno and Benteen have received the blunt of the attack.

Custer has had his share of criticism also. He has been blamed for disobeying Terry's orders and for seeking the glory of defeating the Indians for himself and for the Seventh Cavalry. More to the point was the fact that the colonel handled his men badly when hostilities began. By splitting his forces into four groups, he made it possible for the Indians to inflict severe damage on his elite regiment.[50]

Terry and the men of the summer expedition against the hostiles had suffered a major setback. Crazy Horse and his warriors had defeated Crook on the Rosebud on June 17, and the general had withdrawn to resupply. Eight days later those same Indians, plus many others, had joined to defeat a detachment of Terry's forces. These defeats must not be looked upon so much as defeats of the whites but rather as victories for the hostile Sioux and Northern Cheyennes. The Indians had changed their military tactics from one of hit-and-run to that of all-out warfare by large numbers of warriors. The whites had underestimated the Indians, and the heavily depleted ranks of the Seventh Cavalry gave witness to this fact.

The victory by the warriors actually speeded up the decline of the Sioux rather than delaying it. Terry and the army were more determined than ever to gain a victory over the hostiles, and hundreds of soldiers flooded into the northern plains to bring a hasty end to the freedom of the hostiles. Even in victory at the Little Bighorn, the Sioux were forced to evacuate their village to escape Terry's column moving from the north. The soldiers would not abandon the chase.

NOTES

1. Edgar I. Stewart, *Custer's Luck* (Norman: University of Oklahoma Press, 1955), pp. 121-131.

2. Ibid.

3. Ibid.

4. Marguerite Merington, ed., *The Custer Story: The Life and Intimate Letters of General George A. Custer and His Wife Elizabeth* (New York: Devin-Adair, 1950), pp. 292-293, has copies of letters George to Elizabeth, April 25, 1876, and George to Elizabeth, April 29, 1876.

5. Robert P. Hughes, "The Campaign Against the Sioux in 1876,"

Journal of the Military Service Institution of the United States 18 (January 1896): 9, in William A. Graham, *The Story of the Little Big Horn* (New York: Bonanza Books, 1959).

6. Sherman to Custer, May 4, 1876, LS, Records of the Headquarters of the Army, 1825-1903, RG108, NA.

7. Mark Kellogg, a newspaper reporter who accompanied the soldiers on the Sioux expedition of 1876, described Terry as a "Gentleman soldier" who was a "popular, kind, and considerate commander." Oliver Knight, *Following the Indian Wars* (Norman: University of Oklahoma Press, 1960), p. 202.

8. Terry to Custer, May 6, 1876 and Sheridan to Sherman, May 7, 1876, in Loyd J. Overfield, Ed., *Official Documents of the Little Big Horn* (Glendale, Calif.: Arthur H. Clark Co., 1971), pp. 14-16.

9. Sherman to Terry, May 8, 1876, LS, Records of the Headquarters of the Army, 1825-1903, RG108, NA.

10. Terry to Sheridan, telegram, May 14, 1876, in Hughes, "Campaign Against the Sioux," p. 16.

11. Hughes, "Campaign Against the Sioux," p. 15.

12. Terry to Polly, May 17, 1876, Terry Papers, Yale University Library; Alfred H. Terry, "The Field Diary of General Alfred H. Terry, 1876" (Washington, D.C.: Library of Congress), p. 1.

13. Terry, "Field Diary," p. 1.

14. Terry to Betsey, May 18, 1876, Terry Papers.

15. Ibid.

16. Terry to Fanny, May 23, 1876, Terry Papers; Terry, "Field Diary," pp. 3-10.

17. Terry, "Field Diary," pp. 3-10.

18. Ibid.

19. Ibid.

20. Ibid., pp. 10-12.

21. E. S. Godfrey, diary, Godfrey Papers, pp. 4-5, Library of Congress, Washington, D.C.

22. Terry to the Girls, June 2, 1876, Terry Papers.

23. Ibid.

24. Overfield, *Official Documents,* p. 20.

25. Terry to the Girls, June 2, 1876, Terry Papers.

26. "Custer's Last Battle Mss.," Godfrey Papers, pp. 8-10.

27. Godfrey diary, p. 7.

28. Terry, "Field Diary," pp. 21-17.

29. Annual Report of Terry, November 21, 1876, LR, AGO, RG94, NA; Stewart, *Custer's Luck,* pp. 240-241.

30. Stewart, *Custer's Luck,* pp. 240-241.

31. Joseph Mills Hanson, *The Conquest of the Missouri: Being the Story of the Life and Exploits of Captain Grant Marsh* (Chicago: A. C. McClurg, 1909), pp. 246-247.

32. Annual Report of Terry, 1876, LR, AGO.

33. Ibid.

34. Ibid.

35. Hughes, "Campaign Against the Sioux," pp. 14-15, 32; Stewart, *Custer's Luck,* p. 138. Terry did not hear of Custer's "cut loose" comment until he returned to St. Paul in September 1876.

36. Brisbin to Godfrey, January 1, 1892, Godfrey Papers; Donald F. Danker, ed., *Man of the Plains: Recollections of Luther North, 1856-1882* (Lincoln: University of Nebraska Press, 1961), p. 188.

37. Edward C. Bailly, "Echoes from Custer's Last Fight: Accounts by an Officer Never Before Published," *Military Affairs, Journal of the American Military Institute* 17 (1953): 176. This is taken from Winfield Scott Edgerly's account. Custer visited him on the night of June 21, shortly after Terry's staff meeting.

38. Annual Report of Terry, 1876.

39. Sheridan to Sherman, May 29, 1876; James T. King, *War Eagle: A Life of General Eugene A. Carr* (Lincoln: University of Nebraska Press, 1963), pp. 102, 154-55, give good examples.

40. Annual Report of Terry, 1876.

41. Terry, "Field Diary," pp. 29-31; Brisbin to Godfrey, January 1, 1892, Godfrey Papers.

42. Terry, "Field Diary," pp. 31-34; James H. Bradley, *The March of the Montana Column: A Prelude to the Custer Disaster* (Norman: University of Oklahoma Press, 1961), pp. 144-150.

43. Terry, "Field Diary," pp. 32-34; Bradley, *March of the Montana Column,* pp. 150-151.

44. Terry, "Field Diary," pp. 35-36; Bradley, *March of the Montana Column,* pp. 152-160.

45. Stewart, *Custer's Luck,* p. 465. The author pointed out that it was the Indian custom to leave the belongings of the deceased when camp was broken.

46. "Custer's Last Stand," mss., Godfrey Papers, p. 49.

47. Annual Report of Terry, 1876.

48. Ibid.

49. Robert M. Utley, *Custer and the Great Controversy* (Los Angeles: Westernlore Press, 1962), p. 54.

50. James M. Merrill, *Spurs to Glory: The Story of the United States Cavalry* (Chicago: Rand McNally, 1966), p. 227, has quotes by Sheridan and Grant.

9 Victory over the Hostiles, 1876-1877

Terry realized his worst fears that June day on the banks of the Little Bighorn River in Montana Territory. The terrible defeat at the hands of the hostiles was a terrific shock to those military men who believed that no United States cavalry regiment could be so decisively defeated by Indians. Terry's men had toiled for over a month to reach the hostile camp, only to have the Indians inflict defeat on the soldiers and make their escape.

The general reasoned that there was still time to gain victory over the hostiles before winter returned. He realized that it was rare to win a military success over nomadic natives during the warm weather months when the Indians could outride the slower-moving soldiers. Terry also understood that he must chase and harass the hostiles and whenever possible destroy their camp equipage and food stores. In this way the Indians would not be able to stock up their provisions for the long winter months ahead, and they probably would have to return to their agency to survive. Because of Terry's and Crook's persistence in carrying the fight to the natives during the next year, they were able to gain the elusive triumph over the hostiles and to determine the destiny of the nonreservation Indians on the northern plains.[1]

Victory over the hostiles must have seemed a long way off for Terry as he viewed the hastily abandoned Indian village and the wounded and dead soldiers of his command at the Little Bighorn battle site. The events of the past few days and the reasons for defeat weighed heavily on Terry's mind. Still, he must continue. Terry carefully planned his next moves. The first step was to take care of the dead. On the morning of June 28, he ordered the Seventh Cavalry to the Custer battlefield where he assigned different companies to various sections of the field. The soldiers were fortunate to find shovels in the debris of the Indian village to facilitate their burial duties.[2]

While this grim task was underway, Terry sent out scouts to explore the surrounding area to locate possible survivors of the battle. None were found, and it appeared certain that Custer had lost his entire five companies. Terry ordered an additional company of scouts under the command of Captain Edward Ball to locate the route of the Indian withdrawal. The trail led south toward the Bighorn Mountains. Ball's cavalry followed the trail for about fifteen miles where it divided. The Indians had burned the grass beyond this point, and it was difficult to follow the trail either to the southeast or the southwest. Ball reported back to Terry, who was busy with the wounded.[3]

The general was more concerned about the injured than pursuing the Indians at this time. Late that afternoon he had his entire command ready to move toward the mouth of Little Bighorn and a rendezvous with the *Far West.* It took eight men to carry each litter, and the movement by this means proved to be unsuitable. Litter bearers stepped into holes in the dark, and they jostled the wounded. A small number of the wounded were carried on horse litters, and this method worked much better. After four hours of travel in this manner, the men made camp at 8:00 P.M. Terry, convinced that horse litter transportation was the best for the wounded, ordered some of his men to return to the abandoned Indian camp early the next morning to gather discarded lodge poles to use for horse litters. By 6:30 P.M. the column was ready to march. Terry preferred to travel at night in order to avoid the heat of the day and because the wounded would bear up much better under these conditions. By 2:00 A.M. on June 30, the soldiers reached the boat. The horse litters had proved a great success.[4]

Terry conferred with Captain Grant Marsh, the skipper of the *Far West,* and impressed upon him how important it was to transport the wounded safely to the base at the mouth of the Bighorn. The captain ordered the deck covered with grass to a depth of over a foot and then had his men place tarps over it to make a comfortable mattress. Marsh made a quick and safe trip, and two days later the Reno and Gibbon columns joined them on the Yellowstone. The *Far West* was used to ferry the soldiers across to the north bank of the Yellowstone, and by noon of July 3, the wounded were back on board and on their way to Bismarck. It took Marsh fifty-four hours to cover the 710 miles and bring the sad news of the army's defeat to the grief-stricken people of Bismarck and Fort Abraham Lincoln.[5]

Terry sent one of his aides, Captain Edward W. Smith, on the riverboat to Bismarck to answer any questions that Sheridan or Sherman might have. He also instructed Smith to seek information about General Crook's activities and to ascertain his location, of which Terry was still in doubt. The general further directed Smith to make arrangements to refit the Dakota column, especially in the matter of animal transportation. Terry was unwilling to risk steamers on the low waters of the Bighorn River again so late in the season and indicated that he needed at least one hundred horses to mount the cavalry men he now had with him.[6]

The Dakota column spent most of the month of July in camp on the north bank of the Yellowstone opposite the Bighorn River awaiting supplies. Terry consumed much of the time searching for Indians in the area and waiting for reports from Crook. He utilized the *Josephine* and the *Far West*, when it returned from Bismarck on July 17, to steam back and forth along the Yellowstone between the Bighorn and Powder rivers in search of hostiles. On July 7, he learned from seven Crow scouts about Crook's fight on June 17 with the hostiles. The general, aware that Crook must be in the area, tried to get messages to him on three occasions. The last effort proved successful, and from Crook's reply, he learned of the route of advance the Platte column would follow and their estimation of the location of the Indians. Terry also received dispatches from General Sheridan via Fort Ellis, locating the hostiles on the Rosebud. He was anxious to continue the campaign, but he could do little until he was reinforced and resupplied and had worked out plans with Crook for their concerted troop movements.[7]

Terry sent Captain Hughes on the *Josephine* to Bismarck to make arrangements for the final movements of reinforcements and provisions. The general continued to send out scouting patrols to search for hostiles in the area, but there were also leisure moments. Although some of the soldiers became ill, many fished, played cards, and went swimming. The mosquitoes were bad, and the weather was hot during the day, but during the cooler evenings the officers gathered for pleasant sings. For most life seemed tolerable except for the shortage of vegetables. The officers enjoyed boxes of goods sent from loved ones in Bismarck or Fort Ellis. Terry was constantly thanking his sisters for the pickled mushrooms, asparagus, and other delicacies that they sent.[8]

There were problems in camp, however. Gloom spread through the ranks when it was learned that Captain Lewis Thompson, company commander in the Second Cavalry, had committed suicide. He had been suffering from consumption, which he contracted during the Civil War in a southern prison, and he evidently felt he could not continue to live as he did. Trouble also arose when Colonel Gibbon had Major Reno arrested, supposedly because of a misunderstanding over a scouting detachment but more precisely over the major's aggressive nature. Terry had to soothe the major's ruffled feelings and calm the respected Gibbon.[9]

By late July Terry was in a position to make his advance. Most of his supplies had arrived, and his reinforcements were on the way. He decided to move his camp east along the Yellowstone to the mouth of the Rosebud. Crook would move along that creek from the south, and Terry would approach it from the north. If there was a hostile camp on the banks of the Rosebud as reported, the converging columns might still gain a victory over the Indians. No matter what the results, Terry speculated that this advance would be his last action of the campaign before he started for home.[10]

The troops made camp on the Yellowstone opposite the Rosebud on July 28. Terry employed four river steamers in this operation and eventually concentrated his entire force there. On August 1, the *Carroll* arrived with Lieutenant Colonel Elwell S. Otis, six companies of the Twenty-second Infantry, and their supplies. The next day Colonel Nelson A. Miles with six companies of the Fifth Infantry and 150 recruits arrived on board the *Durfee*. That same day the *Josephine* returned with supplies, guns, and sixty-four horses. The next few days were spent in making final preparations for the campaign. Terry organized his staff so that Colonel Gibbon, Major Reno, and Major Brisbin commanded various units of the column. He left one company of infantry, the dismounted men of the Seventh Cavalry, and three Gatling guns all under the command of Captain Louis Sanger to guard the supply depot.[11]

The day of the advance began with reveille at 3:00 A.M., and the march commenced two hours later. Because the terrain was rough, the column made only nine and a half miles that first day of August 8. The next day the column advanced eleven miles in twelve hours. Reports filtered in from advance scouts that the hostiles were about twelve miles ahead. Terry and his men broke camp the next day at 4:30 A.M. and advanced toward the hostile camp. The confident general felt that his 1,620 men could defeat the Indians, especially since he believed that the natives were not a large body because it was impossible for them to live together in sizable numbers and still find the forage they needed for their animals.

The general feared that he would not be able to surprise the hostiles and that they would escape. He took solace in the fact that if the campaign failed, the misfortune would be lost in the excitement of the presidential campaign and election. Terry pushed aside thoughts of failure and returned to the reality of 109° temperatures and the fact that the spirit of the men was good and that they were determined to revenge their earlier loss to the hostiles.[12]

After nine miles of marching on August 10, scouts reported a large body of hostiles ahead. The Seventh Cavalry formed a skirmish line, and the Dakota column prepared to fight. Their Crow scouts applied war paint to their faces in anticipation of a great battle with their old enemies. Instead a scout, "Buffalo Bill" Cody, from Crook's column approached and gave Terry's men the news that the hostiles had escaped and that it was Crook's soldiers who approached.[13] The combined forces camped along the Rosebud that night, and a disappointed Terry and Crook talked. As the two generals reflected on their position, Crook told Terry what he knew of the past movements of the Indians. The hostiles had left their camp at the base of the Bighorn Mountains, had passed around Crook's right flank, and had descended the Rosebud to a point about where the soldiers were then in camp. They had left the Rosebud at the approach of the soldiers, crossing eastward toward the Tongue River and leaving a broad trail that indicated a very large number of Indians.

Terry felt that the hostiles could still be caught. He knew he could not get his supply wagons across the ridge separating the Rosebud and Tongue, and so he prepared to take a pack train. He saw to it that Crook's troops were supplied, and the remainder of the provisions were taken back to the depot. Terry ordered Miles with his six companies of infantry and the battery to return to the depot on the Yellowstone also. He instructed the colonel to use the steamer to cross the Yellowstone and to patrol the north bank between the Tongue and Powder rivers, leaving detachments to cover the fords and to patrol in the river boats when possible.

On August 11, Terry's and Crook's columns, about thirty-two hundred strong, broke camp and moved eastward with fifteen days of rations. (See map 9.) Terry firmly believed that the combined forces were strong enough "to whip all the Indians on the continent."[14] During the next five days, they followed the Indian trail to the Tongue, down that stream to Pumpkin Creek, and across the Mizpah Creek and the Powder River. Here the trail turned toward Beaver Creek and the Little Missouri River. Terry was

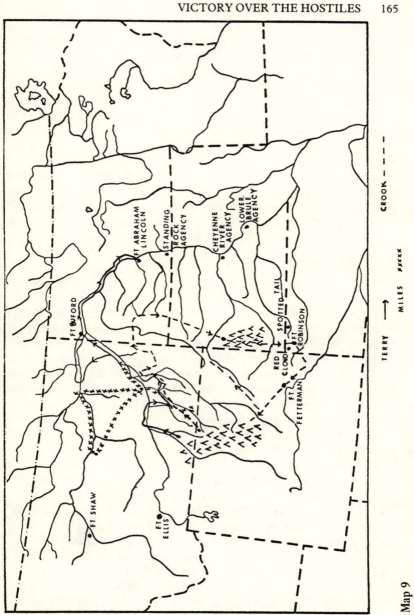

Map 9

CAMPAIGN EXTENDED, 1876-1877

reluctant to continue following the trail because the column would have
to move farther away from their supply depot. The combined columns
thus marched to the mouth of the Powder, where limited amounts of supplies awaited them. Their animals were weak from the long marches, and
the columns waited until August 23 before grain from the Rosebud depot
arrived. Crook's forces were immediately supplied, and they continued
their march, following the Indian trail toward the Little Missouri River.

Terry had received numerous reports of Indians spotted farther up the
Yellowstone, some near Glendive Creek. He realized that the hostiles
probably would not continue to the east very much farther because there
was little forage for them there. Terry reasoned that they must go either
north or south. There seemed a good possibility that some of them had
gone north, and the two generals decided to split their forces. Crook was
pleased to leave Terry and to be in top authority again; Terry, by virtue
of his seniority, had commanded the combined units.[15] Crook was to
follow the trail south, and Terry would patrol the north bank of the Yellowstone and determine the validity of reports he had received from that
vicinity.

Taking four of Miles's infantry companies with him on August 27, Terry
proceeded north along the Yellowstone toward Glendive Creek where additional supplies awaited him. After two more days of travel and scouting,
Terry was not able to locate the hostiles. They were in the area north of
the Yellowstone, but Terry's men had not yet found their trail. The Indians
had crossed in large numbers and then had broken into small groups. They
had burned the grass and left no trail. Terry's scouts could find no sign
of them. On one occasion the general sent Major Reno and the Seventh
Cavalry west along the Missouri but succeeded only in driving the Sioux
toward the Canadian border.

It seemed useless for Terry and his entire command to stay in the field
to hunt the scattered hostiles. The large force consumed provisions as fast
as the supplies arrived. The commander had been campaigning for over
four months, and he and his men were worn.[16] Sheridan ordered him to
have some of his men patrol the Yellowstone during the winter months
and to set up a temporary camp at the mouth of the Tongue. The Yellowstone River was very low at this time, and Terry realized that overland
supply was the only way to keep the camp at the Tongue provisioned. The
general decided to send Gibbon and his column back to the Montana forts
for the winter. Terry ordered Miles and his well-rested Fifth Infantry to

the Tongue, while the rest of the Dakota column returned to their original posts.

Terry had one final task to perform before he could conclude the military campaign. Sheridan had ordered that the reservation Indians at Standing Rock and Cheyenne Agency be disarmed and relieved of their horses. The Indians, reasoned the government, would thus have little choice but to remain peaceful and to cooperate with the whites' efforts to bring civilization to them. As Sheridan put it, "A Sioux on foot is a Sioux no longer."[17]

Terry took twelve hundred infantry and cavalry from Fort Abraham Lincoln and marched down river to the two agencies. The movement was efficiently carried out, and twelve hundred animals from Standing Rock and nine hundred animals from Cheyenne Agency were acquired. Terry suspected that the large force would be sufficient to quell any thought of reprisal on the part of the Indians at the agencies, and he was right. No shots were fired, and no violence was necessary to gain the natives' cooperation. Terry predicted that more ponies would be gained when absent Indians returned to the agencies during the winter. In the meantime the twenty-one hundred horses and ponies were to be sold to whites, and the proceeds were to be used to purchase cows and work oxen for the agency Indians.[18]

Thus the army began in earnest a policy that aimed at settling the problem of the hostile Indians. The natives' days of wandering free from reservation restrictions and purchasing guns and ammunition from agency traders were about to end. Most of the buffalo were gone or would be gone in a few short years, and then the Indians' subsistence would depend entirely on the government. In order for Indians to receive food supplies, they would have to agree to unconditional surrender and to give up their horses and guns. Terry's visit to Grand River and Cheyenne agencies was only the first step toward implementing this policy. General Crook stopped off at Red Cloud and Spotted Tail agencies on the last lap of his long march and dismounted and disarmed the Indians there. Some questioned if the friendly Indians would receive the same treatment as the hostiles, and they learned that the military supported treating all the Indians the same because they believed that the friendly Indians frequently supplied the hostiles with war materials.[19]

Other developments during the fall and winter of 1876 tended to make this a very successful campaign against the hostiles. Columns from Terry's and Crook's armies continued to chase and to harass the hostiles to the point where a large majority of the natives sought peace and safety on the reservations. The first note of success came from Crook's column that had parted with Terry on the Powder and had followed the Indian trail to the east and south. They crossed the Little Missouri River and pushed to the headwaters of the Heart River west of Fort Abraham Lincoln. From this vantage point, Crook reported on September 5, the trail scattered and was impossible to follow. He had but two days of provisions left and decided to march for Custer City in the Black Hills where he ordered that provisions be sent to meet him. Crook sent Captain Anson Mills and 150 cavalry as advance guard, and on the morning of September 9, they stumbled upon the village of American Horse near Slim Buttes. It was a small camp of thirty lodges, and Mills's men gained an initial success, killing Chief American Horse and twenty-seven warriors. The soldiers captured the village and hungrily ate some of the provisions the Sioux had left behind.[20]

Crazy Horse had his camp nearby, and the hostiles soon came to the support of their friends. Crook's main column reached the scene at about the same time, and he was able to hold off the Indians. His men were so worn and tattered from their march that they could not follow up the Indian retreat. Instead they rode captured Indian ponies to the white settlements in the Black Hills. The result of the attack was another step toward the goal of destroying hostile Indian villages and winter provisions.

To the north Colonel Miles of Terry's column also located some hostiles in mid-October and chased them for the rest of the year. The colonel and his men operated out of Tongue River Camp on the Yellowstone. It was a temporary and rather austere camp but well situated for the needs of the soldiers. Miles had received reports that Indians were disturbing a supply train in the vicinity, and he and about four hundred infantry marched rapidly to the troubled area. There they found the village of Sitting Bull situated north of the Yellowstone between the Tongue River and Glendive Creek at a place called Cedar Creek. The chief wanted to negotiate rather than fight, and they held a number of talks. Some conferences were simply ruses to allow the villagers time to escape, but Miles tenaciously followed. Finally, the Indians agreed to return to the agencies. Miles took five chiefs as hostages, but still only the people from forty of an estimated four hundred lodges actually returned to their reservation.

Sitting Bull and about four hundred of his followers moved north and west to the Missouri River and were joined later by Gall and about ninety

lodges. During November and December Miles pursued. In addition he
sent Lieutenant Frank D. Baldwin to the Fort Peck Indian reservation
to seek out Sitting Bull. In mid-December the lieutenant and three infantry companies came upon a large Sioux village. They attacked the surprised Indians and captured 119 lodges, sixty ponies, and an abundance
of camp supplies. The blow was crushing to the Sioux, who had little with
which to survive the coming winter. Many moved to the north toward
Canada. Baldwin's and Miles's worn troops returned to the Tongue River
cantonment for a few days of Christmas conviviality before they returned
to the chase. Thus Terry had the north end of the Yellowstone well
defended. At Fort Buford Colonel William B. Hazen could patrol the
Missouri or Yellowstone rivers with his Sixth Infantry. To the south
Lieutenant Colonel Elwell S. Otis with his Twenty-second Infantry made
temporary camp at Glendive Creek. South of him Colonel Miles stationed
his men at Tongue River cantonment.[21]

In the Department of the Platte, Crook was active. After his march
through western Dakota and the Black Hills, he returned to Fort Robinson in order to dismount and disarm the Indians at Red Cloud and Spotted
Tail agencies. This was completed by late October, and Crook was on his
way to Fort Laramie to meet with Sheridan to plan his winter campaign.
By mid-November Crook had about eight hundred cavalrymen when he
combined his force with that of Colonel Ranald S. Mackenzie. Six hundred and fifty infantry under Colonel Richard I. Dodge marched with
the cavalry from Fort Fetterman across the partially frozen Platte River
and moved north toward the Powder River. Mackenzie and his men com-
pletely surprised Dull Knife's Cheyenne village of 173 lodges on the Powder. They captured and destroyed the village and took five hundred ponies.
The soldiers were unable to follow up their victory, however, and most
of the Cheyennes escaped to join Crazy Horse's camp on the Tongue.[22]

The military made other forays after the Indians but with little further
success other than that of annoyance. Major George M. Randall led a
force of Crow Indians from Fort Ellis through the Bighorn Mountains,
and Colonel Miles located the village of Crazy Horse on the Tongue but
accomplished little. Winter had set in, and it was extremely severe. The
Indians could only hope to survive the season on their meager provisions.
When spring arrived many Indians from hostile camps began to return to
their reservations in hopes of obtaining government provisions. Crazy
Horse and other leading chiefs were persuaded of the wisdom of holding

out no longer. Most of the hostiles eventually returned with the exception of Sitting Bull and Gall and their over one hundred lodges that escaped into Canada.[23] Thus an extensive summer campaign proved unnecessary.

The soldiers were pleased with the results of their year-long campaign against the hostiles. Their overall objective had been to force the Indians back to their reservations, and this they accomplished when many Indians straggled back to the reservations during the spring and summer of 1877. By the fall of 1877 most of the hostiles were at their agencies. The army had been relentless in its pursuit of a numerous and much more mobile enemy. The hostiles had been on the defensive in a country they knew well, while the military had constantly to seek out the enemy in an unfamiliar environment.

Another chapter in the decline of the Sioux had been completed. The luster and magic of Sitting Bull's camp in the Powder and Bighorn regions had vanished. Soon soldiers would be building forts in the area, and white settlers would be planting their crops. Only a glimmer of hope shown from Canada where Sitting Bull and his followers lived in defiance of the United States.

The army's success lay primarily with the aggressive actions of Terry's and Crook's subordinate officers, such as Colonels Merritt, Otis, Mackenzie, Mills, and Miles. These officers had pushed the hostiles to the limit of their endurance and rather than risk their families in continued hostilities during the next summer, the natives had succumbed. The army's victory had not come by killing large numbers of Indians but rather by destroying provisions, camp equipment, and pony herds.[24] Although the hostiles had probably killed more soldiers than they had lost and had won many of the battles, they had lost the campaign. Crook and Terry had lost opportunities to end the campaign earlier, but actions by less distinguished figures like Reynolds and Custer had extended it. To whites the heroic figures were the officers and soldiers who relentlessly pursued the elusive Indians until their will to continue the struggle was broken. Generals Terry and Crook personally led the field commands, and Sheridan served as strategist and coordinator.

The army had won the campaign, but at great expense. Official figures showed that 283 United States soldiers had been killed and 125 wounded.[25] The financial figures were also staggering. The army spent about $2.3 million on the campaign, an astronomical amount from a budget-minded congressional point of view.[26] National attention now focused on winning

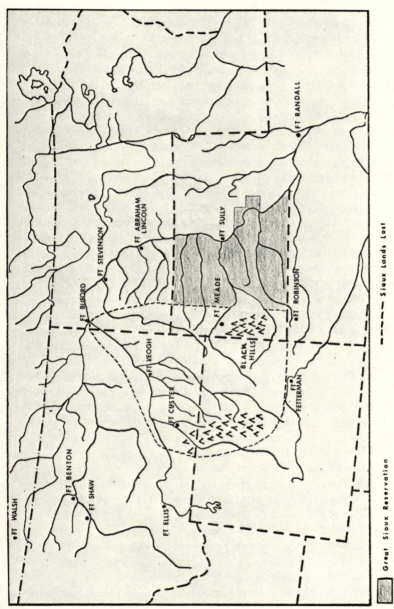

Map 10

SIOUX LANDS IN 1877

treaty settlements with the Indians in order to avoid the necessity of yet another campaign against the hostiles.

The United States, falling back on past experiences, sent two commissions to the Sioux in 1877. One, headed by George W. Manypenny, a former commissioner of Indian affairs, was instructed to inform the Sioux that they would receive no further appropriations from the Indian Department unless they agreed to a significantly reduced reservation. The government policy for the Sioux was clearly one of concentrating the natives along the west bank of the Missouri River between the Cannonball River on the north and the Nebraska state line on the south. In this way the cost of transporting subsistence provisions to the Indians would be minimized by use of the Missouri River and connecting railroads, and the whites could gain the valued Black Hills region to the west. With the realization of a peaceful concentration of Sioux along the Missouri River, the process of Christianization and civilization would stand a better chance of success. Chiefs from Red Cloud and Spotted Tail agencies reluctantly agreed to these terms and then enjoyed generous gifts from the commissioners.[27] (See map 10.)

The one trouble spot for the whites in this encouraging picture was that of Sitting Bull's presence in Canada. Spurred on by Canadian government officials, United States President Rutherford B. Hayes appointed a second commission headed by Terry to deal with Sitting Bull and his people. He called a meeting of the commission for September 11, 1877, at St. Paul. Terry, Judge A. G. Lawrence of Rhode Island, and H. C. Corbin of the United States Army, who served as secretary, were present. They decided that in order to carry out their instructions, they must make the long trek to Canada to visit Sitting Bull. The commissioners left St. Paul on September 14 and traveled through Omaha to Ogden, Utah Territory, on the Union Pacific Railroad. From there they took the Montana stage line to Helena and Fort Benton, high up on the Missouri River in northern Montana. Terry complained of the trip, saying he was too tall for the stage coach and that the travel made him deaf. He did not enjoy the dreary lava beds in Idaho but thrilled to the splendid scenery of Montana with its snow-capped mountains.[28] United States military units escorted them to the Canadian line where they were met by a Royal Mounted Police detachment under Lieutenant Colonel James F. McLeod. From here they made a three-day journey to Fort Walsh and a meeting with Sitting Bull and other Sioux chiefs who had escaped across the national boundary.[29]

The council with the Sioux took place on October 17 at the fort in the presence of Terry, Lawrence, Corbin, McLeod and other Canadian mounted police, and a number of Sioux chiefs. Arrangements were made for interpreters before the Americans seated themselves behind tables in the officers' mess, and the Sioux took their places on buffalo robes spread on the floor in front of the commissioners. The Indians ignored the Americans but displayed warm friendship toward the Canadians. Terry presented the proposition of the United States government to the Sioux. The general explained that this was the only band of Sioux that had not surrendered and returned to the agencies. He promised a full pardon for all and pledged the friendship of the United States to every man, woman, and child. He related that there had been no trouble at the agencies and that all had received sufficient clothes and food. Star, as the Indians called Terry, warned the Sioux that they would have to surrender their horses and guns.

The general's efforts went unheeded. After his speech, a number of Indians spoke and in substance expressed their disbelief of the commander's words. Sitting Bull said that for sixty-four years he had been treated badly by the whites and all he had heard were lies. He shook hands with the British officers and said they were his friends and that he would stay in Canada. Other Indians expressed these same sentiments.

The Canadians explained to the Sioux that their government could take no responsibility for feeding or clothing the Indians. McLeod told the gathering that the Sioux could live in Canada but that they could not raid across the border. If this happened, the Canadians were responsible by international law and would have to attack the Sioux just as the Americans would. No argument could change the minds of the Indians, who were adamant in their determination to stay in Canada.

There was nothing that Terry could say to remove the bitterness that the Sioux felt for the United States. The general did not believe that the Sioux would sever their ties with the agency Indians, and he expected that there would be future dealings with Sitting Bull. For now, the United States government could close the books on this issue and declare Sitting Bull and his band no longer their problem.

Terry and the other commissioners left Fort Walsh the next morning and returned to Fort Benton, but not without incident. While crossing the Teton River, one of their wagons tipped over, and much of their personal baggage and bedding was soaked. Otherwise the trip to Fort Benton was uneventful.[30] At this point they transferred to mackinaw boats and traveled with the current of the Missouri River to Forts Buford and Abraham Lincoln. They switched to the Northern Pacific Railroad and arrived at St. Paul on November 8.

For the commissioners it had been an arduous trip with disappointing results. On the other hand, for the Interior and War departments it meant the end of the problem of the hostiles on the northern plains. It had been about two years since Indian Inspector Watkins had recommended military force as a means of compelling the hostiles to return to their agencies. By the fall of 1877 this had been accomplished. On the reservations the natives did not seek the white man's civilization, nor did they fully comprehend that they had lost the Black Hills, the Powder River basin, and the Big-horn Mountain region. Only with the construction of military posts in these areas and the restrictiveness of the agencies now under military control, did the Sioux slowly begin to realize the extent of their tragedy.

NOTES

1. Terry to Sheridan, July 2, 1876, LR, AGO, RG94, NA.

2. Edgar I. Stewart, *Custer's Luck* (Norman: University of Oklahoma Press, 1955), pp. 474-475.

3. Terry to Sheridan, November 21, 1876, LR, AGO.

4. Ibid.

5. Ibid.; Stewart, *Custer's Luck,* pp. 474-483; Alfred H. Terry, "The Field Diary of General Alfred H. Terry, 1876" (Washington, D.C.: Library of Congress), pp. 36-39; Max E. Gerber, "Steamboat and Indians of the Upper Missouri." *South Dakota History* 4 (Spring 1974): 158-159.

6. Annual Report of Terry, November 21, 1876, LR, AGO.

7. Ibid.

8. Terry to the Girls, July 4, 1876, Terry Family Papers, Yale University Library.

9. Terry to Sisters, July 30, 1876, Terry Family Papers; Godfrey, diary, pp. 23-30, Godfrey Papers, Library of Congress.

10. Terry to Sisters, July 30, 1876.

11. Annual Report of Terry, November 21, 1876, LR, AGO.

12. Terry to Polly, August 1, 1876, and Terry to Sisters, August 7, 1876, Terry Family Papers; Terry, diary, pp. 53-57.

13. Annual Report of Terry, November 21, 1876. The account below is taken from Terry's Annual Report, 1876, except as indicated otherwise.

14. Terry to Sisters, August 10, 1876, Terry Family Papers.

15. Sherman to Sheridan, July 18, 1876, LR, AGO.

16. Annual Report of Sheridan, November 25, 1876, LR, AGO.

17. Ibid.

18. Sheridan to Terry, July 27, 1876, LS, AGO. Annual Report of E. A. Hayt Commissioner of Indian Affairs, November 1, 1877, H. Ex. Doc. 1, 45 Cong., 2 sess., Serial 1800, pp. 410-411.

19. Ibid.; Annual Report of Terry, 1876, LR, AGO.

20. The story of the following military events was taken from Annual Report of Hayt, pp. 410-413.

21. Annual Report of Sheridan, October 25, 1877, LR, AGO; Nelson A. Miles, *Serving the Republic* (New York: Harper & Row, 1911), pp. 146-161.

22. Annual Report of Sheridan, October 25, 1877; Donald F. Danker, ed., *Man of the Plains; Recollections of Luther North, 1856-1882* (Lincoln: University of Nebraska, 1961), pp. 202-204.

23. Annual Report of Sheridan, October 25, 1877; Oliver Knight, "War or Peace: The Anxious Wait for Crazy Horse," *Nebraska History* 54 (Winter 1973): 521-544.

24. Annual Report of Sheridan, November 25, 1876; Joseph Mills Hanson, *The Conquest of the Missouri* (Chicago: A. C. McClurg, 1909), pp. 246-247, 365.

25. *Statement of Casualties*, E. D. Townsend, December 11, 1877, Office of the Adjutant General, S. Ex. Doc. 33, 45 Cong., 2 sess., Serial 1780. No accurate count of Indian casualties can be determined.

26. *Cost of the Sioux War, 1876-1877; Message from President R. B. Hayes, March 25, 1878, to Senate*, S. Ex. Doc. 33, 45 Cong., 2 sess., Serial 1780. The Department of Dakota spent $992,807.78 and the Department of the Platte $1,319,726.46.

27. *J. Q. Smith, Commissioner of Indian Affairs, to Secretary of the Interior*, December 11, 1876, S. Ex. Doc. 17, 44 Cong., 2 sess., Serial 1718; *Report and Journal of Sioux Commission of 1876*, George W. Manypenny, Chairman, S. Ex. Doc. 9, 44 Cong., 2 sess., Serial 1718; James C. Olson, *Red Cloud and the Sioux Problem* (Lincoln: University of Nebraska Press, 1965), pp. 224-230.

28. Terry to Girls, September 14, 1877, Terry Family Papers.

29. *Report of the Commission to Sitting Bull, 1877*, Alfred H. Terry, Chairman, Report of the Commissioner of Indian Affairs, November 1, 1877, H. Ex. Doc. 1, 45 Cong., 2 sess., Serial 1800, pp. 720-728. Unless otherwise cited, this is the source used for the Sitting Bull Commission.

30. Terry to Girls, October 11, 1877, Terry Family Papers.

10 The Final Challenge, 1877-1881

The years following the army's victory over the hostiles witnessed an alteration in military policy and a reorganization in the fort system that reflected changed conditions in the Department of Dakota. No longer did the hostiles roam the areas of the Bighorn Mountains, the Powder River, and the Black Hills. Most had been consigned to reservations on the banks of the Missouri and White rivers. Others had escaped into Canada, where American soldiers could not molest them.

Reflecting the new habitations of the hostiles, the soldiers built forts in the Yellowstone and Black Hills country, and they strengthened their line of forts north of the Missouri River in order to check movements by the hostiles who might stray south of the Canadian line. Posts near the Missouri River agencies were also strengthened in order to protect the peaceful Sioux and to discourage the restless Tetons who longed to join the camps of the hostiles north of the border. The new forts were constructed to hold large numbers of men and illustrated the army's new big-fort policy from which aggressive movements might be initiated. The old policy of numerous small posts scattered along the transportation routes became of secondary importance, and the army abandoned many of these forts during the late 1870s and the 1880s.

White settlement patterns also dictated the desirability for military posts in certain areas. The population of Minnesota climbed from about 440,000 to 781,000 during the 1870s. In northern Dakota Territory the population jumped from 2,000 in 1870 to 37,000 a decade later. Wheat farmers filled much of the central and eastern portions of the territory, and they no longer needed extensive military protection. The growth of other regions in the northern plains was similar. Southern Dakota Territory filled rapidly, as the increase in population from approximately 12,000 to 98,000 during the 1870s illustrated. Farmers and merchants settled the region east of the Missouri, and the mining settlements in the Black Hills explained the growth of that area. Montana Territory also had benefited from the influx of miners and farmers, but its growth was not as great as that of neighboring regions. Although its population rose from 21,000 in 1870 to 39,000 ten years later, the presence of a sizable number of Indians north of the border in Canada and the necessity of maintaining large numbers of troops in the territory illustrated the relatively unsettled status of white civilization in Montana.[1]

To meet the challenge of the years ahead, Sheridan and Terry planned for extensive changes in the fort system (map 11). One of the most important links in the new system had been a cantonment during the past engagement. Supplies had been stored at the mouth of the Tongue River, and Colonel Nelson Miles had operated out of a temporary base at this location during 1876. In that year officials decided to establish a permanent fort there and named it Fort Keogh in honor of one of the most respected leaders of the Seventh Cavalry who had died at the Little Bighorn battle.

The new fort was built of pine shipped in from Fort Buford and brick that was baked at the construction site. It was to be a large post, and when completed it was considered one of the finest in the West. There was barracks space to accommodate about seven hundred men. Terry designated Fort Keogh as the headquarters of the newly created District of the Yellowstone, whose command he gave to Miles to reward the aggressive colonel for his fine work during the year.[2]

Another post in his district, Fort Custer, was constructed in 1877 at the junction of the Little Bighorn and Bighorn rivers. It too was large and was located in a key position to control the Bighorn region and to expel the hostiles if they should elect to return to their old hunting grounds. Miles had only these two forts in his makeshift district, but he concentrated over one thousand men there, and he was equipped to take the offensive against Sitting Bull's hostiles if they should cross the border from Canada to hunt in northern Montana.[3] Miles used Forts Keogh and Custer as effective bases of operations until June 1881, when Sherman transferred him to command the Division of the Columbia. Terry then discontinued the District of the Yellowstone within his department; for organizational purposes he maintained a Montana District, and the rest of the forts were handled as independent posts.[4]

Terry saw to the construction of new forts in Montana also. For years

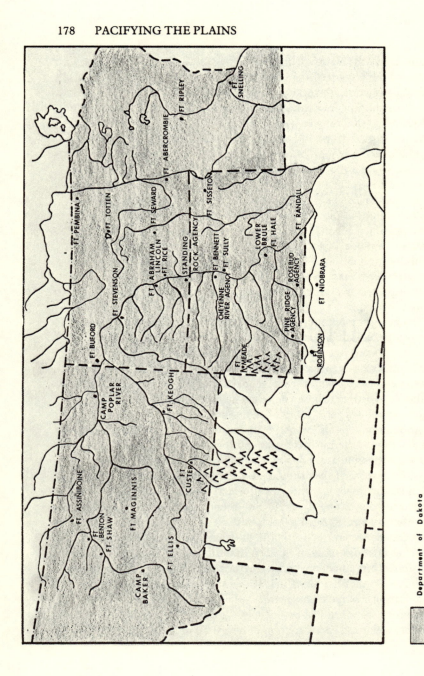

Department of Dakota

Map 11   THE DEPARTMENT OF DAKOTA, 1877-1881

the Judith and Musselshell river regions had been trouble spots for the army. To solve the problem of Indian depredations in the area, Fort Maginnis was constructed in 1880. It was not a large fort, but it was strong enough to protect the settlers of the area.[5] About 125 miles west of Camp Baker, which had been renamed Fort Logan, the army erected Fort Missoula in 1877. It was far to the west of the Fort Shaw-Fort Ellis line of posts and served more to deal with the Indians of the Department of the Columbia, which was part of the Division of the Pacific. It was a small post that could house four companies of troops and also served to police the Indians of the Bitterroot Valley in western Montana.[6] The army constructed a fifth new post in Montana in 1879 in the northern part of the territory. Fort Assiniboine was located on the south bank of the Milk River and served to supply troops who operated in north central Montana. The fort, large and capable of housing six hundred men, became the key post in the district. Colonel Thomas H. Ruger personally oversaw the construction of the brick fort and recommended to Terry that it be expanded from a six- to a twelve-company capacity.[7]

Assiniboine was just one of several forts that Terry and Sheridan planned for the northern border. The generals envisaged a chain of posts stretching from Fort Pembina in extreme northeastern Dakota to Fort Assiniboine in northern Montana. Forts Totten and Buford in Dakota were also part of this plan, but Terry felt it desirable to construct at least one more post located between Assiniboine and Buford, a distance of 250 miles. Terry struggled for two years to gain approval from Congress for the construction of a fort on Frenchman's Creek, a tributary of the Milk River running south from the Canadian border. The cordon of forts was necessary, Terry felt, to eliminate communication between the Missouri River reservations and the hostile Sioux in Canada and to cut off transportation routes between the two regions. A further function would be to enforce the agreements that forbade the Canadian Sioux from hunting or marauding south of the Canadian line. Fort Assiniboine proved a key asset to the military objectives on the border, but the general never achieved the construction of a post on Frenchman's Creek.[8]

While Terry oversaw the construction of the five new posts in Montana during the period 1877-1881, he was also quick to realize that certain forts had outlived their usefulness there. Fort Logan was abandoned in 1880 because white settlers had filled the area, and hostile Indians no longer threatened. A year later he withdrew troops from Fort Benton, which was not well located, and with the establishment of Fort Assiniboine northeast of it, there was little need for the Missouri River post. There was even talk that Fort Shaw was no longer needed because it was located well within the settlements.[9]

The military complexion in Montana had changed since 1877. The old line of forts that had guarded the mining settlements along the east side of the Rocky Mountains was of little significance. Of the four posts, two were abandoned and one was of little value. Only Fort Ellis, which guarded the west end of the Yellowstone, maintained a sizable force and still held strategic importance. In place of the old cordon of posts were Forts Assiniboine, Custer, and Keogh, all capable of sending large detachments of men to push Sitting Bull's people north of the border should they stray into the United States or to discourage reservation Indians from seeking to return to the Yellowstone region in search of their old homes. The military emphasis in Montana had shifted to large posts capable of supporting aggressive actions against hostile Indians. Some defensive thinking remained, however, at forts like Maginnis and Missoula where small forces were located to protect white settlements.[10]

In northern Dakota change also came but in a different way. With the completion of the Northern Pacific Railroad to Bismarck by 1873, population had built up all along the line. No longer were forts needed to protect settlements in the region where the railroad was located. Thus in 1877, Forts Seward and Abercrombie were abandoned. In this same year fire destroyed some of the buildings at Fort Ripley, and the government decided to discontinue the post and open up the military reservation to settlers, a decision long contemplated in the 1870s. A year later the army also abandoned Fort Rice. It was located only twenty-five miles south of the recently constructed Fort Abraham Lincoln at the head of the Northern Pacific, and there was little need for the older post.[11]

Much of the troop strength in this area was located at Fort Yates on the west bank of the Missouri River in the Standing Rock Indian Reservation. The natives from Grand River Agency had been moved there, and Terry kept many soldiers here to carry out his policy of taking guns and horses from the Sioux. If the Tetons tried to escape to the north or west, there were a sufficient number of men at Forts Yates and Abraham Lincoln to cut off their escape routes. Thus the fort system along the northern boundary made up of Forts Pembina, Totten, and Buford, and the Missouri River forts of Buford, Stevenson, Yates, and Abraham Lincoln maintained its control over the Indians. In Minnesota only Fort Snelling remained as the division headquarters.[12]

In southern Dakota Sheridan finally received favorable action on his bid to locate a fort in the Black Hills region. Near Bear Butte in 1878 the army constructed Fort Meade. It was a large post and fitted in the pattern of the new offensive-minded approach. Terry stationed over four hundred men here, and aside from its protection duties to local miners and farmers in the Black Hills region, it was capable of launching a formidable force against Sioux who had designs on their old mountain paradise.[13] On the Missouri River Terry concentrated troops at Fort Bennett on the Cheyenne River Agency lands and Fort Hale on the Lower Brulé Agency grounds. He also stationed units at Forts Sully and Randall, but the strength of the region was located to the west at Fort Meade.[14]

There were other important changes in the South. After visits to Washington, Red Cloud and his people were able to convince the politicians of the wisdom of moving the Indians of Red Cloud's camp from the Missouri River to the west along a tributary of the White River. The agency located in southwestern Dakota was renamed Pine Ridge, and here the Oglala and their kinsmen settled down in 1878. To the east along another tributary of the White River settled Spotted Tail's people at Rosebud Agency. Two forts in the Department of the Platte were located near the new agencies in case of trouble. Fort Robinson on the White River and Fort Niobrara, established in 1880 south of Rosebud Agency, were closer to the agencies than any of the Department of Dakota forts and guarded over these Indians. Thus the Teton Sioux agency system was completed with these two sites on tributaries of the White River and Lower Brulé, Cheyenne River, and Standing Rock on the Missouri.[15]

Terry also was busy with other projects during these years of the late 1870s and early 1880s that helped the army cope with the complex business of managing the Indians. His men worked diligently to erect a telegraph communications complex within the department that would allow for efficiency and intelligence gathering that had been lacking in 1876. It was important not only to build new forts but to stretch telegraph lines throughout the region. His men erected poles, strung lines, and replaced rotten poles with new ones. By 1880 they had strung over 1,650 miles of wire, and the system was basically complete.[16]

On two occasions troops were not available to work on telegraph lines or to perform other duties at their posts because they were needed to put down civilian disturbances. In the summer of 1877 soldiers from the department rushed to Chicago to help quell labor riots. In a similar manner soldiers from Fort Abraham Lincoln marched to nearby Bismarck to protect government property from rioters in 1880. This was no doubt distasteful work for the soldiers, but it was service that was expected of the army.[17]

More important from Terry's viewpoint was furthering the work of the railroad companies in his department. The Chicago and Northwestern had completed its line to Pierre, Dakota Territory, by 1880, and its surveyors had completed their work to Deadwood in the Black Hills. Another railroad, the Chicago, Milwaukee, and St. Paul, had almost reached the Missouri River, and it also planned a branch line to the Black Hills.[18]

Dakota soldiers were generally not involved with the construction efforts of these companies, but in 1879 they continued to offer protection and escort service to the Northern Pacific Railroad employees. The company had completed about 450 miles of track into Dakota and 105 miles on the Pacific coast near Puget Sound when it was forced into bankruptcy by the depression in 1873. Six years later Henry Villard bought his way into the Northern Pacific lines, and with his financial backing, construction on the railroad began in Dakota and Oregon.[19]

The soldiers of Fort Abraham Lincoln were the first to receive a call in 1879 to escort the railroad engineers and protect the construction workers. Terry distributed four infantry companies along the rail line and moved them from point to point as different sections of the work were finished. By the end of September, the roadbed had been extended eighty miles west of Bismarck and the tracks laid for fifty miles.[20]

During the next year, five companies of infantry and three companies of cavalry primarily from Fort Keogh spent the summer and fall guarding the railroad workers and surveyors. The laborers made good progress laying track to the Little Missouri River and preparing the roadbed far to the west toward the Yellowstone River.[21] Terry ordered a two company winter camp established on the south bank of the Yellowstone in October 1880, and Camp Porter was settled three miles above the mouth of Glendive Creek. The troops guarded the working parties and materials of the Northern Pacific at the spot that had served as a favorite supply base during the campaigns of 1876 and 1877. By the fall of 1881 trains were servicing regularly the village of Glendive, and the tracks had reached Miles City on the Yellowstone opposite Fort Keogh. Five years before, the hostiles had controlled this region, and now white men were building villages and bringing trains into the heart of the Yellowstone area. The Dakota army had been the forerunner to this event, forcing the hostiles from their cherished hunting grounds and making the way safe for white settlers.[22]

Terry thought that his department was rid of Indian problems after the victory over the hostiles in 1877. Peace generally prevailed in the five agencies in Montana, the eleven in Dakota, and the one in Minnesota. He could foresee trouble, perhaps, from the hostiles who had escaped across the border into Canada, but little did he expect that trouble would come from the west and the south. These incursions began in 1877 and lasted until 1881.

The first were the Nez Perce who came from the west.[23] These natives had suffered from many of the same injustices that the Sioux had labored under. The whites had discovered gold in the Nez Perce lands of western Idaho, and with the influx of miners and land-hungry farmers, some of the Indians had scattered to other areas. The Nez Perce tried to live in peace with the whites, but by June 1877, the Indians could no longer tolerate their bad treatment and decided to withdraw to the east.

General Oliver O. Howard, a one-armed veteran of the Civil War and commander of the Department of the Columbia, swung into action, leading a force to track down the fleeing Nez Perce. A battle took place at the Clearwater River, but the Nez Perce slipped away, leaving the slow-moving Howard and his men to continue the chase. Terry was warned of the possibility that the Nez Perce might enter Montana, and he in turn alerted Colonel Gibbon, his district commander in Montana. Gibbon quickly moved additional troops to Fort Missoula to cut off the Indians, and in early August he surprised the Nez Perce with a dawn attack on their camp. In this, the Battle of Big Hole, the Indians suffered terribly, losing eighty-nine men, women, and children. About thirty of Gibbon's men were killed, and the sharp-shooting Nez Perce inflicted many wounds, including one to Gibbon.

Howard picked up the chase again and marched into Montana and thus the Department of Dakota. Terry was perturbed that Howard was chasing Indians in his department. A command level higher, Sheridan, as commander of the Division of the Missouri, was concerned that soldiers from the Division of the Pacific under Irwin McDowell would receive credit for victory over the Nez Perce, if indeed this could be achieved. Howard and his men were exhausted and ready to return to their department, but Sherman was adamant that he continue the chase and complete the job he had started, since it would be time-consuming to get another command into the field. Sherman had been touring Yellowstone National Park and was anxious to bring the Nez Perce under control.[24]

The Indians continued their journey, moving through Yellowstone Park and into central Montana toward Canada. They hoped to reach the border in safety and perhaps live with Sitting Bull's people in the British possessions. It was the army's job to stop them before they achieved this goal. Terry alerted Miles that the Nez Perce were in his district, and he immediately set out to stop the Indians' march.

Miles took a force and raced to the north to cut off the Indians. He found their camp near Bear Paw Mountain forty miles from the international border, and in the chilling late September rain, he attacked. A sharp battle ensued but the outcome was indecisive. Miles laid siege to the camp for five days during which time Howard and his force arrived on the battlefield. By October 5, many of the Nez Perce chiefs had been killed, and Chief Joseph was ready to give up. Four hundred Indians surrendered to Miles and Howard, marking the end of the Nez Perce war, although about three hundred of Joseph's people managed to escape the soldiers and flee into Canada to Sitting Bull's camp.[25]

It had been a march of epic proportions, where eight hundred Indian people had traveled seventeen hundred miles, eluding the United States Army at almost every turn in the difficult terrain. One hundred and twenty Nez Perce were dead, but they had killed 180 whites and wounded another 150. The soldiers of Dakota had played a major role in stopping the Nez Perce and without Miles's pursuit, the question of American Indians living north of the border would have been even more complex.

In 1878 a similar development occurred in the northern plains when the Bannock Indians of Idaho invaded the Department of Dakota, trying to reach the sanctuary of Canada and Sitting Bull's camp. Miles was visiting Yellowstone Park with one hundred men when he learned of the Bannocks' approach and immediately deployed his troops to intercept them. There were several small skirmishes before Miles surprised the Indian camp near Heart Mountain, killing eleven and capturing thirty-one, in addition to taking about two hundred mules and ponies. The Bannock threat had been turned back.[26]

For a third time in three years, Terry faced the prospect of Indians coming into his department from the outside. This time it was the Northern

Cheyenne who in 1878 sought to leave the Indian Territory in the south and return to their old homes on the northern plains. These Indians had participated in the campaigns of 1876-1877 and had surrendered only after they had been given hope of gaining a reservation in the north. The commissioner of Indian affairs dashed these dreams when he ordered them to the south shortly after their surrender. Of the 937 Cheyennes who moved to Indian Territory in 1877, only about three hundred were strong enough to fight off disease and live to plan their return to the north.[27]

The trek began in September 1878 when Dull Knife and Little Wolf led their people northward. Troops from the Department of the Missouri and the Department of the Platte gave chase. When the Cheyennes reached Nebraska, Dull Knife succumbed to the bitter cold weather, taking his followers and surrendering at Fort Robinson. Little Wolf led his people on to the north in hopes of settling in the Yellowstone region. Terry learned of the Cheyenne movement and ordered his post commanders in southern Dakota and Montana to prepare to meet the Cheyennes should they enter the department boundaries.[28]

Little Wolf's band of Cheyennes entered the southeast corner of Montana along the Little Missouri River in February, 1879. Lieutenant William Philo Clark and two companies of the Second Cavalry from Fort Keogh went in pursuit, but it was very difficult to locate the Cheyenne. Clark's greatest asset was his four Sioux and seven Cheyenne scouts who knew the area and the ways of their people. The scouts located the Cheyenne camp and were eventually able to convince Little Wolf's people that no harm would come to them if they surrendered. Clark made it clear that they would be required to surrender their arms immediately and their ponies when they reached Fort Keogh. Clark was patient with the Cheyennes and used his scouts wisely to convince Little Wolf to accept peace and to trust the whites. The Indians had little choice since they were outnumbered, out-gunned, and short of food in 33° below zero weather. Little Wolf and his people accepted peace and were allowed to live near Fort Keogh for several years, where they served as scouts for the army. Eventually they received their own agency in Montana along the Tongue River.[29]

Terry's problems with the Nez Perce, Bannocks, and Northern Cheyennes were minor compared to the continuing struggle with Sitting Bull, which came to a head during the winter of 1880-1881. The chief's presence in Canada was important symbolically because his village beckoned to all northern Indians who might seek escape from the United States. He also presented a problem of protection to white settlers in northern Montana, and he caused an international question, which neither Canada nor the United States seemed prepared to meet.[30]

Reports persisted during 1878 that the Sioux were south of the border hunting buffalo. Terry put his troops in northern Dakota and Montana on notice in the event the Tetons had hostile intentions. The Sioux sought only food for their people, and because the buffalo were scarce in Canada, they were forced south of the border. This worked a hardship on the Gros Ventres and Assiniboines, because the Sioux did not allow the buffalo to roam to the headwaters of the Milk River where they lived. Terry received permission to feed these unfortunate Indians from military store-houses to keep them from starving.[31]

Reports continued to arrive in Terry's office telling of the movements of Sitting Bull's hostiles. The Indian agent from Poplar River, Montana, told that the Hunkpapas were dispersed in camps of twelve to one hundred lodges in northern Montana. The agency Indians complained bitterly that the Sioux scattered the buffalo and other game, and when they left the area, they stole horses and drove them north of the boundary.[32]

Terry finally concluded that he must send a strong column from Fort Keogh to clear northern Montana of hostile Sioux. If he did not act soon, the friendly Indians of the area would become desperate for food and perhaps commit depredations. The general planned for a summer campaign in which he would send Miles to separate the friendly from the hostile Indians. Terry received permission for the campaign from the general of the army and immediately contacted Miles. He instructed the colonel to take personal command of the column and to force the hostile Sioux to retreat into Canada by a show of force rather than actual conflict. The general also planned to maintain a summer camp at Poplar River Agency with one or two companies of infantry from Fort Buford. This would serve as a compromise measure for the additional fort that he had desired to erect between Forts Assiniboine and Buford.[33]

Miles's column left Fort Keogh on July 3, 1879, and consisted of 676 soldiers and 143 friendly Indians. When the men reached the south bank of Milk River, they discovered signs that Sioux had been in the area. Lieutenant Clark, who had dealt with the Cheyennes so effectively in 1879, took his Indian scouts ahead of the main column and discovered a camp of about four hundred Sioux warriors on Beaver Creek. In the sharp fight that followed, the Sioux were driven to the north. Miles's soldiers joined the chase, fought the Sioux, and drove them into Canada. At least eight hostiles were killed, and Miles's show of force had convinced Sitting Bull to retire to his sanctuary in the north.[34]

While Miles was still in camp on the border, Major William Walsh of the Northwest Mounted Police visited him and learned of the object of the colonel's mission. Walsh hurried to the hostile camp and five days later paid Miles another visit, this time bringing Long Dog, a respected Hunkpapa chief. Walsh was convinced that the hostiles had committed no depredations and asked the Sioux chief in Miles's presence if he would like to leave Canada and live in the United States. Long Dog assured him he preferred Canada, and Walsh was convinced that no further Sioux parties would cross the border again.[35]

Miles also was convinced that the hostile Sioux would refrain from crossing the border and risking another confrontation with him. The pretentious colonel included in his report to Terry some interesting information about the strength of the hostiles. For the past three years he had been gathering information on the Sioux from traders, half-breeds, Indians, and American and Canadian officials and concluded that the hostiles numbered between six thousand and eight thousand people and twelve thousand to fifteen thousand horses. They were divided into four large camps: the Hunkpapas under Sitting Bull, Black Moon, Long Dog, and Pretty Bear; the Miniconjous under Black Eagle; the Sans Arcs under Spotted Eagle; and the Oglalas under Big Road and Broad Tail. Miles personally was pleased that these, "the worst Indians of the Northwest country," would stay in Canada rather than surrender to the United States and become its responsibility.[36]

The optimism of 1879 faded into the reality of 1880 when it became apparent that there were no longer enough buffalo for the Sioux to subsist on in Canada. Buffalo were scarce even in the area of the United States north of the Missouri River. The Sioux not only crossed the Canadian border but some hunted as far south as the Yellowstone Valley. Miles sent numerous scouting parties out to intercept the hostiles, and for the Sioux the situation seemed critical once again. In September 1,030 Indians surrendered at Fort Keogh. It seemed likely that more would follow. They had not received a reservation in Canada nor had they gained government subsistence goods. The buffalo were gone, and there seemed no alternative except to surrender to the white soldiers, turning over their guns and ponies in exchange for domestic stock. This had been the substance of Terry's offer to Sitting Bull four years ago, and now the Sioux were beginning to accept the reality of their situation.[37]

By December 1880, Miles had won his battle for promotion when he became a brigadier general and commander of the Department of the Columbia.[38] Major Guido Ilges assumed command at Fort Keogh, and from this centrally located fort, he and Terry continued to work for the final subjugation of the hostile Sioux.

Major David H. Brotherton of the Seventh Infantry, commanding at Fort Buford, reported to Terry that he had an interpreter, E. H. Allison, who possessed great influence among the hostile Sioux and who was willing to contact Sitting Bull in order to explain surrender terms to him and persuade him to give up himself and his people. Lengthy negotiations followed, and the Indians promised to surrender at Poplar River. Terry sent four companies of men from Fort Buford and five companies from Fort Keogh under the command of Ilges to receive the Indians at the Poplar River Agency. The troops arrived around Christmastime and immediately began constructing the huts that would serve as their winter quarters.[39]

The hostile Sioux under Chief Gall, who had been so prominent at the Little Bighorn, were camped across the Missouri River from the agency and numbered almost four hundred. They wanted to surrender but not until springtime because it was too cold to travel in the 15° to 50° below zero weather and knee-deep snow. As the Indian camp increased in numbers, they became less peaceful and more arrogant, to the point where they were ready to fight rather than surrender. Major Ilges decided to become more aggressive while there was still time. He gathered a force of three hundred men and advanced on the Hunkpapa camp. Most of the Indians escaped into the nearby woods, though some stayed in the camp to fight. Eight hostiles were killed, and the village was captured. Under a white flag, Gall told Ilges to return to the agency, and he would lead the Indians over the next day. The suspicious major had the Indian camp dismantled, which left the Indians little choice but to surrender. The warriors came out of the woods, and over three hundred surrendered along with about two hundred animals. Sixty hostiles escaped and joined Sitting Bull's camp.[40]

Gall's surrender party was only one of many that came in from January to July 1881. The scout Allison returned with 325 Indians under Crow

King in early February. In March, another 135 Indians under Low Dog surrendered at Fort Buford and during the spring, hostiles came in large and small groups to surrender at the forts. By the end of May, 1,125 Indian prisoners were gathered at Fort Buford awaiting transportation down the Missouri. The Interior Department had authorized five dollars per person for clothing, in addition to which Terry ordered 107 tents, 60 stoves, and 20,000 rations for the Indians. At Fort Keogh more than sixteen hundred hostiles awaited transportation. The government chartered a number of steamers, and the Fort Keogh Indians moved down the Yellowstone to Fort Buford. From there all the hostiles were transported down the Missouri to Standing Rock Agency near Fort Yates.[41]

Sitting Bull had returned to Canada in January and held out as long as he possibly could. Finally on July 19 the reluctant Sioux leader came to Fort Buford and gave himself up. With him came 187 of his followers. Ten days later he and his people boarded the steamer *General Sherman* and made their way to Fort Yates. Sherman ordered the Sioux chief transferred to Fort Randall, where he remained a prisoner for two years before he was allowed to return to his people at Standing Rock.[42]

Terry was relieved that Sitting Bull had surrendered. It had been fifteen years since the general had served on the Indian Peace Commission that had been troubled by the proud, stubborn Hunkpapas. Now the chief was safely in prison. Under the circumstances, it was good for the Sioux that Sitting Bull had surrendered. Conditions had changed and no longer could the plains support the old way of life for which the Indians longed. The buffalo were gone and white settlers were crowding into the northern plains in large numbers. Sitting Bull's surrender was the symbolic end of the traditional ways of the Tetons. The Sioux must begin a new life patterned after the white way. Thirty-five Sioux families were still known to be in Canada, but Terry felt they were too few in number and too broken in spirit to worry about. Eventually they were given small reservations by the Canadian government.[43]

Fittingly, perhaps, while Sitting Bull was making his way to Fort Buford to surrender, a detachment of the Second Cavalry made camp on the Little Bighorn and began to erect a monument on the Custer battlefield site.[44] The white man's symbol of the Indian fighter rose from the heart of the Sioux buffalo country, while the Indian symbol of hope against the white man's civilization had succumbed to the inevitable. Sheridan praised Terry for his good management of the Indian roundup, and they both praised the men who had served so well in the bitter winter weather.[45] The soldiers of the Department of Dakota had met their final significant challenge from the Teton Sioux.

NOTES

1. United States Bureau of the Census, *Historical Statistics of the United States, Colonial Times to 1957* (Washington, D.C.: Government Printing Office, 1960), pp. 12-13.

2. Virginia Weisel Johnson, *The Unregimented General: A Biography of Nelson A. Miles* (Boston: Houghton Mifflin, 1962), pp. 210-221.

3. *Annual Report of Terry,* November 12, 1877, H. Ex. Doc. 1, 45 Cong., 2 sess., Serial 1794, pp. 484-488, 517-518.

4. *Annual Report of Terry,* October 9, 1881, H. Ex. Doc. 1, 47 Cong., 1 sess., Serial 2010, pp. 87-88, 96; Johnson, *Unregimented General,* p. 221; Richard Upton, comp. and ed., *Fort Custer on the Big Horn, 1877-1898: Its History and Personalities as Told and Pictured by Its Contemporaries* (Glendale, Calif.: Arthur H. Clark Co., 1973).

5. *Annual Report of Terry,* October 4, 1880, H. Ex. Doc. 1, 46 Cong., 3 sess., Serial 1952, pp. 61, 65; *Correspondence Relative to Fort Maginnis,* March 21, 1880, S. Ex. Doc. 134, 46 Cong., 2 sess., Serial 1885, pp. 1-3.

6. *Annual Report of Terry,* 1877, pp. 484, 518.

7. *Annual Report of Terry,* October 1, 1879, H. Ex. Doc. 1, 46 Cong., 2 sess., Serial 1903, pp. 49-50, 64-65, 76; *Report Relative to Fort Assiniboine,* S. Ex. Doc. 286, 45 Cong., 2 sess., Serial 1790, pp. 1-5.

8. *Annual Report of Terry,* 1879, pp. 64-66, 76; ibid., 1880, pp. 67, 77.

9. *Annual Report of Terry,* 1880, p. 77; ibid., 1881, pp. 89, 96.

10. Ibid., 1880, p. 61.

11. Francis Paul Prucha, "Fort Ripley: The Post and the Military Reservation," *Minnesota History* 28 (September 1947): 224; Annual Report of Terry, 1879, p. 51.

12. *Annual Report of Terry,* 1877, pp. 484-486; ibid., 1881, pp. 87-88.

13. Ibid., 1879, pp. 49-50; ibid., 1880, pp. 65-66.

14. Ibid., 1881, pp. 87-88.

15. Ibid., 1879, p. 51; George E. Hyde, *Spotted Tail's Folk: A History of the Brule Sioux* (Norman: University of Oklahoma Press, 1961), pp. 256-275; James C. Olson, *Red Cloud and the Sioux Problem* (Lincoln: University of Nebraska Press, 1965), pp. 260-263.

16. *Annual Report of Terry,* 1877, pp. 519-520; ibid., October 4, 1878, H. Ex. Doc. 1, 45 Cong., 3 sess., Serial 1848, p. 70; ibid., 1880, p. 66.

17. Ibid., 1877, p. 486; ibid., 1880, p. 65.

18. *Annual Report of Sheridan,* October 22, 1880, H. Ex. Doc. 1, 46 Cong., 3 sess., Serial 1952, pp. 52-57.

19. Robert E. Riegel, *The Story of Western Railroads, from 1852 Through the Reign of the Giants* (Lincoln: University of Nebraska Press, 1967), pp. 203-206; *House Report of William W. Rice,* April 17, 1878, H. Report 618, 45 Cong., 2 sess., Serial 1824, p. 1.

20. *Annual Report of Terry,* 1879, p. 64.

21. Ibid., 1880, pp. 66-67.

22. Ibid., 1881, pp. 89, 109.

23. The following account of the Nez Perce is taken from ibid., 1877, which contains Miles's report. Also see General Nelson A. Miles, *Personal Recollections and Observations* (1896; reprint ed., New York: Da Capo Press, 1969), pp. 259-268; Oliver O. Howard, *My Life and Experiences Among Our Hostile Indians* (1906; reprint ed., New York: Da Capo Press, 1972), pp. 232-300; and Mark H. Brown, *The Flight of the Nez Perce: A History of the Nez Perce War* (New York: G. P. Putnam's Sons, 1967). A short but accurate synopsis is in Robert M. Utley, *Frontier Regulars: The United States Army and the Indian, 1866-1891* (New York: Macmillan Publishing Co., 1973, pp. 305-330.

24. Sherman to Townsend, August 23, 1877, LS, AGO, RG94, NA.

25. Oliver Otis Howard, *Autobiography of Oliver Otis Howard, Major General United States Army* (New York: Baker & Taylor Co., 1908), pp. 474-475.

26. Annual Report of Terry, 1878, pp. 66-67. A history of the Bannocks is Brigham D. Madsen, *The Bannock of Idaho* (Caldwell, Id.: Caxton Press, 1958).

27. See Mari Sandoz, *Cheyenne Autumn* (New York: McGraw-Hill, 1953).

28. Annual Report of Terry, 1879, pp. 50-51.

29. Ibid., pp. 55-59. This includes Lieutenant Clark's report.

30. For the international complications, see Gary Pennanen, "Sitting Bull: Indian Without a Country," *Canadian Historical Review* 51 (June 1970): 123-140. A biography of Sitting Bull is Stanley Vestal, *Sitting Bull, Champion of the Sioux* (Norman: University of Oklahoma Press, 1957).

31. Annual Report of Terry, 1878, pp. 65-66.

32. Ibid., 1879, pp. 59-61.

33. Ibid.

34. Ibid., pp. 61-62.

35. Ibid., p. 62.

36. Ibid., pp. 62-63.

37. Ibid., pp. 67, 75-77.

38. Utley, *Frontier Regulars,* pp. 296-297; Johnson, *Unregimented General,* pp. 220-221.

39. Annual Report of Terry, 1881, pp. 100-101.

40. Ibid., pp. 101-105.

41. Ibid., pp. 92-98, 101-107; Terry to Brotherton, January 10, 1881, LR, Records of the Bureau of Indian Affairs, RG75, NA; Lt. Gen. Philip H. Sheridan, *Record of Engagements with Hostile Indians Within the Military Division of the Missouri, From 1868 to 1882* (Washington, D.C.: Government Printing Office, 1882), pp. 113-114.

42. *Annual Report of Terry,* 1881, pp. 107-108.

43. Ibid., p. 108.

44. Ibid., p. 97.

45. *Annual Report of Sheridan,* October 22, 1881, LR, AGO.

11 The Job Completed, 1882-1890

After the surrender of Sitting Bull and his people in 1881, the events of the rest of the decade seemed anticlimactic to the soldiers of the Department of Dakota. More important than minor problems with the Indians were the signs of change within the department. Sherman wrote of visits to Yellowstone Park, and Terry expressed enthusiasm over drill practice and other routine activities in his department. There was not much else happening. Forts were abandoned, and troops traveled by train from one point to the next. Gone were the days of large expeditions marching off into little known areas to track Indians or to build forts isolated from civilization. Now Dakota and Montana filled with miners, ranchers, farmers, merchants, and politicians. These developments meant that the army had completed its job of paving the way for white society on the northern plains.

Indians had always been a fact of life for whites in Dakota and Montana, and reservations were a fact of life for these native Americans in the 1880s. With the disappearance of the buffalo, some of the Indians readily accepted the new way of life on the reservations, while others were reluctant to change. Indian Commissioner Hiram Price maintained that it was wrong for the government to spend over one million dollars a year to feed and clothe Indians. He felt they must learn to labor in order to develop "true manhood" and self-sufficiency.[1] Carl Schurz, a reforming secretary of interior from 1877 to 1881, felt the Indian must labor where the earth was fertile. He maintained that concentration was a mistake if it meant moving natives from a place where they were already farming. He favored the distribution of land to individual Indians so that through private ownership farming might be encouraged. He advocated restricting the labor of whites on reservations, and he supported the education of Indians in the use of the English language and other practical knowledge.[2]

In 1879 the Indian Bureau distributed about three thousand cattle to the Sioux, and the natives treated the animals well. Because the Indians seldom killed any, the herd grew rapidly. Still Schurz was skeptical about making cattlemen out of the Sioux because the work would keep only a few natives busy while the majority remained idle. Another idea to keep the Tetons active was to have them haul supplies from the Missouri River to their agencies on the White River tributaries. The Sioux proved efficient, honest, and reliable freighters, and they incorporated about thirty-six hundred wagons in the business in Dakota and Montana. Their success in herding and freighting was encouraging, but farming remained the goal that most government officials had chosen for the approximately sixty thousand Indians of the Department of Dakota.[3]

Some of the Teton adjusted to agriculture remarkably well according to official government reports. By 1881 the Sioux at the Missouri River agencies had erected 718 permanent houses and raised 41,000 bushels of wheat and corn and 12,000 bushels of vegetables. The Oglalas and Brulés on the White River had constructed 700 log houses and cultivated 2,200 acres of land. They owned 300 mules, 5,600 head of cattle, 280 pigs, and thousands of horses. Their crops for the year had been seriously damaged by an early drought, but there was optimism about next year. The Santee Sioux at Sisseton and Devils Lake were virtually self-supporting. They practiced private ownership of land, they lived in houses, and they wore white man's clothes. Government officials foresaw the day when the Tetons also would reach this stage of civilization.[4]

Many of the Indians in Montana were not ready to settle down to the white man's way of life, however. Almost continuous warfare existed between the Crees of Canada and the Montana Indians. Soldiers from Fort Assiniboine repeatedly scouted the Milk River and the surrounding area to drive the Crees back across the border. These Canadian Indians killed the game, thus depriving the American Indians of their subsistence, and they also conducted pony and horse raids on those who lived north of the Missouri River. The army continued its border patrol activities, but it was a frustrating type of endeavor because the troops could not go north of the border.

The soldiers also had problems with Indians who had nothing to do with Canada. The Piegans, Crows, Gros Ventres, and Assiniboines continued to raid each other, and the army had to intervene frequently. These were minor actions but time-consuming for the soldiers.

Generally during the 1880s, however, the Indian frontier was quiet. Year after year Terry's annual reports, and later Ruger's, contained a phrase describing the year as being unusually quiet or uneventful. General of the Army William T. Sherman accurately described conditions in 1883 when he reported to Congress: "I now regard the Indians as substantially eliminated from the problem of the Army. There will be spasmodic and temporary alarms, but such Indian wars as have hitherto disturbed the public tranquillity are not probable."[6]

With the decline in the number of Indian depredations, there was an increase in white efforts to pass legislation that might further clear the way for Indians to follow in the white way. Most of these attempts centered around Indian land and farming. In 1887, Congress passed the Dawes Act, which reformers claimed would bring on a new era for Indian-white relations.

This legislation allotted Indians 160 acres of land for each family head and lesser amounts for others. There were other provisions, but it was significant that the principle of private ownership of land was to be applied to the Sioux. At last, the whites hoped, the stubborn Tetons would turn to farming, and tribal authority would diminish.[7]

Supplementary to the Dawes Act, Congress passed the Sioux Act in 1889, legislation that set aside six separate reservations for the Tetons: Standing Rock, Cheyenne River, Crow Creek, Lower Brulé, Rosebud, and Pine Ridge. The land that was left over in the Great Sioux Reserve, about half the total acreage, was then to be put up for sale to whites. Crook promised the Sioux generous provisions, and he was able to convince them that they would lose the land without much compensation if they did not sign the agreement. Through the most skilled and subtle means, he gained the signatures of three-fourths of the Indians. The Sioux had suffered another severe loss of land.[8]

Terry and Crook had probably done more than any other government officials to force the Teton Sioux into their position of 1889. As generals, they had led their soldiers against the Sioux in the climactic campaigns of 1876 and 1877. As peace commissioners, they made sure that victories won on the battlefield were reflected in the treaties that followed. Terry had been a key figure in the 1868 treaty that set the groundwork for the treaties that followed. Crook was responsible for their grudging acceptance of the 1889 treaty. Neither man hated the natives. Both respected the Indian's position, but in the case of the Sioux, it was not whether the

Indians would lose their lands but what kind of a settlement they would get when the whites greedily partitioned their reservations.

Although the main business of the northern plains army was the management and subjugation of the Indians, there were signs that pointed to a lessened need for the soldier's presence in the region. One was the increasing presence of the railroads. During 1882 and 1883, the army continued its escort service for the Northern Pacific engineers and laborers. The Indians gave little trouble, and the soldiers sometimes enjoyed the break from camp routine. During the first summer's work the labor gangs constructed the road along the south bank of the Yellowstone River, and by the end of the working season the line reached Livingston, 115 miles west of Billings.[9]

During the next year the Northern Pacific pushed northwest out of the Yellowstone Valley and across the Belt Range. The ascent of the mountains proved a challenge for the engineers, but with the construction of the Bozeman tunnel, some 3,610 feet long, the range was conquered. By the end of 1883 the line was joined with the road that was built from the West Coast, and the Northern Pacific became the fourth transcontinental railroad in the United States.[10]

With the railroads came the spread of the white man's way of life. As the Northern Pacific pushed its way through the Yellowstone Valley, settlers poured into the area. The railroad meant population and with it a potential for prosperity. Farmers had a means to ship their crops to market, and goods could be brought from the East at much less cost than before. The railroad meant a great deal to a community that hoped to grow and prosper. The coming of the railroad also meant the decline in the role that the military would play. Numerous scattered forts to protect isolated settlements were no longer necessary. Civilian law enforcement officers would handle local problems, and soldiers could be rushed from large, centrally located posts to troublesome areas.[11]

The Northern Pacific was the key transportation route in the northern plains, but other smaller railroads brought settlements into the mainstream of trade and communication. The Dakota Southern; the Chicago, Milwaukee, and St. Paul; and the Chicago and Northwestern railroads all opened up southern Dakota. The northern division of the Chicago, Milwaukee, and St. Paul did the same for northern Dakota; and the St. Paul, Minneapolis, and Manitoba railroad opened up the northern Missouri River and Milk River region. In 1879 James J. Hill began developing the

Great Northern railroad in this same area. He sought to gain the business of the area north of the Northern Pacific. In 1883 his line reached Devils Lake, and by 1893 it was completed to Seattle. The construction of these lines and many spur roads began to spread a vast network of rails across the northern plains, which meant the demise of the buffalo, Indian, and soldier. In their places were the farmers, ranchers, merchants, and politicians. Civilization had come to Dakota and Montana.[12]

Another sign that the role of the army on the northern plains was decreasing was the concern that government officials had for Yellowstone National Park. Now Terry had time to spend in making preparations for various dignitaries to visit these natural wonders. Secretary of War Belknap had come in 1875, General Sherman in 1877, Secretary of the Interior Schurz in 1880, Sheridan with large parties in 1881 and 1882, and President Chester Arthur in 1883. On most occasions these visitors traveled on the Union Pacific Railroad; and to the commander of the Department of the Platte fell many of the chores of planning. When the Northern Pacific reached Livingston in 1882, however, the dignitaries began to use this shorter route to the park, and Terry was called upon to host these trips.[13]

The most enjoyable trek to the park for Terry was in 1883 when Sherman returned to Yellowstone just prior to his retirement. In late June Terry entertained Sherman and Supreme Court Chief Justice Morrison R. Waite at Fort Snelling. The party then took the train, passing through Brainerd, Bismarck, Glendive, Miles City, and Livingston. Terry was amazed to see the region of the Tongue, Powder, and Bighorn rivers filled with peaceful farmers and cattle ranchers. Only seven years before, this area had been prime buffalo country, and Terry had spent the summer chasing hostile Sioux across the unsettled land.[14]

On July 5 the group entered the park and soon reached the new Mammoth Hotel near the hot springs. Here the party split. Sherman and some of the detachment went to view the geysers and thrilled to see the Giant Geyser and Old Faithful. Terry, Waite, and others viewed Tower Falls and then moved south toward Yellowstone Lake. During this time Justice Waite experienced a fall from his horse and broke two ribs. A physician in a party nearby heard of the accident and came to bandage the injury so that Waite could continue the journey. When the group reached Mount Washburn, several of the men decided to go to the summit some ten thousand feet above sea level. Chief Justice Waite was persuaded not to make the trip, and he waited while Terry, his aide Major Robert Hughes, and others rode horseback to the top. The panorama that unfolded before them was magnificent. After a delightful trip through the park, Terry and Waite returned to the East while Sherman continued his tour to the West Coast and the Southwest.[15] Several years later, in 1888, troops from the Department of Dakota were actually stationed in Yellowstone to oversee the operation of the park.[16]

Upon his return to department headquarters, Terry settled back into the routine of office work. He faced decisions about closing forts and shifting personnel from post to post. In 1882, he moved the Seventh Cavalry headquarters from Fort Abraham Lincoln to Fort Custer. (See map 12.) Lincoln, which Sheridan once had called one of the finest posts in the West, was only a skeleton of the original fort. Although it was not abandoned at this time, others were.[17] Fort Stevenson in 1883 and Fort Hale in 1884, two Missouri River posts of earlier significance, were taken from the list of active forts. In 1886 Fort Ellis, at one time a key post near the Yellowstone River in Montana District, was abandoned, and three years later Fort Sisseton in eastern Dakota near the Lake Traverse Indian Agency was vacated.[18]

These closings were just a prelude to the dismantling of the Department of Dakota fort system that took place in the 1890s. The army, notoriously slow in closing forts, abandoned eleven of them in the 1890s and three more shortly after the turn of the century. The closing of Fort Custer in 1898 was the last of the department closings in the century and seemed to illustrate the point once again that there was little left for the army to do on the northern plains. The last of the forts was not closed until shortly after World War II, but the work of the army in subjugating the Sioux had long since been completed.[19]

Even the decrease in the number of Indian scouts kept by the army in Dakota told the story of its lessening responsibility during the 1880s. Congress had authorized the use of three hundred scouts during the 1870s, but during the 1880s the army used from a low of ten to a high of fifty-nine. Here was an example of another institution that had outlived its usefulness in the rapidly developing northern plains.[20]

Black soldiers made their entrance into the Department of Dakota in 1884. The black infantrymen did well and received Terry's praise. The general was surprised that they could function so well in such a cold climate, but he reported that their desertion figures were less than those

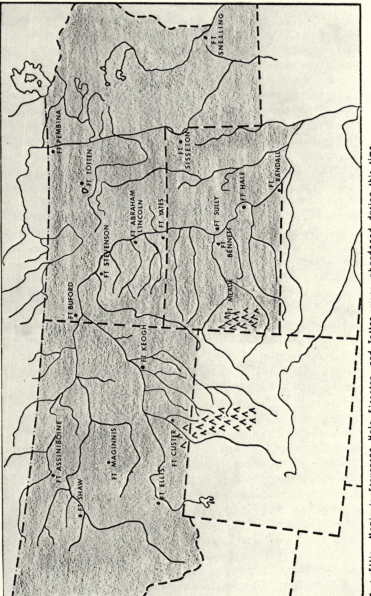

Forts Ellis, Maginnis, Stevenson, Hale, Sisseton and Totten were abandoned during this time.

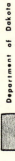 Department of Dakota

Map 12 THE DEPARTMENT OF DAKOTA, 1882-1890

of white soldiers, and their ratio of ill to healthy was much less than that of the white soldiers. Thus another myth about the "buffalo soldiers," as the blacks were called, fell by the wayside.[21]

Terry also took an interest in target practice and marksmanship awards for the soldiers now that there was time. In 1883 he bragged in his reports that more than 25 percent of his men were entitled to wear marksmen's buttons.[22] The percentage got better each year, and the general took great pride in the work his officers and men carried out on the target range.

In 1866 Terry felt some consternation over his military rank. An opening occurred at the major general level, and Terry was anxious for the position, but because of an unusual circumstance, Terry offered to give way for another man. In 1878-1879 he had served on a board of inquiry held at the request of Fitz John Porter, an officer who had been court-martialed and cashiered out of the army in 1863. Colonel Porter was accused of disobeying several of General John Pope's orders at the Civil War battle of Second Bull Run, which took place in 1862. Porter was not able to gain a rehearing until fifteen years after his dismissal. Terry, General John M. Schofield, and Colonel George W. Getty, an artillery officer who had served under Porter, sat on the board, which held a majority of its meetings at West Point, New York. Terry and Schofield were reluctant to serve because they held the preconceived opinion that Porter was guilty. As the case of the defendant unfolded, Terry smoked his cigars and listened with increasing interest. Soon he became convinced of the severe injustice that Porter had suffered, and he was pleased when the board found him innocent and recommended his restoration to his previous rank.[23]

Terry was ashamed that he had prejudged Porter and that the officer had lived for fifteen years under the stigma of the court-martial. He wrote Grant that he "believed that he [Porter] had committed a crime so great that human laws could find no adequate punishment for it. But when it became my duty to examine carefully the facts in the case I found that I had grossly erred. I found that he was not a criminal but a near martyr."[24] It was not until 1886 that President Grover Cleveland reappointed Porter colonel of infantry, the rank he held before his dismissal. With the vacancy in rank at the major-general level, Terry offered to yield his position of seniority to Porter, but the innocent colonel turned it down. Porter was not interested in becoming a soldier again; he wanted only justice.[25]

In April 1886, Terry was raised in rank to major general and promoted to commander of the Division of the Missouri in place of General Schofield, who moved to the Division of the Atlantic. Colonel Thomas Ruger was raised in rank to brigadier general and moved from commander of the Montana District to head the Department of Dakota. At age fifty-nine, Terry had reached a pinnacle in his career and was near the top of the army in rank and seniority. He was still relatively young and looked to have a fine future ahead of him.[26]

He plunged into his new job with much vigor and soon was writing to Sheridan, who was now general of the army, explaining his views of the "new army," which he felt the United States must work toward. His emphasis was on target practice and its importance in connection with the "new army" that the United States must achieve. He explained that during the last twenty years a revolution had taken place in the art of war, second in time but more important than that produced by the invention of gunpowder. Prior to the introduction of firearms, the most important factor in determining the strength of an army, he maintained, was the individual skill in the use of arms by the soldiers. In history were numerous examples where small units of soldiers skilled in the use of their arms had won great victories over much larger masses of untrained men.[27]

The invention of gunpowder had changed all this, he explained, because little skill could be attained on the crude guns of the time. As a consequence, there was little effort made to train soldiers in the skillful use of their arms but rather to teach them to move or act with speed and precision. Thus, as Terry explained it, the emphasis in the past had been to train soldiers in drill rather than rifle practice. With the invention of the breechloading rifle and other improvements in the weapon, it was now reasonable to expect that once again, as in the pregunpowder era, soldiers could become skillful in the use of arms if properly and systematically instructed.

Terry believed that other nations understood the need for new training techniques, and he was determined that the United States should not fall behind or that its army become outdated. Large numbers of untrained men, he reasoned, were an encumbrance in battle, and so he argued forcefully for a target season of several months of theoretical instruction plus four months of actual target practice. This would still leave half the year for the drilling exercises that many officers were reluctant to slight.

Some politicians opposed the idea of building a substantial army skilled in the use of firearms. They argued that it was too costly, and in the long run it might endanger the liberties of Americans. These people believed that the United States had an abundance of soldiers trained during the

Civil War, and in a time of national danger these men could be called upon to form a vast army that was the equal of any in the world. Terry disagreed. The military strength of any nation fell upon the men between the ages of twenty and thirty-five, and even the youngest of Civil War veterans were beyond this age in 1886. They also had little knowledge of the new weapons then being used and thus would be of limited value to the military.

Terry further argued that an army carried out two functions at the outbreak of a war. One was to meet and stop the initial attacks of the enemy, and the second was to train new recruits who would be rushed into the army during the wartime emergency. The general felt that the expense of establishing an adequate peacetime army was the price of freedom, and he further felt that a nation with only one soldier per one thousand population was not in any danger of losing its liberties through army control.

While Terry contemplated his theories on the military, he also looked to his many other responsibilities in his new job as commander of the Division of the Missouri. From his headquarters in Chicago, he oversaw the activities of the four departments under him. He knew well the problems of the Department of Dakota and had worked with General Ruger in the past. In the Department of the Platte, General Crook was in charge; and their main concern was a Ute uprising in 1887 in Colorado, which the department commander handled well. In the Department of the Missouri, there were changes in command from Generals Miles to Ruger to Joseph H. Potter. In the Department of Texas, General David S. Stanley, Terry's former Southeastern District commander in Dakota, was in control. There were aggravating problems with the Apaches but no general uprisings at the time.[28]

It was well that there was comparative quiet in the division, because Terry was not well. He had contracted Bright's disease while in Minnesota shortly before he left his command there. He had been under the care of Major Charles H. Alden, the attending surgeon in the Department of Dakota, since May 1885. The major diagnosed Terry's discomfort as a kidney illness. His case was not advanced, and he continued his duties in St. Paul, but he was in a somewhat weakened condition. The surgeon recommended that Terry take a leave of absence and rest in a warm climate during the winter, but Terry remained in St. Paul and held up well.[29]

In April 1886, Terry moved to division headquarters in Chicago and a new doctor. Major Charles R. Greenleaf saw his new patient in December 1886 and diagnosed Terry's sickness as Bright's disease complicated by gout. The general was very nervous, physically weak, and generally unfit for the duties of his office. Any stress was particularly harmful to Terry, and he had just gone through the trial of the anarchists who were supposedly involved in the Haymarket Square labor riot in Chicago, a Crow disturbance in Montana, and a visit by President Cleveland to Chicago. Terry had responsibilities in all these matters, and they aggravated his condition so much that Major Greenleaf recommended Terry's retirement. The general was unable to sleep, was restless, lacked appetite, had palpitation of the heart and a quick pulse, and was extremely nervous. The only relief for his condition was full rest and a warm climate during the winter to protect him from exposure.[30] Terry traveled to Texas on an inspection tour of some of the forts in that department and even took a short junket to Monterey, Mexico, "to become acquainted with the territory contiguous to the frontier." He was gone about twenty days, but the trip did not improve his health; he was too weak even to write letters.[31]

Next Terry sought the medical advice of his brother, J. Wadsworth Terry, and another New York doctor, J. R. Leaning. Although couched in complicated medical terms, their findings were the same: Bright's disease, gout, enlargement of the heart, nervousness, sleeplessness, and a painful cough.[32] On March 24, 1888, Terry submitted his request for retirement to the army. He had taken a leave of four months and was resting in St. Augustine, Florida, and therefore he did not appear before the retiring board in April. It did not matter because his friend, General Schofield, was president of the board, and he had received documented evidence of Terry's condition. The board granted the retirement.[33] Terry spent some of his retirement in the South and also stayed with his sisters in New Haven. He found it hard to accept retirement and felt cheated out of what should have been more useful years of his life. The rigors of Minnesota winters had taken their toll on the general, but now Terry rested and was free of responsibility. For a while his health improved, but he was still incapable of exertion.[34]

While Terry convalesced on an adequate pension from the government and the wealth he had inherited during his life, political activities on the northern plains came to a head. In Dakota, there had been talk of statehood as early as the 1870s. There was also a great controversy about moving the territorial capital to Bismarck to satisfy the Northern Pacific faction or to Fort Pierre as a midway point. Others talked of dividing the territory into two parts in preparation for statehood. By 1889, President Cleveland signed the omnibus bill creating the four new states of North Dakota, South Dakota, Montana, and Washington. State capitals were located in Bismarck, Pierre, and Helena, places that thirty years before were part of the wilderness stronghold of native Americans. The region had grown rapidly and the 1880s manifested a tremendous population growth. North Dakota had grown from 37,000 to 191,000 over the decade, South Dakota from 98,000 to 349,000, and Montana from 39,000 to 143,000. This represented a jump of about 400 percent and reflected the importance of the new railroads as harbingers of white civilization.[35]

As the plains filled with people and towns, the Indians lived out their miserable lives on the reservation lands that the whites did not take from them. The Tetons' once cherished lands of the Bighorn country, the Powder River region, and the Black Hills were controlled by the whites. This proud minority had been conquered by the soldiers of Dakota during the 1870s, and their culture was shattered during the 1880s. The land was lost, the buffalo were gone, and a way of life had passed. There was a flicker of hope among the Indians in 1890 with the Ghost Dance phenomenon, which promised the return of the old life. A Paiute Indian messiah from far-off Nevada preached that the whites would disappear and the dead Indians and buffalo would return to the plains. But these dreams were shattered on the frozen field of Wounded Knee Creek in South Dakota, when soldiers from the Department of the Platte shot down another 153 Sioux in a meaningless and unfortunate confrontation. The Tetons' fate had already been decided, however, and their retreat into a past that could never live again did not help them to face reality.

The army in the Department of Dakota also faced a new day. It had carried out the work of subjugating and managing the Indians of the northern plains. Terry had been with them most of the way. He did not hate the Indians, nor did he agree with a policy of extermination. The general expressed no great love for the Indians either, but rather his feelings centered around the quest for justice for native Americans. With his background of law and honor, he sought to achieve the best possible solution for both races. Undoubtedly he believed that the Indians had little to offer to the white man's culture, and he believed that native Americans must eventually accept the civilization of the dominate people. In this respect Terry represented the nineteenth-century mentality of white

America. He was an easterner who took his views of law and humanity and moved to the West. Here the rawness and anti-Indian feelings of the region affected him little, but the reality of mixing two races in the crucible of the northern plains led him to seek justice for Indians in the context of white American culture.

During the 1880s Terry became somewhat involved with eastern human-itarians who sought to bring Christianity and justice to the American Indians. It was strange that an army general would be found in this com-pany, but he was much sought after as a speaker for missionary and church groups who supported a humanitarian approach to the native American problem. One member of the American Missionary Association described Terry as "a cultured man, an honored soldier and a Christian gentleman." On another occasion H. L. Wayland, editor of the *National Baptist Journal,* described Terry "as a friend of the Indians . . . whose hands are free from stain of Indian murders, and one who will be as he has been, wise, just, humane, brave, in dealing with our red wards."[36]

The Sioux and the army had been the main characters in the drama on the northern plains for years. The importance of both dwindled dur-ing the 1880s and came to a symbolic end in 1890. Sitting Bull, the man who stood staunchly in the path of the whites and represented the freedom and culture of Sioux life, met his death on the morning of December 15, 1890. On that day Indian police came to his wooden hut at Standing Rock Agency to arrest him. Agent James McLaughlin believed that the old chief must be removed from the reservation because he found it difficult to accept the new way of life on the reservation and he negatively influenced others. The police surrounded the cabin and the chief was awakened. His people crowded to his side, a scuffle broke out, gunshots followed, and the fifty-nine year old Hunkpapa fell to the ground, his chest and head broken by bullets from guns held by younger Sioux of a newer generation.[37]

Hundreds of miles from the South Dakota Indian reservation in a com-fortable house in New Haven, Connecticut, the flicker of life faded slowly from Alfred Terry. The end came to the sixty-one year-old soldier less than twenty-four hours after his old northern plains adversary had passed away.[38] Their deaths signaled the end of an era in the northern plains. Indeed a period in American history had come to a close. By 1890 the frontier had receded before the onslaught of white civilization, and the dawn of a new day had come to the West.

NOTES

1. *Annual Report of Price,* December 24, 1881, H. Ex. Doc. 1, 47 Cong., 1 sess., Serial 2018, p. 3.

2. *Annual Report of Schurz,* November 1, 1878, H. Ex. Doc. 1, 45 Cong., 3 sess., Serial 1850, p. iii; ibid., November 1, 1880, H. Ex. Doc. 1, 46 Cong., 3 sess., Serial 1959, pp. 3-4.

3. Ibid., November 15, 1879, H. Ex. Doc. 1, 46 Cong., 2 sess., Serial 1910, pp. 6-7, 23-24; Annual Report of Price, 1881, p. 31; Robert M. Utley, *The Last Days of the Sioux Nation* (New Haven: Yale University Press, 1963), pp. 25-26.

4. *Annual Report of Schurz,* 1880, pp. 28-29. For a contradictory view of the Santee, see Roy W. Meyer, *History of the Santee Sioux* (Lincoln: University of Nebraska Press, 1967).

5. *Annual Report of Terry,* October 6, 1882. H. Ex. Doc. 1, 47 Cong., 2 sess., Serial 2091, pp. 89, 94, 95.

6. *Annual Report of Sherman,* 1883, H. Ex. Doc. 1, 48 Cong., 1 sess., Serial 2181, p. 46.

7. Utley, *Last Days of the Sioux Nation,* pp. 43-45; Loring Benson Priest, *Uncle Sam's Stepchildren: The Reformation of United States Indian Policy, 1865-1887* (1942; reprint ed., New York: Octagon Books, 1969), pp. 193-197, 217-252.

8. Herbert S. Schell, *History of South Dakota* (Lincoln: University of Nebraska Press, 1968), pp. 323-324; Utley, *Last Days of the Sioux Nation,* pp. 44-55.

9. *Report on Transcontinental Railways,* 1883, Col. O. M. Roe, October 1, 1883, H. Ex. Doc. 1, 48 Cong., 1 sess., Serial 2182, pp. 262-269; *Annual Report of Terry,* 1882, pp. 84-88.

10. *Annual Report of Terry,* 1882, pp. 84-88.

11. Annual Report of Sheridan, October 20, 1882, LR, AGO, RG94, NA.

12. *Annual Report of Ruger,* September 22, 1887, H. Ex. Doc. 1, 50 Cong., 1 sess., Serial 2533, p. 138; Robert E. Riegel, *The Story of the Western Railroads* 1926; (reprint ed., Lincoln: University of Nebraska Press, 1964), pp. 212-214.

13. Hiram M. Chittenden, *The Yellowstone National Park* (Cincinnati: Robert Clarke Co., 1895), pp. 105-107.

14. *Report of Journey Made by General W. T. Sherman in the Northwest and Middle Parts of the United States in 1883,* October 27, 1883, H. Ex. Doc. 1, 48 Cong., 1 sess., Serial 2182, pp. 203-252; Sherman to Robert T. Lincoln, July 29, 1883, LS, Records of the Headquarters of the Army, RG108, NA.

15. Sherman to Lincoln, July 29, 1883.

16. H. Duane Hampton, *How the U.S. Cavalry Saved Our National Parks* (Bloomington: Indiana University Press, 1971), p. 92.

17. Annual Report of Terry, 1882, p. 89.

18. See Annual Reports of Terry, Department of Dakota, appropriate date; Francis Paul Prucha, *A Guide to the Military Posts of the United States, 1789-1895* (Madison: State Historical Society of Wisconsin, 1964), pp. 73, 108-109.

19. Prucha, *Guide to the Military Posts,* pp. 55, 57, 60-61, 63, 69, 82, 90-92, 96, 98, 100, 107, 108, 110, 112, 118. The following forts were closed: Forts Totten and Maginnis in 1890; Bennett, Abraham Lincoln, and Shaw in 1891; Randall in 1892; Camp Poplar River in 1893; Sully in 1894; Buford and Pembina in 1895; Custer in 1898; Yates in 1903; Keogh in 1908; Assiniboine in 1911; and Missoula, Meade, and Snelling after World War II.

20. See the annual reports for the 1880s for the facts on the Indian scouts.

21. *Annual Report of Terry,* October 6, 1884, H. Ex. Doc. 1, 48 Cong., 2 sess., Serial 2461, pp. 119-120.

22. Ibid., 1883, p. 117.

23. See *Board of Inquiry, Fitz John Porter,* April 12, 1878-March 19, 1879, S. Ex. Doc. 37, 46 Cong., 1 sess., Serial 1871 and 1872, for the complete testimony of the hearing. See also Otto Eisenschiml, *The Celebrated Case of Fitz John Porter* (Indianapolis: Bobbs Merrill Co., 1950).

24. Terry to Grant, November 19, 1882, Terry Papers.

25. Eisenschiml, *Celebrated Case of Fitz John Porter,* pp. 304, 313.

26. *Annual Report of Terry,* September 10, 1886, H. Ex. Doc. 1, 49 Cong., 2 sess., Serial 2461, pp. 119-120.

27. For Terry's philosophy of the "new army," see ibid., pp. 120-122.

28. Ibid., p. 116.

29. ACP: Alfred H. Terry, AGO, RG94, NA, Proceedings of an Army Retiring Board, April 4, 1888, Washington, D.C., Major General John M. Schofield, President.

30. Ibid.

31. Ibid.; Terry to Sheridan, March 3, 1887, ACP, Terry, AGO.

32. ACP, Terry, Army Retiring Board, April 4, 1888.

33. Ibid.; Terry and Schofield were close friends. Schofield described Terry as a "ripe scholar, a thorough lawyer, a very laborious student of the art and science of war, more so than most West Point graduates." In 1880 there was a question of foul play at West Point, and Terry was offered the job to succeed Schofield as superintendent of the academy. Terry

refused the appointment when he learned that Schofield was innocent. John M. Schofield, *Forty-six Years in the Army* (New York: Century Co., 1897), pp. 445-447, 535.

34. Terry to William C. Endicott, Secretary of War, March 24, 1888, ACP, Terry, AGO.

35. Howard Roberts Lamar, *Dakota Territory, 1861-1889: A Study of Frontier Politics* (New Haven: Yale University Press, 1956), pp. 177-273; Schell, *History of South Dakota,* pp. 189-222; Elwyn B. Robinson, *History of North Dakota* (Lincoln: University of Nebraska Press, 1966), pp. 197-216; James McClellan Hamilton, *History of Montana: From Wilderness to Statehood* (Portland: Binfords and Mort, 1957), pp. 524-600; United States Bureau of the Census, *Historical Statistics of the United States, Colonial Times to 1957* (Washington, D.C.: Government Printing Office, 1960), pp. 12-13.

36. Rev. M. E. Strieby to Terry, October 5, 1882, and Wayland to Terry, March 8, 1886, Terry Papers.

37. Stanley Vestal, *Sitting Bull: Champion of the Sioux* (1957; reprint ed., New York: Houghton Mifflin, 1932), pp. 293-307; Utley, *Last Days of the Sioux Nation,* pp. 146-166.

38. Sitting Bull died about 5:35 A.M., December 15, 1890. Alfred Terry died at 4:00 A.M., December 16, 1890. Utley, *Last Days of the Sioux Nation,* p. 158; Hughes to Schofield, December 16, 1890, ACP, Terry AGO; Hughes to AGO, December 22, 1890, ACP, Terry AGO; *New York World,* December 17, 1890.

Bibliography

RECORDS IN THE NATIONAL ARCHIVES

Record Group 48: Records of the Office of the Secretary of the Interior. This has excellent material on the Peace Commission of 1867-1868 and is a key source for this period.

Interior Department Territorial Papers: Dakota, 1863-1889.

Interior Department Territorial Papers: Montana, 1867-1889.

Office of Secretary of Interior, Indian Division, Separated Correspondence, Indian Treaty Commissions, 1867-1868.

Office of Secretary of Interior, Indian Division. Transcript of the Minutes and Proceedings of the Indian Peace Commission Appointed by an Act of Congress Approved July 20, 1867.

Record Group 59: General Records of the Department of State. This collection contains material relative to territorial-military relations with correspondence between military officers and territorial officials important for this study.

State Department Territorial Papers: Dakota, 1861-1873.

State Department Territorial Papers: Montana, 1864-1872.

Record Group 75: Records of the Bureau of Indian Affairs. This source comprises correspondence between army and Indian Bureau officials concerning the handling of local Indian problems.

Records of the Bureau of Indian Affairs. Minutes of Special Commission: Proceedings, 1868.

Record Group 94: Records of the Adjutant General's Office. These records were extremely helpful in matters of rank, promotion, leaves, retirement, orders of the War Department, military expeditions, annual reports of department and division commanders, army installations, and Indian affairs and constitute a major source for this work.

Appointment, Commission and Personal Branch: Robert Patterson Hughes.

Appointment, Commission and Personal Branch: Alfred Howe Terry.

Record Group 108: Records of the Headquarters of the Army, 1825-1903. This contains letters sent and received by the Commanding General of the Army and his subordinates in the field. Information on military campaigns, troop movements, and inspections were pertinent to this study.

Headquarters of the Army. Letters Sent: 1866-1869, 1873-1890.

Headquarters of the Army. Letters Received: 1866-1869, 1873-1878, 1883-1887.

Record Group 153: Records of the Office of the Judge Advocate General. Here may be found information on army discipline, court-martial proceedings, and army hearings which took up a great deal of General Terry's normal working day.

Annual Reports for the Department of Dakota, 1866-1891.

Record Group 393: Records of the U.S. Army Continental Commands, 1821-1920. This collection contains valuable correspondence on the departmental and divisional level and constitutes a major source for this work.

Department of Dakota. Letters Received: December 1879-December 26, 1890.

Department of Dakota. Letters Sent: 1866-1869, 1874-1875, 1887-1888.

Department of Dakota. Letters Sent by Headquarters Field: June-September 1867 and April-July 1868.

Division of the Missouri. Letters and Telegrams Sent: 1884-1888.

Division of the Missouri. Letters and Telegrams Received: 1886-1888.

GOVERNMENT PUBLICATIONS

U.S. Commissioner of Indian Affairs. Annual Reports. 1866-1891.
U.S. Congress. *Congressional Globe,* 39-42 Cong. (1866-1873).
_____. *Congressional Record,* 43-51 Cong. (1873-1891).

U.S. Congress. House of Representatives. H. Ex. Doc. 1, 39 Cong., 1 sess.,
Serial 1248. *Report of Governor Newton Edmunds, Dakota Territory.*
October 14, 1865.
_____. H. Ex. Doc. 23, 39 Cong., 2 sess., Serial 1288. *Protection Across
the Continent.* December 6, 1866.
_____. H. Ex. Doc. 1, 40 Cong., 2 sess., Serial 1326. *Report of P. J. de
Smet, Special Indian Agent.* June 1, 1867.
_____. H. Ex. Doc. 76, 40 Cong., 2 sess., Serial 1332. *Report of Destitu-
tion of Sioux Near Devil's Lake, Dakota Territory.* January 7, 1868.
_____. H. Ex. Doc. 97, 40 Cong., 2 sess., Serial 1337. *Report of Indian
Peace Commissioners.* January 7, 1868.
_____. H. Ex. Doc. 1, 40 Cong., 3 sess., Serial 1366. *Report of the Indian
Peace Commissioners.* January 7, 1868.
_____. H. Ex. Doc. 121, 41 Cong., 2 sess., Serial 1417. *Montana Militia.*
February 7, 1870.
_____. H. Ex. Doc. 96, 42 Cong., 3 sess., Serial 1566. *Condition of the
Teton Sioux.* January 10, 1873.
_____. H. Ex. Doc. 213, 42 Cong., 3 sess., Serial 1569. *Erection of Mili-
tary Posts Along the Northern Pacific Railroad.* February 19, 1873.
_____. H. Ex. Doc. 144, 43 Cong., 2 sess., Serial 1648. *An Amendment
to Indian Appropriation Bill to Extinguish Rights to Hunt under
1868 Treaty.* April 29, 1868.
_____. H. Mis. Doc. 33, 43 Cong., 2 sess., Serial 1653. *Dakota Legislature
Asks Black Hills Be Opened for Settlement.* January 11, 1875.
_____. H. Ex. Doc. 125, 44 Cong., 1 sess., Serial 1689. *Expense of Geo-
logical Exploration of the Black Hills.* February 14, 1876.
_____. H. Ex. Doc. 184, 44 Cong., 1 sess., Serial 1691. *Military Expedi-
tion Against the Sioux Indians.* July 15, 1876.
_____. H. Mis. Doc. 126, 44 Cong., 1 sess., Serial 1702. *Amount of Ex-
penses for Fulfilling Treaty with the Sioux.* June 30, 1876.
_____. H. Mis. Doc. 181, 44 Cong., 1 sess., Serial 1706. *Statement on
Distribution of Troops.* July 10, 1876.
_____. H. Report 240, 44 Cong., 1 sess., Serial 1708. *Transfer of Indian
Bureau.* March 14, 1876.
_____. H. Ex. Doc. 55, 45 Cong., 2 sess., Serial 1806. *Distribution of
U.S. Troops as of June 30, 1877.*
_____. H. Report 618, 45 Cong., 2 sess., Serial 1824. *Report of William
W. Rice.* April 17, 1878.
U.S. Congress. Senate. S. Ex. Doc. 3, 39 Cong., 2 sess., Serial 1276. *Re-
port of General M. C. Meigs, Quartermaster General of U.S. Army.*
November 30, 1866.

_____. S. Report 156, 39 Cong., 2 sess., Serial 1279. *Condition of the Indian Tribes.* January 26, 1867.

_____. S. Mis. Doc. 26, 40 Cong., 2 sess., Serial 1319. *Memorial of the Legislature of Minnesota.* January 30, 1868.

_____. S. Ex. Doc. 51, 41 Cong., 3 sess., Serial 1440. *The Yellowstone Expedition of 1870.* August 21, 1870.

_____. S. Ex. Doc. 16, 42 Cong., 3 sess., Serial 1545. *Indian Interference with Northern Pacific Railroad.* July 2, 1872.

_____. S. Mis. Doc. 45 Cong., 2 sess., Serial 1546. *Exploration of Dakota.* January 24, 1873.

_____. S. Ex. Doc. 32, 43 Cong., 2 sess., Serial 1629. *Report of the Expedition to the Black Hills Under Bvt. Maj. Gen. George A. Custer.* August 2, 1874.

_____. S. Ex. Doc. 51, 44 Cong., 1 sess., Serial 1664. *Mineral Wealth, Climate, and Rain Fall and Natural Resources: The Jenney Report on the Black Hills.* April 15, 1876.

_____. S. Ex. Doc. 4, 44 Cong., 2 sess., Serial 1718. *Removal of the Sioux from Treaty Reservation to Indian Territory.* December 11, 1876.

_____. S. Ex. Doc. 9, 44 Cong., 2 sess., Serial 1718. *Report of Indian Commissioner J. Q. Smith.* December 11, 1876.

_____. S. Ex. Doc. 9, 44 Cong., 2 sess., Serial 1718. *Report and Journal of Sioux Commission of 1876, George W. Manypenny, Chairman.* December 18, 1876.

_____. S. Ex. Doc. 33, 45 Cong., 2 sess., Serial 1780. *Statement of Casualties.* December 11, 1877.

_____. S. Ex. Doc. 33, 45 Cong., 2 sess., Serial 1780. *Cost of the Sioux War, 1876-1877.* December 7, 1877.

_____. S. Ex. Doc. 286, 45 Cong., 2 sess., Serial 1790. *Correspondence Relative to Fort Assiniboine.* March 28, 1878.

_____. S. Ex. Doc. 1, 46 Cong., 1 sess., Serials 1871 and 1872. *Proceeding and Report of the Board of Army Officers in the Case of Fitz John Porter.* April 12, 1878.

_____. S. Report 708, 46 Cong., 2 sess., Serial 1899. *Report of Select Committee to Examine into the Circumstances Connected with the Removal of the Northern Cheyennes from the Sioux Reservations to the Indian Territory.* June 8, 1880.

_____. S. Ex. Doc. 1, 46 Cong., 3 sess., Serial 1952. *Correspondence Relative to Fort Maginnis.* November 19, 1880.

_____. S. Ex. Doc. 123, 47 Cong., 1 sess., Serial 1990. *Cost to Government of Indian Wars.* January 24, 1882.

_____. S. Report 911, 47 Cong., 2 sess., Serial 2087. *General Sheridan's Report on Yellowstone Park.* January 5, 1883.

_____. S. Ex. Doc. 33, 50 Cong., 1 sess., Serial 2504. *Indian Operations on the Plains.* February 11, 1887.

U.S. Department of Commerce. *Historical Statistics of the United States, Colonial Times to 1957.* Washington, D.C.: Government Printing Office, 1960.

U.S. Secretary of War. Annual Reports of the Secretary of War, General of the Army, Commander of the Division of the Missouri, and the Commander of the Department of Dakota, 1866-1891.

MANUSCRIPTS

Burt, Elizabeth J. "Forty Years in the U.S. Regular Army, 1862-1902." Library of Congress, Washington, D.C.

Faulk, Andrew Jackson. Papers, 1817-1896. Yale University Library, New Haven, Connecticut.

Ghent, William James. Papers. Library of Congress, Washington, D.C.

Godfrey, Edward Settle. Papers. Library of Congress, Washington, D.C.

Sheridan, Philip H. Papers. Library of Congress, Washington, D.C.

Sherman, William Tecumseh. Papers. Library of Congress, Washington, D.C.

Terry, Alfred Howe. Diary, 1876-1877. Library of Congress, Washington, D.C.

_____. Family papers, letters, diaries, newspaper clippings, and photographs. Yale University Library, New Haven, Connecticut.

THESES AND DISSERTATIONS

Bowler, Mary Jane. "The Sioux Indians and the United States Government, 1862-1878." Master's thesis, Washington University, 1944.

Marino, Carl William. "General Alfred Howe Terry: Soldier from Connecticut." Ph.D. dissertation, New York University, 1968.

Mitten, Hamilton F. "Army Life on the Plains During the Indian Wars." Master's thesis, University of Nebraska, 1930.

Parrish, Cora Hoffman. "The Indian Peace Commission of 1867 and the Western Indians." Master's thesis, University of Oklahoma, 1948.

Van Huizen, George Harry. "The United States Government and the Sioux Indians, 1878-1891." Master's thesis, Washington University, St. Louis, 1950.

Waddell, William S. "The Military Relations Between the Sioux Indians and the United States Government in the Dakota Territory, 1860-1891." Master's thesis University of South Dakota, 1931.

Waltmann, Henry G. "The Interior Department, War Department and Indian Policy, 1865-1887." Ph.D. dissertation, University of Nebraska, 1962.

NEWSPAPERS

Bismarck Tribune, 1873-1890.
Chicago Times, 1865-1890.
Helena Herald, 1866-1890.
New York Herald, 1876, 1890.
New York Sun, 1890.
New York Times, 1868, 1876, 1881, 1890.
New York World, 1890.
Richmond Examiner, 1865-1866.
Saint Paul Daily Dispatch, 1873-1886.
Saint Paul Pioneer Press, 1873-1880.
Yankton Press and Dakotaian, 1873-1877.

ARTICLES

Anderson, Harry H. "Indian Peace-Talkers and the Conclusion of the Sioux War of 1876." *Nebraska History* 40 (December 1963): 233-254.
Antrei, Albert. "Father Pierre Jean DeSmet." *Montana, The Magazine of Western History* 13 (April 1963): 24-43.
Athearn, Robert G., ed. "A Winter Campaign Against the Sioux." *Mississippi Valley Historical Review* 35 (September 1948): 272-284.
_____. "Early Territorial Montana: A Problem in Colonial Administration." *Montana, The Magazine of Western History* 2 (July 1951): 15-22.
_____. "The Fort Buford 'Massacre.' " *Mississippi Valley Historical Review* 41 (March 1955): 675-684.
_____. "Frontier Critics of the Western Army." *Montana, The Magazine of Western History* 5 (Spring 1955): 16-30.
_____. "War Paint Against Brass: The Army and the Plains Indians." *Montana, The Magazine of Western History* 6 (Summer 1956): 11-22.
Bailly, Edward C. "Echoes from Custer's Last Fight: Accounts by an Officer Never Before Published." *Military Affairs Journal of the American Military Institute* 17 (1953): 170-180.

Baird, George W. "General Miles' Indian Campaigns." *Century Magazine* 20 (1891): 351-370.

Barrett, John G. "Sherman and Total War in the Carolinas." *North Carolina Historical Review* 37 (July 1960): 367-381.

Briggs, Harold E. "The Black Hills Gold Rush." *North Dakota Historical Quarterly* 5 (1930-1931): 71-99.

Brown, Lisle G. "Yellowstone Supply Depot." *North Dakota History* 40 (Winter 1973): 24-33.

Conard, Jane. "Charles Collins: The Sioux City Promotion of the Black Hills." *South Dakota History* 3 (Spring 1972): 131-171.

Cox, John E. "Soldiering in Dakota Territory in the Seventies: A Communication." *North Dakota History* 6 (October 1931): 65.

Daniel, Forrest W. "Dismounting the Sioux." *North Dakota History* 41 (Summer 1974): 9-13.

Dippie, Brian W. "What Will Congress Do About It? The Congressional Reaction to the Little Big Horn Disaster." *North Dakota History* 37 (Summer 1970): 160-189.

Ellis, Richard N. "The Humanitarian Generals." *Western Historical Quarterly* 3 (April 1972): 169-178.

_____. "The Humanitarian Soldiers." *Journal of Arizona History* 10 (Summer 1969): 53-66.

Ericksson, Erik McKinley. "Sioux City and the Black Hills Gold Rush, 1874-1877." *Iowa Journal of History and Politics* 20 (July 1922): 319-347.

Fite, Gilbert C. "The United States Army and Relief to Pioneer Settlers, 1874-1875." *Journal of the West* 6 (January 1967): 99-107.

Fridley, Russell W. "Fort Snelling, from Military Post to Historic Site." *Minnesota History* 35 (December 1956): 178-192.

Gerber, Max E. "Custer Expedition of 1874: A New Look." *North Dakota History* 40 (Winter 1973): 4-23.

_____. "Steamboat and Indians of the Upper Missouri," *South Dakota History* 4 (Spring 1974): 139-160.

Gibbon, John. "Hunting Sitting Bull." *American Catholic Quarterly Review* 2 (October 1877): 665-694.

_____. "Last Summer's Expedition Against the Sioux." *American Catholic Quarterly Review* 2 (April 1877): 271-304.

Green, Charles Lowell. "The Indian Reservation System of the Dakotas to 1889." *South Dakota Historical Collections* 14 (1928): 307-415.

Hughes, Robert P. "The Campaign Against the Sioux." *Journal of the Military Service Institution of the United States* 18 (January 1896), reprinted in W. A. Graham. *Story of the Little Big Horn.* Harrisburg: Stackpole Co., 1945.

Johnson, Roy P. "The Siege at Fort Abercrombie." *North Dakota History* 24 (January 1957): 1-77.

Knight, Oliver. "War or Peace: The Anxious Wait for Crazy Horse." *Nebraska History* 54 (Winter 1973): 521-544.

Kroeker, Marvin. "Deceit About the Garden: Hazen, Custer and the Arid Lands Controversy." *North Dakota Quarterly* 38 (Summer 1970): 5-21.

Larsen, Arthur J., ed. "The Black Hills Gold Rush." *North Dakota Historical Quarterly* 6 (July 1932): 302-318.

Luvaas, Morten Jay. "The Fall of Fort Fisher." *Civil War Times Illustrated* 3 (August 1964): 4-9, 31-35.

_____. "Johnston's Last Stand—Bentonville." *North Carolina Historical Review* 33 (July 1956): 332-358.

McDermott, Louis M. "The Primary Role of the Military on the Dakota Frontier." *South Dakota History* 2 (Winter 1971): 1-22.

McElroy, Harold L. "Mercurial Military: A Study of the Central Montana Frontier Army Policy." *Montana, The Magazine of Western History* 4 (Autumn 1954): 9-23.

McLaird, James D., and Turcher, Lesta V. "Exploring the Black Hills, 1855-1875: Reports of the Government Expeditions." *South Dakota History* 3 (Fall 1973): 359-389.

Mahnken, Norbert. "The Sidney-Black Hills Trail." *Nebraska History* 30 (September 1949): 203-225.

Mardock, Robert W. "The Plains Frontier and the Indian Peace Policy, 1865-1880." *Nebraska History* 49 (Summer 1968): 187-201.

Mattison, Ray H. "The Army Posts on the Northern Plains, 1865-1885." *Nebraska History* 35 (March 1954): 1-27.

_____. "Fort Rice—North Dakota's First Missouri River Military Post." *North Dakota History* 20 (April 1953): 87-109.

_____. "Indian Reservation System on the Upper Missouri, 1865-1890." *Nebraska History* 36 (September 1955): 141-172.

_____. "Old Fort Stevenson—A Typical Missouri River Military Post." *North Dakota History* 18 (April-July 1951): 53-91.

"Notes and Documents." *North Dakota Historical Quarterly* 6 (July 1932): 306-307.

Paulson, Howard W. "The Allotment of Land in Severalty to the Dakota Indians before the Dawes Act." *South Dakota History* 1 (Spring 1971): 132-153.

Pennanen, Gary. "Sitting Bull: Indian Without a Country." *Canadian Historical Review* 51 (June 1970): 123-140.

Phillips, George H. "The Indian Ring in Dakota Territory, 1870-1890." *South Dakota History* 2 (Fall 1972): 345-376.

Prucha, F. Paul. "Fort Ripley: The Post and the Military Reservation."
   Minnesota History 28 (September 1947): 205-224.
Radabaugh, J. S. "Custer Explores the Black Hills, 1874." *Military
   Affairs* 26 (1962): 162-170.
Rolston, Alan. "The Yellowstone Expedition of 1873." *Montana, The
   Magazine of Western History* 20 (April 1970): 20-29.
Stanley, Henry M. "A British Journalist Reports the Medicine Lodge
   Peace Councils of 1867." *Kansas Historical Quarterly* 33 (Autumn
   1967): 249-320.
Stewart, Edgar I. "Major Brisbin's Relief of Fort Pease: A Prelude to the
   Bloody Little Big Horn Massacre." *Montana, The Magazine of Western
   History* 6 (Summer 1956): 23-27.
_____, and Luce, E. S. "The Reno Scout." *Montana, The Magazine of
   Western History* 10 (Summer 1960): 22-28.
Sully, Langdon. "The Indian Agent: A Study in Corruption and Avarice."
   American West 10 (March 1973): 4-9.
Swift, Lester L., ed. "The Recollections of a Signal Officer." *Civil War
   History* 9 (March 1963): 36-54.
Thane, James L., Jr. "The Montana Indian War of 1867." *Arizona and
   the West* 10 (Summer 1968): 153-170.
Unrau, William E. "The Civilian as Indian Agent: Villain or Victim?"
   Western Historical Quarterly 3 (October 1972): 408-420.
Utley, Robert M. "The Celebrated Peace Policy of General Grant."
   North Dakota History 20 (July 1953): 121-142.
Walker, James F. "Old Fort Berthold As I Knew It." *North Dakota History*
   20 (January 1953).
Wemett, W. M. "Custer's Expedition to the Black Hills in 1874." *North
   Dakota Historical Quarterly* 6 (July 1932): 292-301.
Wright, Dana. "The Fort Totten-Fort Stevenson Trail." *North Dakota
   History* 20 (April 1953): 110-131.

BOOKS

Andrist, Ralph K. *The Long Death: The Last Days of the Plains Indians.*
   New York: Macmillan Co., 1964.
Atkin, Ronald. *Maintain the Right: The Early History of the North West
   Mounted Police, 1873-1900.* New York: John Day Company, 1973.
Athearn, Robert G. *Forts of the Upper Missouri.* Englewood Cliffs, N.J.:
   Prentice-Hall, 1967.
_____. *Thomas Francis Meagher: An Irish Revolutionary in America.*
   Boulder: University of Colorado Press, 1949.
_____. *William Tecumseh Sherman and the Settlement of the West.* Nor-
   man: University of Oklahoma Press, 1956.

Baldwin, Alice Blackwood. *Memoirs of the Late Frank D. Baldwin, Major General, U.S.A.* Los Angeles: Wetzel Publishing Co., 1929.

Berthrong, Donald J. *The Southern Cheyennes.* Norman: University of Oklahoma Press, 1963.

Bonney, Orrin H., and Bonney, Lorraine. *Battle Drums and Geysers: The Life and Journals of Lt. Gustavus Cheyney Doane, Soldier and Explorer of the Yellowstone and Snake River Regions.* Chicago: Swallow Press, 1970.

Bordeaux, William J. *Conquering the Mighty Sioux.* Sioux Falls: n.p., 1929.

Bourke, John G. *On the Border with Crook.* New York: Charles Scribner's Sons, 1892.

Bradley, James H. *The March of the Montana Column: A Prelude to the Custer Disaster.* Norman: University of Oklahoma Press, 1961.

Brady, Cyrus Townsend. *Indian Fights and Fighters.* New York: Doubleday & Co., 1923.

_____. *Northwestern Fights and Fighters.* New York: McClure Co., 1907.

Brininstool, E. A. *Fighting Red Cloud's Warriors.* Columbus: Hunter-trader-trapper Co., 1926.

_____. *Indian Fighting Warriors.* Harrisburg: Stackpole Co., 1953.

_____. *Troopers with Custer.* Harrisburg: Stackpole Co., 1952.

Brininstool, E. A., and Hebard, Grace R. *The Bozeman Trail.* 2 vols. Cleveland: Arthur H. Clark Co., 1922.

Brown, Dee. *Fort Phil Kearny: An American Saga.* New York: G. P. Putnam's Sons, 1962.

Brown, Mark H. *The Flight of the Nez Perce.* New York: G. P. Putnam's Sons, 1967.

_____. *The Plainsmen of the Yellowstone: A History of the Yellowstone Basin.* New York: G. P. Putnam's Sons, 1961.

Bruce, Robert. *The Fighting Norths and Pawnee Scouts.* Lincoln: Nebraska State Historical Society, 1932.

Burdick, Usher L. *Tales from Buffalo Land: The Story of Fort Buford.* Baltimore: Wirth Brothers, 1940.

Burlingame, Merrill G. *The Military Indian Frontier in Montana, 1860-1890.* Iowa City: University of Iowa Press, 1938.

Butterworth, W. E. *Soldiers on Horseback: The Story of the United States Cavalry.* New York: W. W. Norton and Co., 1967.

Byrne, Patrick E. *Soldiers of the Plains.* New York: Minton, Balch & Co., 1926.

Carpenter, John A. *Sword and Olive Branch, Oliver Otis Howard.* Pittsburgh: University of Pittsburgh Press, 1964.

Carroll, John M., ed. *General Custer and the Battle of the Little Big Horn:*

The Federal View. New Brunswick, N.J.: Garry Owen Press, 1976.

Carter, William Harding. *From Yorktown to Santiago with the Sixth U.S. Cavalry.* Baltimore: Lord Baltimore Press, 1900.

Chandler, Melbourne C. *Of Garry Owen to Glory: The History of the Seventh United States Cavalry Regiment.* Annandale, Va.: Turnpike Press, 1960.

Chittenden, Hiram Martin. *History of Early Steamboat Navigation of the Missouri River.* New York: Francis P. Harper, 1903.

———, ed. *Life, Letters, and Travels of Father De Smet.* 4 vols. 1905. Reprint ed., New York: Arno Press, 1969.

———. *The Yellowstone National Park.* Cincinnati: Robert Clarke Co., 1895.

Coutant, Charles Griffin. *The History of Wyoming.* Laramie: Chaplin, Spafford & Mathison, 1899.

Crook, George. *General George Crook, His Autobiography.* Norman: University of Oklahoma Press, 1960.

Custer, Elizabeth B. *Boots and Saddles, or Life in Dakota with General Custer.* New York: Harper & Brothers, 1885.

Custer, George A. *My Life on the Plains.* 1874. Reprint ed., Lincoln: University of Nebraska Press, n.d.

Danker, Donald F., ed. *Man of the Plains: Recollections of Luther North, 1856-1882.* Lincoln: University of Nebraska Press, 1961.

Downey, Fairfax. *Indian Fighting Army.* New York: Charles Scribner's Sons, 1941.

Dunn, Jacob Piatt, Jr. *Massacres of the Mountains: A History of the Indian Wars of the Far West, 1815-1875.* New York: Harper & Brothers, 1886.

Duratschek, Sister Mary Claudia. *Crusading Along Sioux Trails: A History of the Catholic Missions of South Dakota.* Yankton: Benedictine Convent of the Sacred Heart, 1947.

Dustin, Fred. *The Custer Tragedy.* Ann Arbor: Edwards Brothers, 1939.

Ege, Robert J. *"Tell Baker to Strike Them Hard!" Incident on the Marias, 23 January 1870.* Bellevue, Nebr.: Old Army Press, 1970.

Eisenschiml, Otto. *The Celebrated Case of Fitz John Porter: An American Dreyfus Affair.* Indianapolis: Bobbs-Merrill Company, 1950.

Ellis, Richard N. *General Pope and U.S. Indian Policy.* Albuquerque: University of New Mexico Press, 1970.

Finerty, John F. *War-Path and Bivouac, or the Conquest of the Sioux.* Norman: University of Oklahoma Press, 1961.

Fiske, Frank. *The Taming of the Sioux.* Bismarck: Bismarck Tribune, 1917.

Foner, Jack D. *The United States Soldier Between Two Wars: Army Life and Reforms, 1865-1898.* New York: Humanities Press, 1970.

Forsyth, George Alexander. *The Story of the Soldier.* New York: D. Appleton & Co., 1900.

Fowler, Arlen L. *The Black Infantry in the West, 1869-1891.* Westport, Conn.: Greenwood Publishing, 1971.

Fritz, Henry Eugene. *The Movement for Indian Assimilation, 1860-1890.* Philadelphia: University of Pennsylvania Press, 1963.

Ganoe, William Addleman. *The History of the United States Army.* New York: D. Appleton & Co., 1924.

Gibbon, John. *Gibbon on the Sioux Campaign of 1876.* Bellevue, Nebr.: Old Army Press, 1969.

Goetzmann, William H. *Exploration and Empire.* New York: Alfred A. Knopf, 1966.

_____. *Army Exploration in the American West, 1803-1863.* New Haven: Yale University Press, 1959.

Graham, William A. ed. *The Custer Myth: A Source Book of Custeriana.* Harrisburg: Stackpole Co., 1953.

_____. *The Reno Court of Inquiry: Abstract of the Official Record of Proceedings.* Harrisburg: Stackpole Co., 1953.

_____. *The Story of the Little Big Horn.* Harrisburg: Military Service Publishing Co., 1941.

Grant, Ulysses S. *Personal Memoirs of U.S. Grant.* 2 vols. New York: Century Co., 1885.

Gray, John S. *Centennial Campaign: The Sioux War of 1876.* Fort Collins, Colo.: Old Army Press, 1976.

Greever, William S. *The Bonanza West: The Story of the Western Mining Rushes, 1848-1900.* Norman: University of Oklahoma Press, 1963.

Grinnell, George B. *The Fighting Cheyennes.* New York: Charles Scribner's Sons, 1915.

_____. *Two Great Scouts and Their Pawnee Battalion.* Cleveland: Arthur H. Clark Co., 1928.

Hafen, LeRoy R., and Young, Francis M. *Fort Laramie and the Pageant of the West, 1834-1890.* Glendale, Calif.: Arthur H. Clark Co., 1938.

_____, eds. *Powder River Campaigns and Sawyers Expedition of 1865.* Glendale: Arthur H. Clark Co., 1961.

Hagan, William Thomas. *Indian Police and Judges: Experiments in Acculturation and Control.* New Haven: Yale University Press, 1966.

Hagemann, E. R., ed. *Fighting Rebels and Redskins: Experiences in Army Life of Colonel George B. Sanford, 1861-1892.* Norman: University of Oklahoma Press, 1969.

Hamilton, James McClellan. *History of Montana: From Wilderness to Statehood.* Portland: Binfords & Mort, 1957.

Hammer, Kenneth M. *The Springfield Carbine on the Western Frontier.* Bellevue, Nebr.: Old Army Press, 1970.

Hampton, H. Duane. *How the U.S. Cavalry Saved Our National Parks.* Bloomington: Indiana University Press, 1971.

Hancock, Mrs. Winfield S. *Reminiscences of Winfield Scott Hancock.* New York: Charles L. Webster & Co., 1887.

Hans, Frederick Malon. *The Great Sioux Nation.* Chicago: M. A. Donohue & Co., 1907.

Hanson, Joseph Mills. *The Conquest of the Missouri: Being the Story of the Life and Exploits of Captain Grant Marsh.* Chicago: A. C. McClurg, 1909.

Hart, Herbert M. *Old Forts of the Northwest.* Seattle: Superior Publishing Co., 1963.

Hassrick, Royal B. *The Sioux: Life and Customs of a Warrior Society.* Norman: University of Oklahoma Press, 1964.

Hedges, James Blaine. *Henry Villard and the Railways of the Northwest.* New Haven: Yale University Press, 1930.

Heitman, Francis B. *Historical Register and Dictionary of the United States Army.* 2 vols. Washington, D.C.: Government Printing Office, 1903.

Hoig, Stan. *The Sand Creek Massacre.* Norman: University of Oklahoma Press, 1961.

Hoopes, Alban W. *The Road to the Little Big Horn—and Beyond.* New York: Vantage Press, 1975.

Howard, Oliver Otis. *Autobiography of Oliver Otis Howard, Major General United States Army.* 2 vols. New York: Baker & Taylor Co., 1908.

_____. *My Life and Experiences Among Our Hostile Indians.* Hartford: A. D. Worthington & Co., 1907.

Howe, Mark Anthony DeWolfe. *The Life and Labors of Bishop Hare, Apostle to the Sioux.* New York: Sturgis and Walton Co., 1911.

Hyde, George E. *Red Cloud's Folk: A History of the Oglala Sioux Indians.* Norman: University of Oklahoma Press, 1937.

_____. *A Sioux Chronicle.* Norman: University of Oklahoma Press, 1956.

_____. *Spotted Tail's Folk: A History of the Brulé Sioux.* Norman: University of Oklahoma Press, 1961.

Ingersoll, L. D. *A History of the War Department of the United States.* Washington, D.C.: Francis B. Hohun, 1879.

Jackson, Donald. *Custer's Gold: The United States Cavalry Expedition of 1874.* New Haven: Yale University Press, 1966.

Jackson, W. Turrentine. *Wagon Roads West: A Study of Federal Road Surveys and Construction in the Trans-Mississippi West, 1846-1869.* Berkeley: University of California Press, 1952.

Johnson, Dorothy M. *Warrior for a Lost Nation: A Biography of Sitting Bull*. Philadelphia: Westminster Press, 1969.

Johnson, Virginia Weisel. *The Unregimented General: A Biography of Nelson A. Miles*. Boston: Houghton Mifflin Co., 1962.

Johnson, W. Fletcher. *Life of Sitting Bull*. Edgewood, S.D.: Edgewood Publishing Co., 1891.

Jones, Douglas C. *The Treaty of Medicine Lodge: The Story of the Great Treaty Council As Told by Eyewitnesses*. Norman: University of Oklahoma Press, 1966.

Jones, Robert Huhn. *The Civil War in the Northwest*. Norman: University of Oklahoma Press, 1960.

Kane, Lucile M., trans. and ed. *Military Life in Dakota: The Journal of Philippe Regis de Trobriand*. St. Paul: Alvord Memorial Commission, 1951.

Kappler, Charles J., ed. *Indian Affairs: Laws and Treaties*. 2 vols. 1904. Reprint ed., London: AMS Press, 1971.

Kimball, Maria Porter Brace. *A Soldier-Doctor of Our Army, James P. Kimball, Late Colonel and Assistant Surgeon-General, U.S. Army*. Boston: Houghton Mifflin Co., 1917.

King, Charles. *Campaigning with Crook, and Stories of Army Life*. New York: Harper & Row, 1890.

King, James T. *War Eagle: A Life of General Eugene A. Carr*. Lincoln: University of Nebraska Press, 1963.

Knight, Oliver. *Following the Indian Wars: The Story of the Newspaper Correspondents Among the Indian Campaigners*. Norman: University of Oklahoma Press, 1960.

Koury, Michael J. *Diaries of the Little Big Horn*. Bellevue, Nebr.: Old Army Press, 1968.

———. *Military Posts of Montana*. Bellevue, Nebr.: Old Army Press, 1970.

Krause, Herbert, and Olson, Gary. *Prelude to Glory: A Newspaper Accounting of Custer's 1874 Expedition to the Black Hills*. Sioux Falls: Brevet Press, 1974.

Kroeker, Marvin E. *Great Plains Command: William B. Hazen in the Frontier West*. Norman: University of Oklahoma Press, 1976.

Kuhlman, Charles. *Did Custer Disobey Orders at the Battle of the Little Big Horn?* Harrisburg: Stackpole Co., 1957.

Lamar, Howard Roberts. *Dakota Territory, 1861-1889: A Study of Frontier Politics*. New Haven: Yale University Press, 1956.

Lass, William E. *A History of Steamboating on the Upper Missouri*. Lincoln: University of Nebraska Press, 1962.

Leckie, William H. *The Military Conquest of the Southern Plains*. Norman: University of Oklahoma Press, 1963.

Lounsberry, Clement A. *Early History of North Dakota.* Washington, D.C.: Liberty Press, 1919.

Lowie, Robert Harry. *Indians of the Plains.* New York: McGraw-Hill Book Co., 1954.

McClernand, Edward J. *With the Indian and the Buffalo in Montana, 1870-1878.* Glendale, Calif.: Arthur H. Clark, 1969.

McDonough, James L. *Schofield: Union General in the Civil War and Reconstruction.* Tallahassee: Florida State University Press, 1972.

McGillycuddy, Julia B., *McGillycuddy: Agent.* Palo Alto: Stanford University Press, 1941.

McLaughlin, James. *My Friend the Indian.* Boston: Houghton Mifflin Co., 1926.

Madsen, Brigham D. *The Bannock of Idaho.* Caldwell, Id.: Caxton Press, 1958.

Manypenny, George W. *Our Indian Wards.* Cincinnati: Robert Clarke & Co., 1880.

Mardock, Robert Winston. *The Reformers and the American Indian.* Columbia: University of Missouri Press, 1971.

Merrill, James M. *Spurs to Glory: The Story of the United States Cavalry.* Chicago: Rand McNally & Co., 1966.

Merrington, Marguerite, ed. *The Custer Story: The Life and Intimate Letters of General George A. Custer and His Wife Elizabeth.* New York: Devin-Adair Co., 1950.

Meyer, Roy W. *History of the Santee Sioux: United States Indian Policy on Trial.* Lincoln: University of Nebraska Press, 1967.

Miles, Nelson A. *Personal Recollections.* New York: Werner Co., 1896.
_____. *Serving the Republic.* New York: Harper & Row, 1911.

Mills, Anson. *My Story.* Washington, D.C.: Byron H. Adams, 1918.

Monaghan, Jay. *Custer: The Life of General George Armstrong Custer.* Boston: Little, Brown, 1959.

Mulford, Ami Frank. *Fighting Indians in the 7th United States Cavalry.* Corning, N.Y.: Paul Lindsley Mulford, 1879.

Murray, Robert A. *Military Posts in the Powder River Country of Wyoming, 1865-1894.* Lincoln: University of Nebraska Press, 1968.

Nadeau, Remi. *Fort Laramie and the Sioux Indians.* Englewood Cliffs, N.J.: Prentice-Hall, 1967.

Niven, John. *Connecticut for the Union: The Role of the State in the Civil War.* New Haven: Yale University Press, 1965.

Olson, James C. *Red Cloud and the Sioux Problem.* Lincoln: University of Nebraska Press, 1965.

Osterweis, Rollin G. *Three Centuries of New Haven, 1638-1938.* New Haven: Yale University Press, 1953.

Overfield, Loyd J., ed. *Official Documents of the Little Big Horn.* Glendale, Calif.: Arthur H. Clark Co., 1971.

Parker, Watson. *Gold in the Black Hills.* Norman: University of Oklahoma Press, 1966.

Peattie, Roderick, ed. *The Black Hills.* New York: Vanguard Press, 1952.

Priest, Loring Benson. *Uncle Sam's Stepchildren: The Reformation of United States Indian Policy, 1865-1887.* 1942. Reprint ed., New York: Octagon Books, 1969.

Prucha, Francis Paul. *American Indian Policy in Crisis: Christian Reformers and the Indian, 1865-1900.* Norman: University of Oklahoma Press, 1976.

_____. *A Guide to the Military Posts of the United States, 1789-1895.* Madison: State Historical Society of Wisconsin, 1964.

Rahill, Peter J. *The Catholic Indian Missions and Grant's Peace Policy, 1870-1884.* Washington, D.C.: Catholic University of America Press, 1953.

Richardson, James D., comp. *A Compilation of the Messages and Papers of the Presidents, 1789-1897.* 10 vols. Washington, D.C.: Government Printing Office, 1896-1899.

Rickey, Don, Jr. *Forty Miles a Day on Beans and Hay: The Enlisted Soldier Fighting the Indian Wars.* Norman: University of Oklahoma Press, 1963.

Riegel, Robert E. *The Story of Western Railroads: From 1852 Through the Reign of the Giants.* 1926. Reprint ed., Lincoln: University of Nebraska Press, 1967.

Rister, Carl Coke. *Border Command: General Phil Sheridan in the West.* Norman: University of Oklahoma Press, 1944.

Robinson, Doane. *A History of the Dakota or Sioux Indians. South Dakota Historical Collections* (1904). Reprint ed. Minneapolis: Ross & Haines, 1956.

Robinson, Elwyn B. *History of North Dakota.* Lincoln: University of Nebraska Press, 1966.

Roe, Frank Gilbert. *The Indian and the Horse.* Norman: University of Oklahoma Press, 1955.

Sage, Leland Livingston. *William Boyd Allison: A Study in Practical Politics.* Iowa City: State Historical Society of Iowa, 1956.

Sandoz, Mari. *Cheyenne Autumn.* New York: McGraw-Hill Book Co., 1953.

_____. *Crazy Horse.* New York: Alfred A. Knopf, 1942.

Schell, Herbert S. *History of South Dakota.* Lincoln: University of Nebraska Press, 1961.

Schmeckebier, Laurence F. *The Office of Indian Affairs, Its History,*

Activities, and Organization. Baltimore: The Johns Hopkins Press, 1927.

Schofield, John M. *Forty-six Years in the Army.* New York: Century Co., 1897.

Scott, Hugh Lenox. *Some Memories of a Soldier.* New York: Century Co., 1928.

Sheridan, Philip H. *Report of an Exploration of Parts of Wyoming, Idaho, and Montana in August and September, 1882.* Washington, D.C.: Government Printing Office, 1882.

_____. *Outline Descriptions of the Posts in the Military Division of the Missouri.* 1876. Reprint ed., Bellevue, Nebr.: Old Army Press, 1969.

_____. *Personal Memoirs of P. H. Sheridan.* 2 vols. New York: Charles L. Webster & Co., 1888.

_____. *Record of Engagements with Hostile Indians Within the Military Division of the Missouri, from 1868 to 1882, Lieutenant-General P. H. Sheridan, Commanding.* Washington, D.C.: Government Printing Office, 1882.

Sherman, William Tecumseh. *The Sherman Letters, Correspondence Between General Sherman and Senator Sherman from 1837 to 1891.* 1894. Reprint ed., Da Capo Press, 1969.

_____. *Memoirs of General W. T. Sherman.* 2 vols. New York: Webster & Co., 1891.

Spence, Clark C. *Territorial Politics and Government in Montana, 1864-89.* Urbana: University of Illinois Press, 1975.

Stanley, David S. *Personal Memoirs of Major-General David S. Stanley, U.S.A.* Cambridge: Harvard University Press, 1917.

Stanley, Henry M. *My Early Travels and Adventures in America and Asia.* 2 vols. New York: Charles Scribner's Sons, 1895.

Stewart, Edgar I. *Custer's Luck.* Norman: University of Oklahoma Press, 1955.

Strong, William E. *A Trip to the Yellowstone National Park in July, August, and September, 1875.* Norman: University of Oklahoma Press, 1968.

Terrell, John Upton, and Walton, George. *Faint the Trumpet Sounds: The Life and Trial of Major Reno.* New York: David McKay Co., 1966.

Thian, Raphael P., comp. *Legislative History of the General Staff of the Army of the United States . . . from 1775 to 1901.* Washington, D.C.: Government Printing Office, 1901.

Tucker, Glenn. *Hancock the Superb.* Indianapolis: Bobbs-Merrill Co., 1960.

Turner, John Peter. *The Northwest Mounted Police, 1873-1893.* Ottawa:

Edmond Cloutier, 1950.

Upton, Richard, comp. and ed. *Fort Custer on the Big Horn, 1877-1898: Its History and Personalities as Told and Pictured by Its Contemporaries.* Glendale: Arthur H. Clark Co., 1973.

Utley, Robert M. *Custer and the Great Controversy: The Origin and Development of a Legend.* Los Angeles: Westernlore Press, 1962.

_____. *Frontier Regulars: The United States Army and the Indian, 1866-1890.* New York: Macmillan Co., 1973.

_____. *Frontiersmen in Blue: The United States Army and the Indian, 1848-1865.* New York: Macmillan Co., 1967.

_____. *The Last Days of the Sioux Nation.* New Haven: Yale University Press, 1963.

Van de Water, Frederick Franklin. *Glory Hunter: A Life of General Custer.* Indianapolis: Bobbs-Merrill, 1934.

Vaughn, Jesse Wendell. *Indian Fights: New Facts on Seven Encounters.* Norman: University of Oklahoma Press, 1966.

_____. *Reynold's Campaign on Powder River.* Norman: University of Oklahoma Press, 1961.

_____. *With Crook at the Rosebud.* Harrisburg: Stackpole, 1956.

Vestal, Stanley. *New Sources of Indian History, 1850-1891.* Norman: University of Oklahoma Press, 1934.

_____. *Sitting Bull: Champion of the Sioux.* Boston: Houghton Mifflin, 1932.

_____. *Warpath and Council Fire.* New York: Random House, 1948.

Waldo, Edna L. *Dakota, An Informal Study of Territorial Days.* Bismarck: Capital Publishing Co., 1932.

Walker, Judson Elliott. *Campaigns of General Custer in the Northwest and the Final Surrender of Sitting Bull.* New York: Jenkins & Thomas, 1881.

Weigley, Russell F. *History of the United States Army.* New York: Macmillan Co., 1967.

Wellman, Paul I. *Death in the Prairie.* New York: Macmillan Co., 1934.

White, Lonnie J. *Hostiles and Horse Soldiers: Indian Battles and Campaigns in the West.* Boulder: Pruett Publishing Co., 1972.

Whitman, S. E. *The Troopers: An Informal History of the Plains Cavalry, 1865-1890.* New York: Hastings House, 1962.

Wormser, Richard. *The Yellowlegs: The Story of the United States Cavalry.* Garden City, N.Y.: Doubleday & Co., 1966.

Index

About the Author

JOHN W. BAILEY is Chairman of the History Department at Carthage College, Kenosha, Wisconsin. A specialist in the American West, he has had articles published in *Maryland Historical Magazine* and *Nebraska History*.